City Dog
San Francisco
The Bay Area

ISBN 1-933068-01-9

Editor: Cricky Long
Content Manager: Bryce Longton
Production Coordinator: Jamie Wetherbe
Cover Illustration: Bill Kheel
Cover Design: Jennifer L. Ciminillo
Copy Editor: David Skaugerud
San Francisco Editor: Heather Shouse
San Francisco Writers: Kate Beale, Cheryl Koehler

City Dog

4311 Wilshire Blvd, Ste 608
Los Angeles, California 90010
(323) 857-5217 (phone)
(323) 857-5216 (fax)
www.citydog.net

The purpose of the guidebook is to inform and to entertain. Every effort was made to ensure that all information contained in this guidebook was accurate and up-to-date at the time of publication. However, the authors, editor and City Dog Publishing, LLC shall have neither liability nor responsibility to any person or entity with respect to any loss or damage caused, or alleged to have been caused, directly or indirectly, by the information contained in this book. It is recommended that you call ahead to confirm business information.

Acknowledgments

This book would not have been possible without the tireless efforts of everyone involved, especially Bryce, Cheryl, Eric, Hal, Jamie and Kate. Gus, Robert, Betty and Henry also deserve special thanks for all of their advice and support.

Table of Contents

How to Use This Guide

City Dog has been broken down by area. The Table of Contents includes a list of area directories, which contain the following information:

• Emergency Pet Transport Companies

• Animal Emergency Facilities

• City Dog Picks

• Categorical/Neighborhood Indexes

• General Listings

In addition to the area directories, you will also find the Greater Bay Area Directory. This is where you can check out dog trainers, mobile groomers, shuttle services and other mobile businesses that cover a wide service area. If you are unsure whether a business is listed in a particular area or in the Greater Bay Area Directory, you can check the alphabetical index in the back of this guidebook.

Introduction

Think of what a place this world could be if only we would all be the people our dogs think we are.

City Dog, the urban dog-o-phile's personal 411 to all things dog, is unique. It is the only dog guide singularly devoted to helping city-dwellers find the dog-care resources they need. This is not a book about people-places that permit dogs, but rather a book about places that are specifically for dogs.

The purpose of this guidebook is to help you make your dog the happiest and healthiest he can possibly be.

City Dog's A-to-Z directory includes not only the address, phone number, hours of operation and payment information for each listing, but also an original review of each business. This means you can get the inside scoop, without having to make a personal visit. A service that one dog owner may deem essential might seem utterly frivolous to another. City Dog has covered it all. So please, take from this guidebook what you need, use what works for you, and consider the rest entertainment.

The emergency listings, located at the beginning of each section, are essential for middle-of-the-night ailments. And the appendixes—which include the Puppy Starter Kit,* Lost Dog Help and When Dogs Go to Heaven—are indispensable for first-time dog parents.

*The Puppy Starter Kit contains a list of resources for new pet owners. It does not contain any information on puppy sales. City Dog is opposed to the sale of puppies and kittens in pet stores.

Legend

For those of you who don't like to read the fine print, we have created icons to make it easy for you to see at a glance who offers what services.

Emergency
Facility

Alternative
Product/Service

Dog
Boarding

Dog
Day Care

Dog
Grooming

Grooming—
Self-Serve

Dog
Park

Shuttle
Service

Pet-Supply
Store

Dog
Training

On-Site
Pet Adoptions*

Dog Hikes &
Socials

Dog-Centric
Resource

Dog Walking/
Pet-Sitting

Cat Services/
Products
Available

Anesthesia-
Free Teeth
Cleaning*

Low-Cost
Vaccination
Clinics*

Poop-Removal
Service

$ = Inexpensive

$$ = Average

$$$ = Expensive

(S) = Shuttle service to and from business

* This service is usually offered on a monthly basis.

Greater Bay Area

EMERGENCY PET TRANSPORT

AMERS Animal Ambulance
(877) 426-3771 (emergency)
(925) 261-9111 (office)
www.animalmedics.com
Hours: Every Day 24 Hours
Payment: Credit Cards, Checks
Emergency Fee: $175

Pet Taxi
Bay Area
(415) 386-2534
Hours: Every Day 7 A.M. – 7 P.M.
Emergency Hours: Every Day 24 Hours
Payment: Checks
Price Range: $$/$$$

ANIMAL POISON HOTLINE

ASPCA Animal Poison Control Center
(888) 4ANI-HELP
Hours: Every Day 24 Hours
Payment: Credit Cards
Consultation Fee: $45

ADOPTION

Mobile *Bad Rap*
Willits *Milo Foundation*

ALTERNATIVE PRODUCTS/SERVICES
Rohnert Park *Feed This, Inc!*

DOG BOARDING
Mobile *Fetch! Pet Care, Inc.* **(S)**

DOG TRAINING
Mobile *Molly Harris' Chilipepper Dog Training*
• *Sirius Puppy Training* • *Thinking Dog*

DOG WALKING/PET-SITTING
Mobile *Fetch! Pet Care, Inc.* **(S)** • *For the Love of Dogs* **(S)**
• *O'Brien's Animal Transport Service*

PET-SUPPLY STORES
Rohnert Park *VIP Petcare Services*

VACCINATIONS—LOW-COST
Rohnert Park *VIP Petcare Services*

CITY DOG PICKS
Mobile *O'Brien's Animal Transport Service*

General Listings

Bad Rap
(510) 414-6461
www.badrap.org
Payment: No Charge
Bad Rap (Bay Area Doglovers Responsible About Pitbulls) is a nonprofit group dedicated to educating people about pitbulls, offering rescue resources and supporting owners. The group provides referrals to pitbull-friendly trainers, shelters, kennels and day-care facilities, as well as groups and organizations that cover just about everything you need to know about responsible pitbull ownership. The website also lists pups available for rescue. Bad Rap is as responsible about pitbull adoption as it is about owner education, requiring a hearty commitment and airtight references.

Feed This, Inc!
(707) 887-1122
www.feedthis.com
Hours: See website for schedule
Payment: Credit Cards, Checks
Price Range: $$$
Cathy and Tiffany say raw food is the way to go for optimal canine and feline health. Feed This offers 11 menus to choose from, including puppy-specific fare. And you can order up to four weeks of raw chow at a time. Their service is pricey. But according to a chart on their website, compared to what you might spend on drugs and veterinary care if your dog has to live out her life on standard kibble, you come out ahead. Delivery service is available in Sonoma, Napa, Marin, Mendocino, Alameda, Contra Costa and San Francisco counties.

Fetch! Pet Care, Inc.

(866) 338-2463
www.fetchpetcare.com
Hours: By Appt
Payment: Credit Cards, Checks
Price Range: $$

What can you say about a company that donates a percentage of every sale to the local humane society? How about, "You're hired!" With over a half-dozen locations in Northern California, Fetch! offers 30-minute neighborhood walks, social group outings (about four dogs at a time), home visits and overnight stays in either the sitter's home or your house. They'll even take your dog to the vet or the groomer and deliver pet supplies to your doorstep.

For the Love of Dogs

(877) 285-2885
www.fortheloveofdogs.com
Hours: Mon - Sun 10 A.M. - 4 P.M.
Payment: Credit Cards, Checks
Price Range: $$$

From the routine to the particular, this team of professional pet sitters does it all. Their services include dog walking (limited to two leashed dogs at a time), daily home visits and overnight stays with dogs. For the Love of Dogs will also bathe your dog, administer his medication or give him a massage. Name it, and they'll do it. They'll follow your directions to the letter.

Milo Foundation

(707) 459-4900
P.O. Box 500
Willits, California 95490
www.milofoundation.org

Hours: By Appt
Payment: Checks
Price Range: $$

For the past 10 years, Lynne Tingle has run this no-kill animal sanctuary that's located on 283 acres in Mendocino County. Named for Lynne's deaf and blind Australian Shepherd, the foundation rescues and places more than 1,000 cats and dogs a year, pulling animals from overcrowded California shelters and stepping in when mundane decisions ("I have too much homework to keep my dog") threaten an animal's life. Looking to adopt? Milo's mobile adoption units appear regularly in and around Berkeley.

Molly Harris' Chilipepper Dog Training

(415) 661-7750
www.chilipepperdogtraining.com
Hours: By Appt
Payment: Checks
Price Range: $$

A glutton for punishment, Molly likes to take on challenging cases. She particularly relishes rowdy adolescents who are a little too hot to handle. Her specialty is training toy breeds, especially those with barking issues or those skittish around bigger dogs and people. Molly helps people learn how to safely exercise and socialize their small-fry off leash. She's willing to travel if she feels she's a good match for your dog.

O'Brien's Animal Transport Service

(650) 348-0547
www.animaltransportation.com
Hours: By Appt
Payment: Checks
Price Range: $$$

OATS has been making reservations and seeing off your pooch in air-conditioned style for the last 40 years. Airline regulations differ from airline to airline and from country to country, so OATS takes the guesswork out of the process and ensures that you and your pet will be in compliance. One call to their office will put you at ease because your pet's safety is clearly their main concern. The company is based in Burlingame but can arrange travel plans and offers 24-hour service worldwide.

Pet Express
(415) 821-7111
(866) PETMOVE
www.petmove.com
Hours: By Appt
Payment: Checks
Price Range: $$

Pet Express can take the stress out of your pet's move, even if you're tearing your hair out. To help alleviate anxiety, they can pick up your pooch before the movers arrive and drop him off at your new pad after you've unpacked his bed and treats. The company handles all documentation, flight arrangements and ground transportation. And they're equipped to deal with unforeseen weather and flight problems. They discourage recreational travel with your pet, recommending you use a local boarding facility instead.

Pet Taxi
(415) 386-2534
Hours: Every Day 7 A.M. to 7 P.M.
Payment: Checks
Price Range: $$$

Pet Taxi has been in the business of ferrying pets for six years, taking them to the vet, grooming salon, doggie day care and even to ex-spouses for visits. Run by Joe, a former cab driver, and his wife, Roberta, Pet Taxi attracts most of its fares through referrals from vets and groomers. In their PT Cruiser, they transport one dog—or one household of dogs—at a time, charging a set fee within the city and a per-mile rate everywhere else. They're even willing to accommodate customers after hours for an additional fee.

Sirius Puppy Training

(800) 419-8748

www.siriuspup.com

Hours: See website for class schedules

Payment: Credit Cards, Checks

Price Range: $$

Veterinarian and animal behaviorist Dr. Ian Dunbar established Sirius more than 20 years ago, after being told that his new puppy was too young to start school. With its emphasis on food and toy lures, games and early socialization, Sirius has become one the most popular training methods in the country. Sirius training books and videos are available to help owners reinforce what their pets learn in class. Dunbar also founded the Association of Pet Dog Trainers, which offers national certification to qualified dog trainers.

Thinking Dog

(415) 515-8985

www.shelterworks.us

Hours: By Appt

Payment: Checks

Price Range: $$$

Dogs who don't like to share their toys, who pick fights at the park or who snarl at anyone who approaches their bowl can count on Shannon Cummings to help them work through their feelings. She works one-on-one with aggression clients and offers a full slate of puppy, basic obedience and manners classes. An SF SPCA Academy graduate, Shannon, along with SF SPCA Rehabilitation Coordinator Gina Phairas, runs ShelterWorks, a consulting company aimed at improving the lives of shelter animals and educating animal-care professionals.

Tidy Turf

(800) 989-9667

www.tidyturf.com

Hours: By Appt

Payment: Credit Cards, Checks

Price Range: $

This pet-waste removal company has been serving the Sonoma, Marin, San Francisco and Peninsula regions since 1998. Owner George Gadda's clientele varies from single-family homes to kennels and dog parks, and even includes a few celebrities. George will come by and clean up after your pooch, depositing the waste in your own garbage receptacle. A bit of canine attention, including filling water bowls and offering a biscuit, is also promised. His rates start at $12 per week, making this service affordable for many dog owners.

VIP Petcare Services

(800) 427-7973

www.vipvaccine.com

Hours: Call or check the website for clinic times and locations

Payment: Credit Cards, Checks

Price Range: $

VIP Petcare Services has been providing mobile vaccination clinics at pet and feed stores throughout the Bay Area for almost 10 years. In addition to dog and cat vaccinations, VIP provides microchipping services; blood and fecal testing; deworming; and carries flea, tick, and heartworm products. VIP offers dog and puppy packages in addition to single vaccinations. Check the website for information on mobile clinics in your area.

San Francisco Proper

EMERGENCY PET TRANSPORT

AMERS Animal Ambulance
(877) 426-3771 (emergency)
(925) 261-9111 (office)
www.animalmedics.com
Hours: Every Day 24 Hours
Payment: Credit Cards, Checks
Emergency Fee: $175

Pet Taxi
Bay Area
(415) 386-2534
Hours: Every Day 7 A.M. – 7 P.M.
Emergency Hours: Every Day 24 Hours
Payment: Checks
Price Range: $$/$$$

ANIMAL EMERGENCY FACILITIES

All Animals Emergency Hospital
(415) 566-0530
1333 9th Ave
(between Irving & Judah sts)
San Francisco, California 94122
Hours: Mon - Fri 6 P.M. – 8 A.M.,
Sat - Mon 12 P.M. – 8 A.M.
Payment: Credit Cards, Checks
Price Range: $$

Pets Unlimited

(415) 563-6700
2343 Fillmore St
(@ Washington St)
San Francisco, California 94115
www.petsunlimited.org
Hours: Every Day 24 Hours
Payment: Credit Cards, Checks
Price Range: $$/$$$

ANIMAL POISON HOTLINE

ASPCA Animal Poison Control Center

(888) 4ANI-HELP
Hours: Every Day 24 Hours
Payment: Credit Cards
Consultation Fee: $45

ADOPTION

Mobile *Rocket Dog Rescue*
Castro, The *Best in Show* • *Grateful Dog Rescue* • *One at a Time Rescue* • *Pets Unlimited*
Mission *San Francisco SPCA*
Noe Valley *Noe Valley Pet Co.*

ALTERNATIVE PRODUCTS/SERVICES

Mobile *Canine Romp Around* • *Jennifer Murray Photography*
Bay View *Pet Camp*
Bernal Heights *Bernal Beast*
Castro, The *Best in Show* • *Jeffrey's* • *PuppyCat*
Glen Park *Critter Fritters*
Haight Ashbury *Cole Valley Pets*
Hayes Valley *Babies*
Inner Richmond *B&B Pet Supplies*
Marina, The *Bella and Daisy's*
Noe Valley *Noe Valley Pet Co.*
Parkside *Fishelson, Barbara Fishelson, DVM* • *Petcetera*
Presidio Heights *Drew's K-9 Korner*

San Francisco *Bow Wow Meow*
Soma *Pawtrero Hill Bathhouse and Feed Co.*
West Portal *Happy Pets*

ANESTHESIA-FREE TEETH CLEANING

Castro, The *PuppyCat*
Inner Richmond *B&B Pet Supplies*
Presidio Heights *Drew's K-9 Korner*
Richmond *Cal's Pet Supply*
Soma *Pawtrero Hill Bathhouse and Feed Co.*

DOG BOARDING

Mobile • *Dogwalks.com* • *RUFF 'N READY*
• *Smilin Dogs* **(S)**
Bay View *Pet Camp* • *Pooches' Playtime*
Mission, The *Reigning Dogs & Cats* • *Fog City Doggie Day
Care* **(S)** • *SF Hound Lounge*
Outer Richmond *SF Barking Station*
Parkside *Petcetera*
Paruside *Parkside Pet Grooming*
Soma *O'Paws*

DOG DAY CARE

Mobile *Bark to Basics* **(S)** • *Bone-afide* • *Citizen Kanine
Dogwalking* • *K9to5* • *Malvestiti, Scott* • *puppyDog*
• *RUFF 'N' READY* • *Smilin Dogs* **(S)**
Bay View *Pet Camp* • *Pooches' Playtime*
Mission, The *Reigning Dogs & Cats* • *Fog City Doggie Day
Care* **(S)** • *SF Hound Lounge*
Outer Richmond *SF Barking Station*
Soma *O'Paws*

DOG GROOMING

Mobile *Hodge, Keith* • *K9to5*
Bay View *Pet Camp*

Bernal Heights *Bernal Beast*
Castro, The *Little Ark Grooming Shop, The* • *San Francisco Pet Grooming*
Inner Richmond *Silver Poodle Pet Grooming*
Mission, The *Reigning Dogs & Cats* • *Fog City Doggie Day Care* **(S)** • *Bernie's Pet Supplies and Grooming* • *By George*
Nob Hill *Groom Room* • *Wags*
Noe Valley *VIP Grooming*
Parkside *Petco*
Paruside *Parkside Pet Grooming*
Potrero *Petco*
Russian Hill *Russian Hill Dog Groomers*
San Francisco *Bow Wow Meow*
Sunset *Bill's Doggie Bath-O-Mat*
West Portal *Beauty and the Beasts*
Western Addition *Dunk-N-Dogs* • *Kate's Dog and Cat Salon*

DOG GROOMING—SELF-SERVE
Bernal Heights *Bernal Beast*
Nob Hill *Wags*
Soma *Pawtrero Hill Bathhouse and Feed Co.*
Sunset *Bill's Doggie Bath-O-Mat*

DOG HIKES & SOCIALS
Mobile *DOGMA: The Urban Dog Social Club* • *Dogwalks.com*
Park Merced *Fort Funston*

DOG PARKS—OFF LEASH
Bernal Heights *Bernal Heights Park*
Diamond Heights *Glen Canyon Park* • *Upper Noe Recreation Center*
Haight Ashbury *Buena Vista Park* • *Corona Heights Park* • *Eureka Valley Recreation Center*
Hayes Valley *Alamo Square*
Inner Richmond *Mountain Lake Park*
Marina, The *Fort Mason* • *Marina Green* • *Dolores Park*
Mt Davidson *Mount Davidson*
Noe Valley *Upper Douglass Park*

North Beach *Washington Square*
Outer Richmond *Land's End/Lincoln Park*
Outer Sunset *Ocean Beach*
Pacific Heights *Alta Plaza Park* • *Lafayette Park*
Paradise *Stern Grove*
Park Merced *Fort Funston* • *Lake Merced*
Potrero *McKinley Square*
Presidio *Baker Beach* • *Crissy Field* • *Golden Gate Park*
• *Presidio of San Francisco, The*
Visitacion Valley *McLaren Park*

DOG TRAINING

Mobile *A Better Way Dog Training*
• *Attention to D'tail* • *Bark to Basics* **(S)** • *Citizen Kanine
Dogwalking* • *Dog Gone Good Dog Training* • *Doggie Do
Right Dog Training* • *DOGMA: The Urban Dog Social Club*
• *K9Chops Dog Training* • *Malvestiti, Scott* • *McNamara's
Dog Training* • *Pooch Coach* • *puppyDog*
Parkside *Petco*
Soma *Perfect Paws* • *Carpe Doggum*

DOG WALKING/PET-SITTING

Mobile *Attention to D'tail* • *Ball and Chain, The* • *Bark to
Basics* **(S)** • *Behrends, Dawn* • *Bone-afide*
• *Canine Romp Around* • *Citizen Kanine Dogwalking*
• *Dog Man Walking* • *Dog Nanny* **(S)**
• *Doggy Style* • *DOGMA: The Urban Dog Social Club*
• *Dogwalks.com* • *Dr. Doolittle's Pet Care* • *Hodge, Keith*
• *In-Home Pet Care* • *K-9 Safari* • *K9to5* • *Malvestiti, Scott*
• *On the Go Pet Care* • *puppyDog* • *Ruffhouse Dogs* **(S)**
• *Stenstrom, Elizabeth* • *Urbanhound*
Castro, The *Best in Show*
Marina, The *Fog City Doggie Day Care* **(S)**
Nob Hill *Wags*
Noe Valley *Noe Valley Pet Co.*
Parkside *Petcetera*
Soma *O'Paws*

PET-SUPPLY STORES

Bernal Heights *Bernal Beast*
Castro, The *Pets Unlimited* • *PuppyCat*
Glen Park *Critter Fritters*
Haight Ashbury *Cole Valley Pets*
Hayes Valley *Babies*
Inner Richmond *B&B Pet Supplies*
Marina, The *Amore Animal Supply* • *Animal Connection*
• *Bella and Daisy's* • *Bernie's Pet Supplies and Grooming*
Nob Hill *Wags*
Noe Valley *Noe Valley Pet Co.*
North Beach *North Beach Pet Supplies*
Pacific Heights *Barry for Pets*
Parkside *Petcetera* • *Petco*
Potrero *Petco*
Presidio Heights *Drew's K-9 Korner* • *Pet Source*
• *Urban Pet, The*
Richmond *Cal's Pet Supply* • *Pet Source*
San Francisco *Bow Wow Meow*
Soma *Pawtrero Hill Bathhouse and Feed Co.*
Sunset *Animal Connection*
West Portal *Happy Pets*
Western Addition *George*

VACCINATIONS—LOW-COST

Castro, The *Best in Show*
Glen Park *Critter Fritters*
Inner Richmond *B&B Pet Supplies*
Mission *San Francisco SPCA*
Noe Valley *Noe Valley Pet Co.*
Parkside *Petco*
Potrero *Petco*

CITY DOG PICKS

Mobile *Hodge, Keith*
Hayes Valley *Babies*
Inner Richmond *B&B Pet Supplies*
Marina, The *Fog City Doggie Day Care*
Noe Valley *Noe Valley Pet Co.*
Parkside *Fishelson, Barbara, DVM*
Presidio Heights *Drew's K-9 Korner*
Soma *O'Paws* • *Pawtrero Hill Bathhouse and Feed Co.*
• *Perfect Paws*
Western Addition *George*
West Portal *Beauty and the Beasts*

General Listings

A Better Way Dog Training
(415) 648-DOGS
Hours: By Appt
Payment: Checks
Price Range: $$

Dog trainer Bob Guttierez is the former animal behavior coordinator for the San Francisco SPCA and studied under famed dog trainer Ian Dunbar, the founder of Sirius Puppy Training. He uses whatever tools are necessary to redirect bad behavior, as long as it's humane for the dog. He offers everything from competition obedience to aggressive dog classes. Group classes take place at his Ace Dog Sports facility in Brisbane. He is also available for private classes in circumstances where issues are better addressed at home, such as severe aggression and intense separation anxiety.

Alamo Square
(415) 831-2700
Hayes St @ Steiner St
San Francisco, California 94117

Alamo Square may be a well-known tourist attraction; sightseers come from all over the world for a view of the Painted Ladies Victorians. However, it has also become a popular destination for neighborhood dog owners, who come here for the camaraderie of fellow dog walkers. Despite the leash law, there are always plenty of people with dogs. Come in the morning or the evening for the most active dog scene, and avoid the 12-acre park after dark when the area can get a bit dicey. Water fountains and poop bags are available.

Alta Plaza Park

Jackson St @ Steiner St
San Francisco, California 94115

This terraced park in Pacific Heights attracts well-heeled owners and well-behaved dogs to its official off-leash area. There are plenty of trees for shade, benches for weary guardians and water for panting hounds. Peace is a priority, and an active group of park regulars are on the lookout for aggressive or disruptive dogs. For a peak outdoor experience, visit the park in the morning or late afternoon.

Amore Animal Supply

(415) 436-9788
696 Valencia St
(@ 18th St)
San Francisco, California 94110

Hours: Mon - Fri 10 A.M. - 6:30 P.M., Sat 10 A.M. - 5:30 P.M., Sun 11 A.M. - 5:30 P.M.
Payment: Credit Cards
Price Range: $$

This basic neighborhood pet store located in The Mission is handy if you live around the corner and run out of dog food, but otherwise probably not worth the trip. They have a very limited selection of dog food and supplies. Of course, if you're having your hair done at Garbo—the salon that shares the space—you can pick up some kibble while you're waiting for your color to set.

Animal Connection

Marina Location

(415) 567-5335
2419 Chestnut St
(@ Divisadero St)
San Francisco, California 94123
Hours: Mon - Fri 11 A.M. - 6:30 P.M., Sat 10 A.M. - 5 P.M.,
12 P.M. - 5 P.M.

Sunset Location

(415) 564-6482
2550 Judah St
(@ 31st Ave)
San Francisco, California 94122
Hours: Mon - Fri 10 A.M. - 6:30 P.M., Sat 10 A.M. - 5 P.M.,
Sun 12 P.M. - 5 P.M.

Nob Hill Location

(415) 673-0473
1677 Washington St
(@ Polk St)
San Francisco, California 94109
Hours: Mon - Fri 10 A.M. - 6:30 P.M., Sat 10 A.M. - 5 P.M.,
Sun 12 P.M. - 5 P.M.

Payment: Credit Cards, Checks
Price Range: $$

Animal Connection was established in 1983, and each one of
its stores specializes in something different. The Chestnut
Street location is broken into two storefronts—one for dogs
and one for cats and each stocks adorable toys and basic sup-
plies. The Washington Street store is for pet supplies only. The
Judah Street location is where you go for birds, fish, reptiles
and hamsters (dwarf and teddy bear). You'll know your sense
of smell is working the second you walk in their front door.

Attention to D'tail

(415) 675-0280

www.attentiontodtail.com/dogtraining.htm

Hours: By Appt

Payment: Checks

Price Range: $$

Trainer Youngblood Harris is a standout when it comes to group and one-on-one dog training, adoption evaluation and behavior modification, especially with aggressive dogs. He also offers police dog, schutzhund and AKC obedience training. Particularly convenient is Youngblood's "walk and train" service: He'll pick up your hound for an hour during the day, so she can do her business while he does his business.

B&B Pet Supplies

(415) 221-7711

4820 Geary Blvd

(between 12th & Funston aves)

San Francisco, California 94118

Hours: Tue - Sat 9 A.M. - 8 P.M.

Payment: Credit Cards, Checks

Price Range: $

Making regular appearances in *SF Weekly's* "Best of..." lists, local fave B&B Pet Supplies has a cult following in the city. Offering an extensive selection of pet gear and food, including raw brands like Prairie and Grandad's, B&B's prices are exceptionally competitive. Check with them for a schedule of their low-cost vaccinations, and don't leave the store without buying one of the freakishly popular squeaky balls you'll see on the counter. Your dog will love it!

Babies

(415) 701-7387
235 Gough St
San Francisco, California 94102
www.babiessf.com
Hours: Mon - Fri 11 A.M. - 8 P.M., Sat 11 A.M. - 6 P.M.,
Sun 12 P.M. - 5 P.M.
Payment: Credit Cards
Price Range: $$

The ultimate dog boutique, Babies has what is arguably the largest collar and leash selection in San Francisco: everything from black studded collars to silk brocade gentle leaders. You can also choose from a variety of beds, carriers and clothes to completely outfit your little hipster hound. If you're looking for gifts, Babies has dog-themed shower curtains, drawer knobs and other hard-to-find tchotchkes. In addition to a selection of premium food, they also stock raw foods and will special order anything they don't have on hand.

Baker Beach

Bowley St
(@ Lincoln Blvd)
San Francisco, California 94129
Hours: Apr - Oct 6 A.M. - 10 P.M.; Oct - Apr 6 A.M. - 7 P.M.

Burning Man is what put Baker Beach on the map. The original festival took place at this clothing-optional beach. However, this stretch of sand is currently in the spotlight because it falls within the highly contentious GGNRA, where dogs who were formerly allowed to run free are now required to be on leash. Nonetheless, the view of the Golden Gate Bridge and the geographically desirable beach make Baker a winner with dogs and their owners. Avoid the area on sunny summer days when parking is impossible, and the beach is packed. Water is available in the restrooms.

Ball and Chain, The
(415) 215-9923
Hours: By Appt
Payment: Checks
Price Range: $$$

About 99 percent of the time walking your dog is no burden. The other 1 percent—say when you'd like to go out after work instead of going home to take him out—he becomes the proverbial ball and chain. Dog walker Laurie Page can cut you loose. Loving, attentive and experienced, Page groups her charges by size and attitude when she takes them to the park for an hour of exercise. She'll work with your dog's trainer to ensure that she's reinforcing positive habits, and she's available for pet-sitting.

Bark to Basics
(415) 387-7877
www.bark-to-basics.com
Hours: By Appt
Payment: Checks
Price Range: $$

Shura Kelly gives power to the little pooches with her dog daycare service and training. Dogs must be under 20 pounds to qualify for her fun-filled activities, which include field trips to area parks, play sessions in her backyard, and of course, naps. Between romps, pups are put through their training paces by Shura herself, a graduate of the SF SPCA training program. She also offers pick-ups and drop-offs, as well as transportation to the vet or groomer.

Barry for Pets

(415) 346-8899
1840 Fillmore St
(between Bush & Sutter sts)
San Francisco, California 94115
Hours: Mon - Sat 10 A.M. - 6 P.M., Sun 11 A.M. - 5 P.M.
Payment: Credit Cards, Checks
Price Range: $$

This Fillmore Street pet-supply shop is a handy neighborhood resource in an area known more for boutiques than for basics. It has just about everything you might need, packed from floor to ceiling, including beds, carriers, bowls and toys as well as the ever-essential Giants and 49ers sports jerseys for your hound. And if you're in the market for canine sustenance, the store stocks premium, all-natural foods.

Beauty and the Beasts

(415) 681-6346
537 Taraval St
(between 15th & 16th aves)
San Francisco, California 94116
Hours: Tue - Fri 8:30 A.M. - 5:30 P.M., Sat 8:30 A.M. - 4 P.M.
Payment: Checks
Price Range: $$

Dogs have free run of the place while they wait for their turn in the tub at this popular 37-year-old institution that is renowned for its canine styling. Dogs are mostly fluffed dry, then cage-dried for the last 10 minutes. Call ahead for appointments because the shop is busy. They book up to a month in advance during the holiday season, but their long list of loyals seem perfectly happy to wait as long as necessary to get an appointment in this friendly salon.

Behrends, Dawn

(415) 609-4478
Hours: By Appt
Payment: Checks
Price Range: $

A professional dog walker since 1998, Dawn keeps her groups small and varies her destinations according to the needs of the group so dogs don't get overstrained or under-exercised. She minimizes travel time—dogs get a full 60 minutes outside. And Dawn concentrates on her charges, not on chit-chat, to ensure that her dogs get all the attention they need and deserve. She also offers dog-sitting. Areas covered: Bernal Heights and Potrero Hill.

Bella and Daisy's

(415) 440-7007
1750 Union St
(between Octavia & Gough sts)
San Francisco, California 94123
www.bellaanddaisys.com
Payment: Credit Cards, Checks
Price Range: $$

Offering fabulous high-end accessories as well as healing and pampering alternative treatments, this newcomer to the city's dog-boutique scene has quickly made a name for itself. Bella also offers fresh-baked dog treats: Tasty choices include martini glass-shaped cookies and custom birthday cakes. If you're looking for something a little more substantial, check out the selection of all-natural, homeopathic and raw foods. Alternative-therapy treatments are along the lines of acupuncture, Reiki, touch therapy and massage-type spa services.

Bernal Beast

(415) 643-7800
509 Cortland Ave
(@ Andover St)
San Francisco, California 94110
Hours: Mon - Fri 11 A.M. - 7 P.M., Sat 10 A.M. - 6 P.M.,
Sun 11 A.M. - 5 P.M.
Payment: Credit Cards, Checks
Price Range: $$

Bernal Beast was voted Best Pet Store in the *San Francisco Bay Guardian's* 2003 "Best of..." issue, and it's easy to see why. Employees are knowledgeable, the store stocks hard-to-find supplies, specializes in premium and raw foods, and holistic and homeopathic supplements. They will also special order whatever they don't stock. You can take advantage of the self-service bathing facilities or drop off your pal for a professional 'do. Groomer Sylvia dries your dog according to your wishes. If you need a sitter or walker, the Beast offers a binder full of referrals.

Bernal Heights Park

(415) 831-2700
Bernal Heights Blvd
(@ Carver St)
San Francisco, California 94110
Hours: Mon - Fri 10 A.M. - 5 P.M., Sat - Sun 9 A.M. - 5 P.M.

It stands to reason that one of the most dog-friendly neighborhoods in the city would feature a park where dogs can run free. The top of Bernal Hill and the section bounded by Bernal Heights Boulevard is the official off-leash area. Come for spectacular city views and friendly company in addition to canine companionship. However, the park offers little in the way of amenities, so bring water and poop bags. Also, be on the lookout for poisonous foxtails.

Bernie's Pet Supplies and Grooming

(415) 550-2323
1367 Valencia St
(between 24th & 25th sts)
San Francisco, California 94110
www.berniesgrooming.net
Hours: Mon - Thu 8 A.M. - 6:30 P.M., Fri - Sat 8 A.M. - 6 P.M.
Payment: Credit Cards, Checks
Price Range: $$

Bernie's is part pet-supply store, part groomer and part mural extravaganza. They stock healthy quantites of food, treats, beds, collars, toys and even vacuum cleaners with enough muscle to suck up pet hair. Grooming takes place in a back room where dogs' coats and skins are evaluated to ensure that the proper shampoos are used. All dogs are dried by hand. For special grooming requests, your best bet is to speak with Bernie himself.

Best in Show

(415) 863-7387
300 Sanchez St
(@ 16th St)
San Francisco, California 94114
www.bestinshowsf.com
Hours: Mon - Fri 11 A.M. - 8 P.M., Sat 10 A.M. - 6 P.M.,
Sun 11 A.M. - 5 P.M.
Payment: Credit Cards, Checks
Price Range: $$$

Owners George and Richard come from a design background, and it shows. Their sleek shop is packed with premium dog-food brands and a terrific—if expensive—selection of bowls, carriers, beds and collars: an estimated 300 of them, from everyday rhinestone numbers to $100 Swarovski-crystal stunners. You can even sign your dog up with the store's gift registry. Regularly scheduled events include Milo Foundation adoptions as well as pet psychic readings and portrait render-ings. Pet-sitting and dog-walking services are also available.

Bill's Doggie Bath-O-Mat
(415) 661-6950
3928 Irving St
(between 40th & 41st aves)
San Francisco, California 94122
Hours: Tue - Sat 7:30 A.M. - 5 P.M.
Payment: Checks
Price Range: $$
Owner Bill Ceragioli, a 16-year veteran groomer, couldn't have picked a better location for his grooming salon. When you can see Ocean Beach from your front door, you can count on a constant stream of sandy pups getting into the tubs. Bill offers both self- and full-service grooming. He offers all-natural shampoos and uses hand dryers only. Dogs waiting for to be groomed get free run of the shop, along with Bill's sidekicks Molly and Nino. All breeds are welcome.

Bone-afide
(415) 845-6867
Hours: By Appt
Payment: Checks
Price Range: $$
Partners Lorrie Baranco and Rachel Porter hold two, hour-long structured playgroups a day and pride themselves on their ability to put together groups of dogs that get along with one another. Dogs in their care tend to be of the larger variety, and they don't shy away from pitbulls. If you need someone to care for your canine while you're away, they will cater to your pup's every need—in your home or theirs. Bone-afide covers The Mission, Bernal Heights and Potrero Hill.

Bow Wow Meow

(415) 440-2845
2150 Polk St
(between Broadway & Vallejo sts)
San Francisco, California 94109
Hours: Mon - Fri 10 A.M. - 8 P.M., Sat - Sun 10 A.M. - 6 P.M.
Payment: Credit Cards, Checks
Price Range: $$

Both locations of Bow Wow Meow—the wildly popular SF newcomer and the Peninsula staple—carry high-end food, an enormous selection of beds and all sorts of little accessories. Bow Wow also stocks plenty of gift-type items for the animal lover in your life. Offerings include full-service grooming, and their experienced groomers get raves. They bring in trainers for consultations and specialists, such as doggie dentists.

Buena Vista Park

(415) 831-2700
Haight St
(between E & W Buena Vista)
San Francisco, California 94117

Buena Vista features scenic views, beautiful woods, and best of all, a leash-free zone for your dog. However, many say it's worth leashing up to venture beyond the official off-leash area that is bounded by Central and Haight streets. Avoid grassy areas in the spring because of foxtails and stick to the trails to avoid run-ins with the area's homeless population. There are no facilities, so come equipped.

By George
(415) 648-4846
2979A 21st St
(between Folsom & Treat sts)
San Francisco, California 94110
Hours: Tue - Sat 8 A.M. - 5 P.M.
Payment: Credit Cards
Price Range: $$
Groomer George has hung his hat for over 22 years in this old blue pioneer-style building that's located in The Mission. And he still clips his pups the old-fashioned way—with a pair of scissors. He uses all-natural shampoos, and his charges are lovingly dried by hand. George doesn't turn away any breeds—or cats for that matter.

Cal's Pet Supply
(415) 386-1720
5950 California St
(between 21st & 22nd aves)
San Francisco, California 94121
Hours: Mon - Fri 10 A.M. - 7 P.M., Sat 10 A.M. - 6 P.M.,
Sun 10 A.M. - 5 P.M.
Payment: Credit Cards, Checks
Price Range: $$
In business for 18 years, Cal's is a nuts-and-bolts pet-supply store that stocks brands, such as California Natural and Newman's Own as well as a variety of gourmet treats. If your pet needs a new bed or bowl, you'll find that here too. The store's bulletin board features pictures of local adoptable pups. And for those who prefer their dogs to have kissably fresh breath, Cal's offers anesthesia-free teeth cleaning on the first Saturday of every month.

Canine Romp Around

(415) 279-6344

www.canineromparound.com

Hours: By Appt
Payment: Checks
Price Range: $$

Dog walker and pet-sitter Josie Allen likes to give her all to the dogs in her charge, so she restricts her packs to five dogs per walk. You can also ante up for her solo dog-walking service. Josie will board pups at her house or move into yours for the night. If you choose the latter, she'll tend to your mail, trash and plants. She's not squeamish and will administer medications and injections for an extra fee. In case of emergency, medical attention is close at hand—Josie's husband is a vet.

Carpe Doggum

(415) 385-8425

www.dogslife.biz

Hours: By Appt
Payment: Checks
Price Range: $$

Jacqueline, who is the training and programs manager at A Dog's Life, wants to help you seize the day with your new dog or perhaps even help you seize the perfect dog to fit your lifestyle. She can help you screen candidates at one of the local rescue organizations, and then she will suggest ways to rearrange your home for the transition. She'll probably suggest you read Dr. Ian Dunbar's book *Before and After You Get Your Puppy*, not just because her own shelter dog Studebaker Hawk is the cover pup, but also because she thinks the book gets everything right. She also resolves on-leash aggression issues.

Citizen Kanine Dogwalking

(415) 845-8299
Hours: By Appt
Payment: Checks
Price Range: $$

Voted Best Dog Walker in the *San Francisco Bay Guardian's* 2003 Best of the Bay issue, Jennifer Joyce offers a variety of dog services, including off-leash playgroups (for dogs up to 50 pounds), dog-sitting, private walks and training. She's a recent graduate of the SF SPCA Academy of Dog Training and includes herding dogs among her specialties. For dog walking and pet-sitting, her service area includes Noe Valley, Bernal Heights, Twin Peaks, Diamond Heights, Inner Sunset and the Castro. For training, she covers the entire Bay Area. Keep an eye out for a company name change in the near future.

Cole Valley Pets

(415) 564-8811
910 Cole St
(@ Carl St)
San Francisco, California 94117
Hours: Mon - Sun 10 A.M. - 8 P.M.
Payment: Credit Cards, Checks
Price Range: $$

This general store for pets is a neighborhood staple. It survived the dot-com bust by continuing to do what it does very well: provide good service from an informed staff. Manager Elizabeth has a knack for linking pet owners with local walkers, trainers and pet-sitters. Cole Valley stocks a wide variety of gear and supplies, including certified organic food lines such as Newman's Own. The frequent-shopper program offers discounts to repeat customers.

Corona Heights Park

(415) 831-2700
Roosevelt Way @ Museum Way
San Francisco, California 94114

There is plenty of room for pups to play at Corona Heights Park while owners take in the incredible view of the city. This off-leash dog run, nestled at the foot of the Randall Museum, is actually fenced in, so you don't have to worry about your dog wandering off. The mud can get a bit out of control during the winter, and foxtails and poison oak can rear their ugly heads the rest of the year, so tread carefully. And it can get breezy, so bundle up.

Crissy Field

(415) 561-4323
Mitchell St @ Mason St
San Francisco, California 94129

A favorite among dog lovers, Crissy Field is in the midst of a heated leash debate. For the time being, dogs must be leashed, but that won't get in the way of the magnificent views as you walk along the beach or on one of the maintained paths. Many choose to defy the leash laws, but if you join them, be aware that rangers ticket offenders without impunity. Weekends are busy with windsurfers and families, but you often have the beach to yourself on weekdays. You may want to take advantage of the showers, water fountains and poop bags.

Critter Fritters

(415) 239-7387
670 Chenery St
(@ Diamond St)
San Francisco, California 94131

Hours: Mon - Fri 10 A.M. - 7 P.M., Sat 10 A.M. - 6 P.M.,
Sun 11 A.M. - 5 P.M.
Payment: Credit Cards, Checks
Price Range: $$

This Glen Park pet-supply store has been a neighborhood
institution for over 15 years, referring customers to local
services and supporting rescue groups with a large bulletin
board on the front door of the store. They stock a healthy
variety of premium dog foods, including raw foods, holistic
concoctions and vegetarian kibble. Critters also offers a variety
of pet supplies, including bulk biscuits, and will special order
items. Check for a schedule of their low-cost vaccinations.

D5Dog

www.d5dog.org
Payment: Credit Cards
Price Range: $

D5Dog—the San Francisco District 5 Dog Ownership
Group—is an advocacy, outreach, service and education
group in the city's Haight, Western Addition and Inner Sunset
neighborhoods. The group holds training classes, seminars,
fundraisers and park cleanup days to encourage responsible dog
ownership and positive community interaction. A $20 member-
ship fee gives you access to discussion groups, e-mail updates
and special events. Check out the website for a calendar of
upcoming events and helpful dog-related links.

Dog Gone Good Dog Training

(415) 437-0848
www.doggonegood.org
Hours: By Appt
Payment: Checks
Price Range: $$

Trainer Mike Wombacher tackles all dog issues. He mainly uses
positive reinforcement but also employs corrections if a dog—
especially one with behavioral problems—needs them. He

believes strongly in owner participation and follow-through. He's been known to cut short training with unwilling human participants. Mike has written two dog-training books, *There's a Baby in the House!* and *There's a Puppy in the House!*, and is following up their success with companion videos.

Dog Man Walking

(415) 661-1332
Hours: By Appt
Payment: Checks
Price Range: $$

Dog walker Jerry Howe has been in the biz for over four years and clearly he has found his calling. He knows how to keep things fun on his hour-long walks to Alamo Square or Bernal Hill, and he welcomes dog-walking charges into his home for overnights when owners are out of town. If you have any doubts about his affinity for dogs, check out the calendar he's produced featuring his animal friends. His covers Cole Valley, Noe Valley, the Haight and Alamo Square.

Dog Nanny

(650) 994-4144
www.nannydogma.com
Hours: By Appt
Payment: Checks
Price Range: $$$

Lynn, the Dog Nanny, provides group and solo dog-walking, pet-sitting and pet-limo services. Group walks are at least an hour long. She doesn't call it a day until everyone's had enough fun. Her philosophy is to give her charges the same love and attention they get from their owner. Her service area ranges from Millbrae to San Francisco.

Doggie Do Right Dog Training

(415) 786-9157
www.doggie-do-right.com
Hours: By Appt
Payment: Checks
Price Range: $$

SF SPCA Academy of Dog Training graduate, Sue Minsuk focuses on teaching people how their dogs learn, better equipping them to train their pups. She shows how to use positive reinforcement to help you build a relationship with your dog based on trust and respect. Sue provides in-home obedience training, puppy training, private on-leash training and socialization for pups with behavioral problems. Her service area covers all of San Francisco proper and the northern Peninsula.

Doggy Style

Hours: By Appt
Payment: Checks
Price Range: $$

Pet-sitter Lisa Walsh isn't big on dog runs, preferring instead to give her canine clients a full hour of vigorous exercise in a large park. Walsh's packs are limited to six dogs, and she knows how to handle an emergency should it arise: She's certified in pet first aid and CPR. As if she doesn't do enough walking on the job, Walsh also regularly volunteers her time to walk dogs at the ACC and SPCA.

DOGMA: The Urban Dog Social Club

(415) 307-6263
Hours: By Appt
Payment: Checks
Price Range: $$

Partners Al and Dianne take pups on two-to-three-hour day hikes at Fort Funston. Most of their charges have been lifelong friends, which is what makes the Urban Dog Social Club so congenial. They also take special-needs dogs on solo walks and offer training and puppy-proofing services. Their service area includes Potrero Hill, SOMA, The Mission, the Castro and West Portal.

Dogwalks.com
(415) 673-8684
www.dogwalks.com
Hours: By Appt
Payment: Checks
Price Range: $$

Dogwalks.com can just about do it all when it comes to caring for your pooch. Owner Julia and her team take play groups of four to six dogs to the park, where they get a minimum of 45 minutes park time, not including travel time. Pups under 25 pounds have their own special playgroup. Dogwalks also sits and offers limited boarding; dog-walking clients are given priority for their limited boarding space. In-home pet-sitting services consist of morning, afternoon and two evening walks. The most recent addition to their services is pre-parvo puppy daycare. Their service area includes Russian Hill, Nob Hill, North Beach, Pacific Heights, Marina, Presidio Heights, Laurel Village, Western Addition, Upper Haight and Cole Valley.

Dolores Park
(415) 554-9529
19th St
(@ Dolores St)
San Francisco, California 94110

It's no surprise that Dolores Park was voted Best Dog Park in the *San Francisco Bay Guardian* 2003 Best of the Bay issue. Located in The Mission, the park boasts an active and colorful dog population. The official off-leash area is south of the tennis courts, between Church and Dolores streets, although pups don't always adhere to these boundaries. The fountain will help refresh your pooch while the Dolores Park Cafe will handle pick-me-ups for humans.

Dr. Doolittle's Pet Care

(415) 595-3667
Hours: By Appt
Payment: Checks
Price Range: $$

There are actually two Dr. Doolittles—Eleanor and Jennifer—and they provide house calls. They've been in business for seven years, picking up dogs and taking them for 30-to 50-minute walks at Mountain Lake Park. They restrict their pack size to seven dogs, which makes for more manageable off-leash walks. Dr. Doolittle's also provides dog-sitting services for their regular dog-walking clients. Doolittle serves Pacific Heights, Laurel Heights and Marina.

Drew's K-9 Korner

(415) 221-0060
3518 Geary Blvd
(between Stanyan St & Arguello Blvd)
San Francisco, California 94118
Hours: Mon - Sat 10 A.M. - 5 P.M.
Payment: Credit Cards, Checks
Price Range: $$

This store may be the Bay Area's holistic jackpot. In business for eight years, owner Drew sells only organic, raw and holistic (whole grain and whole vegetable) pet foods; he also stocks more commercial brands like Solid Gold and Wellness. (Even though they're cooked, they're still holistic.) He has recently added a new dehydrated raw food called Honest Kitchen. Though his focus is on solving pet health problems at home, Drew works closely with many holistic vets. Monthly anesthesia-free teeth cleaning is also available at the store.

Dunk-N-Dogs

(415) 931-1108
2178 Bush St
(@ Fillmore St)
San Francisco, California 94115
Hours: Mon - Sat 9 A.M. - 5:30 P.M.
Payment: Credit Cards, Checks
Price Range: $$

Dunk-N-Dogs has been sprucing up pups for 10 years. Dogs are greeted by name and ushered into the store, where they get the run of the place until it's their turn in the tub. The groomers will take on any breed. However, aggressive dogs don't get the same roaming privileges. Hypoallergenic shampoos are the norm, and dogs get dried mostly by hand.

Eureka Valley Recreation Center

(415) 554-9528
100 Collingwood St
(@ 19th St)
San Francisco, California 94114

Once entirely off-leash, Eureka Valley Recreation Center is now one of the city's many dog parks that is under review— meaning its off-leash status could get yanked at any time. For the time being, you can find the fenced-in, off-leash area east of the baseball diamond. It even includes a tennis court, minus the net.

Fishelson, Barbara DVM

(415) 664-4204
3620 Wawona St
(@ Great Hwy)
San Francisco, California 94116

Hours: Tue 10 A.M. - 6 P.M., Wed 12 A.M. - 8 P.M.,
Thu 10 A.M. - 4 P.M.
Emergencies Hours: By Appt
Payment: Credit Cards, Checks
Price Range: $$

Dr. Fishelson is the city's foremost classical homeopathic vet.
Instead of using medications to suppress symptoms (the
Western way), she works to restore the system's natural balance
through homeopathic remedies and nutrition. However, Dr.
Fishelson has also studied Western medicine and is clear on
the parameters of what can be treated with homeopathy. And
she'll work with Western practitioners in areas such as surgery
and radiology. If you can't get to her office, she provides home
consultations. She also performs home euthanasia, believing a
pet shouldn't spend her final moments in a vet's office.

Fog City Doggie Day Care

(415) 409-3647
1488 Lombard St
(@ Franklin)
San Francisco, California 94123
www.fogcitydog.com
Hours: Mon - Fri 7 A.M. - 7 P.M.
Payment: Credit Cards, Checks
Price Range: $$$

Fog City is the preferred day-care choice for posh pups in
the city's northern neighborhoods. The facility is only a stick's
throw from Fort Mason and the staff takes advantage of the
close proximity with daily walks to the park. Owners with
separation anxiety can check in on their pups via Fog City's
webcam. And if you live nearby, you can take advantage of
their $10 pick-up and drop-off services. Fog City also provides
bathing services for those who don't want their dog to bring
home any dirt from the day's play.

Fort Funston

(415) 239-2366
Skyline Blvd
(near John Muir Dr)
San Francisco, California 94132
Hours: Dawn to Dusk

Fort Funston is a popular spot for hikes and beach play with your pup. It's a testament to its glory that people continue to come here in droves even though dogs are now required to be leashed. The leash issue is an ongoing battle between dog owners and the National Park Service, and rangers ticket violators enthusiastically. Nevertheless, it's worth the effort to scramble down the dune trails or the stairs to the beach. Be careful to avoid unstable areas and closed wildlife zones. Also, make sure to fill up on water at the parking lot before heading down to the ocean.

Fort Mason

(415) 561-4700
Bay St
(@ Franklin)
San Francisco, California 94123

This popular dog-walking spot, perched atop a hill, gives you the perfect vantage point to take in Marina Green, the Golden Gate Bridge and the western expanse of the city. Although leashes are the law, some owners—after carefully looking for rangers—can't resist letting their dogs off leash for a game of catch. Of particular note to male dogs is the yellow fire hydrant planted in the middle of the park—perfect for territory marking. And all dogs will enjoy the ground-level doggie water fountain, located by the bathrooms.

George

(415) 447-5248
2411 California St
(@ Fillmore St)
San Francisco, California 94115
www.georgesf.com
Hours: Mon - Fri 11 A.M. - 6 P.M., Sat 10 A.M. - 6 P.M.,
Sun 11 A.M. - 6 P.M.
Payment: Credit Cards, Checks
Price Range: $$$

When George opened its doors more than 12 years ago, it instantly became the prototype for posh pet boutiques. The store has a loyal following that can't get enough of the perennially hip, quality products. George's two Bay Area locations are styled like classic general stores, filled with homemade treats, toys and highbrow dog fashions. If you can't get to either of the stores, browse their website or check your local pet boutique for genuine George accessories.

Glen Canyon Park

(415) 337-4705
Bosworth St
(@ O'Shaughnessy St)
San Francisco, California 94131
Hours: Every Day 9 A.M. to 9 P.M.

The good news is you will quickly forget you're in an urban area—and adjacent to a shopping center—when you're in the midst of Glen Canyon. The bad news is that the rolling hills, dense brush and rock formations make this park a challenging dog-walking spot. Dogs must be on leash, which will help protect them and you from the bountiful poison oak in the area. There is no water in the park, so fill up your canteen at the playground before heading off.

Golden Gate Park

(415) 831-2700
Fulton St, Lincoln Way & Stanyon St
(bounded by Great Hwy)
San Francisco, California 94117
www.parks.sfgov.org
Hours: Dawn to Dusk

Within the more than 1,000 acres of Golden Gate Park are four official off-leash dog walking areas: the area bounded by Lincoln Way, King Drive, 2nd and 7th avenues; the northeast corner of the park at Stanyan and Grove streets; the fenced area bounded by King Drive, Middle Drive, 34th and 38th avenues; and the fenced-in dog training area at 38th Avenue and Fulton Street. Although an oasis by urban park standards, there are certainly obstacles to avoid, including traffic, homeless people, foxtails, leftover garbage from littering picnickers and the bison herd (no danger to you, but your pup may be caught a little off-guard).

Grateful Dog Rescue

(415) 587-1121
P.O. Box 411013
San Francisco, California 94141
www.doctorhu.tripod.com/gratefuldogs
Hours: By Appt
Payment: Checks
Price Range: $

Michelle Parris, a former San Francisco Animal Care and Control volunteer, found it impossible to leave so-called unadoptable pets at the shelter to be euthanized, so she founded Grateful Dog Rescue in an effort to save as many animals as possible. After leaving the shelter, dogs are fostered by volunteers and are spayed or neutered before adoption. All adoptees must go through an application, interview and home-inspection process to ensure that pets don't end up back in the system. Check out the website for pictures of adoptable dogs.

Groom Room

(415) 571-5248
1437 Pacific Ave
(between Larkin & Hyde sts)
San Francisco, California 94109
Hours: Tue - Sat 8 A.M. - 6 P.M.
Payment: Credit Cards, Checks
Price Range: $$$

The Groom Room has stood the test of time. It's been around for 40 years, and the current groomer and manager, Dave Passey, has been at it for 12 years. He will handle any breed of dog (cats and birds are also welcome) with a variety of shampoos on hand to treat any skin or coat condition. And after a cut—hand scissoring is Dave's specialty—your pup will be hand dried.

Happy Pets

(415) 566-2952
709 Taraval St
(between 17th & 18th aves)
San Francisco, California 94116
Hours: Mon - Sat 11 A.M. - 6 P.M., Sun By Appt
Payment: Credit Cards, Checks
Price Range: $$

Happy Pets is not only the source for hormone-free, "human consumable" (a step up from "human grade") pet foods like Grandad's, it's also home to San Francisco's only organic canine bakery. Organic sweet potato bars and the pup-tart (a pastry shell stuffed with simmered barley) are hot items; crispy sesame garlic hearts are so good they're often consumed in the store by dog owners. The all-time favorite? A 15-piece canine confection called the Gold Box. Rodent and other small-animal treats are also available.

Hodge, Keith

(415) 812-6115
Hours: By Appt
Payment: Checks
Price Range: $

If you're looking for an alternative to impersonal kennels, take your pooch over to Keith Hodge's house. Keith and his partner Patrick provide short-and long-term pet-sitting with all the comforts of home. They even welcome dogs with special needs. With a dog park a block away, your dog will get in plenty of playtime. And Keith is a professional dog groomer at VIP Groomers, so you may find your pup cleaner when you pick her up than when you left her.

In-Home Pet Care

(415) 806-9479
www.in-homepetcare.com
Hours: By Appt
Payment: Checks
Price Range: $$

Anne of In-Home Pet Care will give your pet lots of TLC in a stress-free environment—your own home. She's also a vet tech, so she definitely knows what she's doing when it comes time to administer medications and injections to special-needs pets. Her pet-sitting services include making your house look lived in by rotating lights and bringing in the mail, and she'll even water the plants.

Jeffrey's

(415) 864-1414
3809 18th St
(@ Church St)
San Francisco, California 94112
Hours: Mon - Sun 10 A.M. - 9 P.M.

Payment: Credit Cards, Checks
Price Range: $$

Jeffrey has done so well with his fresh, organic, vet-approved raw dog food that he has opened his own store. In addition to his own concoctions, his store stocks a variety of premium organic and all-natural foods, as well as homeopathic reme- dies. Jeffrey's also carries attractive dog accessories, beds, carriers, shampoos and toys. And for a minimum $50 purchase, Jeffrey's will deliver anywhere in the city.

Jennifer Murray Photography

(415) 509-1492

www.mphotography.com

Hours: By Appt
Payment: Checks
Price Range: $$$

There's more to Jennifer and her photographs than meets the eye. Not only is she a gifted photographer, but she's a SF SPCA-certified dog trainer. She finds that knowing the right approach to take with her subjects helps her get the shot she wants. You have the option of choosing from three standard packages to capture your pup on film or creating a custom package. A portion of her income is donated to the SF SPCA, PAWS and the Milo Foundation, among other groups.

K-9 Safari

(415) 305-5424

Hours: By Appt
Payment: Checks
Price Range: $$

Husband-and-wife duo Jay and Megan have been tag-team dog walkers for three years, specializing in tiring your high- energy dogs through off-leash walks in Buena Vista Park, Stern Grove and Fort Funston. They restrict the number of dogs per walk to six, and will pick up pups from Lower Pacific Heights to the Castro (west of Gough to the ocean).

K9Chops Dog Training

(415) 751-9941
San Francisco, California
www.k9chops.com
Hours: By Appt
Payment: Credit Cards, Checks
Price Range: $$

Trainer Joanie Levin-Yarlick specializes in shy, fearful and aggressive dogs. She's seen plenty of them as a behavior evaluator for animals pending vicious-dog hearings at Animal Care and Control. If your pup's in need of a few basic commands, she's got the credentials for that too. She's an AKC Canine Good Citizen Evaluator and a graduate of the esteemed SF SPCA Dog Training Academy. Ask about her discounts for shelter and rescue dogs.

K9to5

(415) 227-4729
90 Welsh St
(@ 4th St)
San Francisco, California 94107
www.k9to5.com
Hours: Mon - Fri 7 A.M. - 7 P.M.
Payment: Credit Cards, Checks
Price Range: $$$

Want your dog happy and exhausted at the end of the day? K9to5 can make it happen. For nearly eight years, city dogs have burned off steam in this pleasant, no-frills dog day-care center. Large or energetic pups cavort on the ground floor, while small, shy or aging dogs have an upper room to themselves. A single visit is $32; the bargain is the $455 monthly package. For a modest additional fee, K9's staff will feed your dog or take him for an outside walk.

Kate's Dog and Cat Salon

(415) 563-5283
1333 Fulton St
(@ Divisadero St)
San Francisco, California 94117
Hours: Mon - Tue 8 A.M. - 6 P.M., Thu - Fri 8 A.M. - 6 P.M.,
Sat 9 A.M. - 5 P.M.
Payment: Credit Cards, Checks
Price Range: $$

The philosophy here is definitely quality over quantity. Kate, who has been grooming for almost 20 years, employs seven groomers in her shop. They take their time and tailor their grooming styles and tools to the temperament of each dog. Their methodical manner means they are able to take all breeds, even dogs other groomers turn away. Kate's uses a variety of non-toxic shampoos, depending on the coat and sensitivity of your dog's skin. If your pooch has fleas or has been skunked, Kate's can help. All dogs are hand dried.

Lafayette Park

(415) 831-2700
Sacramento St
(@ Octavia St)
San Francisco, California 94115

This Pacific Heights park gets a lot of dog traffic, particularly in the mornings and evenings. The official leash-free zone is off of Sacramento Street, between Octavia and Laguna streets. Make sure your pup is well trained because there are a lot of distractions—from babies to sunbathers to traffic. Come prepared with poop bags and water; neither are available at the park. Pups must be 30 pounds or less.

Lake Merced

(415) 831-2700
Lake Merced Blvd
(@ Sunset Blvd)
San Francisco, California 94132

Were it not for the questionable water quality, this spring-fed fresh water lake would be the ideal place to take your dog for a dip. It's only at this municipal park's northern end—where Lake Merced Boulevard meets Middlefield Drive—that your dog can ditch his leash. However, there's a 4.4 mile trail that's pleasant to walk on, and there is beach access to the lake. Technically, the water is off limits, but many people look the other way when water-loving dogs slip into the lake for a swim.

Land's End/Lincoln Park

(415) 561-4700
El Camino Del Mar
(@ Point Lobos Ave between Geary & 25th sts)
San Francisco, California 94121

Hours: Dawn to Dusk

You can take your leashed pup on the coastal trail from Lincoln Park to Land's End, explore the ruins of the Sutro Baths, or frolic at Fort Miley, all at this spectacular park in the city's northwest corner. Should you be tempted to unleash your dog, be aware that park rangers regularly issue citations. Be careful on the trails because there are some steep drop-offs due to cliff erosion. And bring plenty of water because you'll be hard-pressed to find any in the park.

Little Ark Grooming Shop, The

(415) 626-7574
748 14th St
(@ Belcher St)
San Francisco, California 94114
Hours: Tue 8 A.M. - 6 P.M., Thu - Sat 9 A.M. - 6 P.M.
Payment: Credit Cards, Checks
Price Range: $$

You can't miss The Little Ark, which received the *SF Weekly's* award for Best Pet Grooming. Just look for piles of tennis balls and rawhide bones in the windows, and inside you'll find owner Barbara Wood enjoying the constant interaction with her clients, with not a cage in sight. She uses all-natural shampoos and hand dryers, that is unless your dog is too timid to be dried by hand. Barbara, who's been grooming almost 30 years, gives back to the community by contributing her services to PAWS.

Malvestiti, Scott

(415) 431-3648
www.sfdogwalkers.com
Hours: By Appt
Payment: Checks
Price Range: $$$

Recommended by both trainers and dog owners, Scott has been in the dog-walking, training and day-care business for six years. A graduate of the Marin Humane Society's Dog Training Academy, Scott has ample time to flex his training muscle during his daily walks with dogs of every disposition. He'll even take on fearful, undersocialized and aggressive types.

Marina Green

Marina Blvd
(between Scott & Buchanan sts)
San Francisco, California 94123
Extending from Fort Mason to the Presidio, Marina Green
serves as the backyard of many Marina residents and their
dogs. Technically, dogs are required to be leashed. Not all
locals abide by this law, but be aware: The park borders busy
Marina Boulevard and is a large multi-use space, so make sure
your dog is well behaved and under voice control. The Safeway
on the east end and a little snack bar on the west end of the
green are good places to stock up on snacks and water.

McKinley Square

(415) 831-2700
20th St
(@ Vermont St)
San Francisco, California 94107
This Potrero park, which affords scenic vistas of both the city
and Highway 101, is a popular dog-walking spot, especially
now that a fence blocks the hazardous cliff leading down to
the freeway. The off-leash area is on the western slope of the
park, near San Bruno Avenue and 20th Street. Outside the
playground is a grassy area that dogs particularly enjoy. It also
offers a ground-level water fountain for thirsty dogs.

McLaren Park

(415) 831-2700
(@ Mansell St)
San Francisco, California 94134
Hours: Dawn to Dusk

True, McLaren Park is in a dodgy part of town. And yes, the busy Mansell Street does bisect it. Nonetheless, it has a lot to offer the city's dog population. The park is popular with dog walkers, so there's plenty of canine companionship, and because it's the second-largest park in San Francisco, it doesn't take long to feel like you're off the beaten track. The off-leash areas are at Shelly Drive and Mansell Street and the area adjacent to Geneva or Sunnydale streets.

McNamara's Dog Training

(415) 334-5523
Hours: By Appt
Payment: Checks
Price Range: $$

Jim McNamara, who has been schooling dogs for 18 years, is also known for training hearing dogs for the deaf through the SPCA. Jim prefers to train on his own turf and will take on all breeds and all problems, including aggression. Jim offers two training options: The first is a six-week program involving you and your dog. The second is a 12-class curriculum in which he takes your pup for six classes alone and you join in for the other six. He's a proponent of positive reinforcement, but he prefers to use treats only for his shyer pupils.

Mount Davidson

Dalewood Way
(@ Lansdale Ave)
San Francisco, California 94127

Crowned with a controversial 80-foot concrete cross at the top, Mount Davidson affords a panoramic view of the city from several spots in the park. There are a multitude of trails to explore with your leashed pup, some a little more rigorous than others. The popular fire road will take you on a loop trail of almost a mile, so bring water and a sense of adventure.

Mountain Lake Park

8th Ave
(@ Lake St)
San Francisco, California 94118

Enter Mountain Lake Park at 8th Avenue and follow the sound of joyful barking to the mostly dirt off-leash area that's popular with local owners and dog walkers. Ample room for high-speed chases among the trees and plenty of drinking water satisfy dogs' needs, while benches make this park appealing for socializing dog owners. The actual lake, part of the National Park Service's Presidio, is off-limits to dogs, although there are always a few pups who find the muddy water too tempting to pass up.

Noe Valley Pet Co.

(415) 282-7385
1451 Church St
(@ Cesar Chavez)
San Francisco, California 94131
www.noevalleypet.com

Hours: Mon - Fri 10 A.M. - 8 P.M., Sat - Sun 10 A.M. - 6 P.M.
Payment: Credit Cards, Checks
Price Range: $/$$/$$$

This pet-sitting service gone pooch boutique is located in what looks like an old-fashioned general store—albeit a fabulous one that's stocked with funky dog gear: Ella Dish striped dog collars abound, premium and raw foods (Nature's Variety and Primal), and a wide variety of pet-advice books are a few of the hot items. The store offers low-cost vaccinations and hosts monthly pet-adoption days. Dog-walking services include trips to Fort Funston or Pine Lake Park—all for an incredibly inexpensive $16 a day.

North Beach Pet Supplies
(415) 885-0550
801 Greenwich St
(@ Mason St)
San Francisco, California 94133
Payment: Credit Cards, Checks
Price Range: $$$
If there's no kibble in the cupboard or you find yourself without some other essential staple, North Beach Pet Supplies carries a modest selection of supplies, treats, collars and food. But the prices are high, so you may want to stock up on staples somewhere else. Passersby will appreciate the water bowl on the sidewalk and the friendly treat-bearing store owners.

O'Paws
(415) 431-6729
1 Rausch St, Ste D
(@ Howard St)
San Francisco, California 94103
www.o-paws.com
Hours: Mon - Fri 7 A.M. - 7 P.M., Sat - Sun By Appt
Payment: Credit Cards, Checks
Price Range: $$$
The philosophy is quality over quantity, where at O'Paws day care fewer dogs definitely means more time for individual pooch pampering. Pups enjoy a full day of walks, fresh-baked treats, baths and naps, returning home socialized and stress-free. Owners Jonathan and Clodel also offer a bed-and-breakfast option for a limited number of lucky dogs. To ensure compatibility, pups must go through a two-interview process before being admitted to O'Paws.

Ocean Beach

(415) 556-8371
Great Hwy
(between the Cliff House & Fort Funston)
San Francisco, California 94121

A longtime favorite for off-leash fun, Ocean Beach is part of the controversial GGNRA (Golden Gate National Recreation Area). Therefore, dogs are now required to be on leash. With four miles of surfside fun, many dog owners can't resist letting their pooches run free in a secluded area. But watch for rangers, because they will ticket. You'll find free parking on side streets and water near the various restrooms. Beware of the life-threatening riptides that pose a threat to both you and your dog.

On the Go Pet Care

(415) 359-6959
(415) 672-2299
www.onthegopetcare.com
Hours: By Appt
Payment: Checks
Price Range: $$$

Mari and Keri offer basic dog walking, but it's their pet-sitting service that really shines—they go all out for you and your pooch, even keeping a pet log to ensure that you don't miss out on anything. They will even provide reasonable house-keeping services for overnight clients. The incredibly accom-modating duo is a good bet when it comes to special and last-minute requests.

One at a Time Rescue

(415) 519-3250
1388 10th Ave
San Francisco, California 94122
www.oneatatimerescue.org
Hours: By Appt
Payment: Checks
Price Range: $$

One at a Time Rescue was founded in 2002 when Jen Richardson, working as an animal control officer, saw the number of dogs and cats who were euthanized because they couldn't pass the rigorous behavioral and medical exams performed by the shelters. One at a Time rescues animals from shelters, sends them to foster homes and makes sure they receive the necessary medical attention and socialization they need. Pets are spayed/neutered before adoption. An adoption fee of $150 for dogs and $75 for cats helps defray some of their costs. The organization is always looking for donations and volunteers, so contact them if you have the means to help. Check out their website for pictures of adoptable dogs.

Parkside Pet Grooming

(415) 665-2924
2239 Taraval St
(between 32nd & 33rd sts)
San Francisco, California 94116
Hours: Tue - Sat 7 A.M. - 3 P.M.
Payment: Credit Cards, Checks
Price Range: $$

Between owner Malinda and groomer Tina, Parkside offers 30 years of dog-grooming experience. Dogs enjoy nontoxic shampoos and hand dryers, although air drying suffices on warm days. Because the store is small with streetcar tracks out front, the groomers keep dogs safely in their crates to avoid any disasters. Giant breeds and particularly furry hounds are excluded from Parkside's services. Grooming clients can take advantage of Malinda's new boarding facility at her house in Novato.

Pawtrero Hill Bathhouse and Feed Co.

(415) 863-7297
199 Mississippi St
(@ Mariposa St)
San Francisco, California 94107
www.pawtrero.com
Hours: Mon - Fri 11 A.M. - 7 P.M., Sat 11 A.M. - 6 P.M.,
Sun 12 P.M. - 5 P.M.
Payment: Credit Cards, Checks
Price Range: $$

Step into this Potrero Hill establishment and you may feel you've stepped into a frontier saloon. The store stocks all-natural and raw foods, homeopathic supplements, grooming tools, collars and gifts. For $15, you can make full use of their self-service bathhouse. If there's a wait, hang out in the backyard. Pawtrero is a valuable resource for information on walkers, sitters and groomers. In addition, they provide monthly anesthesia-free teeth cleaning services and have hosted various specialists, including an animal communicator and a massage therapist.

Perfect Paws

(415) 647-8000
251 6th St
(between Howard & Folsom sts)
San Francisco, California 94103
www.perfectpaws.org
Hours: By Appt
Payment: Credit Cards, Checks
Price Range: $$

This renowned Bay Area institution, which has been around 20-plus years, was one of *San Francisco* magazine's Best of the Bay Area picks in 2002. In addition to puppy- and basic-training classes, the organization provides clicker, agility and competition training as well as specific classes to resolve such issues as digging, barking and jumping. Private lessons are available for pups with bigger problems, including aggression, biting and destructive behavior.

Pet Camp

(415) 282-0700
525 Phelps St
(@ Evans St)
San Francisco, California 94124
www.petcamp.com
Hours: Mon - Fri 7 A.M. - 6 P.M., Sat 8 A.M. - 11 A.M.,
Sun 3 P.M. - 6 P.M.
Payment: Credit Cards, Checks
Price Range: $$$

This day-care and boarding facility is definitely more of a
retreat than a kennel. Pet Camp offers sublime diversions for
dogs and cats. Indoor and outdoor play areas accommodate
every age, size and temperament of dog: puppies, seniors,
active dogs, gentle dogs and little white fluffy dogs. Between
the twice-a-day, hour-long play sessions, your pooch can
enjoy a grooming session at the spa or a swim in Pet Camp's
dog pool. This environmentally friendly company generates its
own energy through a roof-top solar power system. The energy
provides soothing music 24 hours a day and a radiant heating
system in its private dog runs that keeps the temperature comfy.

Pet Source

Presidio Heights Location

(415) 831-8688
2900 Geary Blvd
(2 blocks from Masonic Ave)
San Francisco, California 94118

Richmond Location

(415) 831-1799
5221 Geary Blvd
(between 16th & 17th aves)
San Francisco, California 94118

Hours: Mon 10 A.M. - 7 P.M., Tue - Sat 10 A.M. - 8 P.M.,
Sun 10 A.M. - 7 P.M.

Payment: Credit Cards, Checks
Price Range: $$

Pet Source has been in business for nine years, and some of its supplies look as though they've been around even longer. The stores carry the more basic commercial to speciality dog-food brands, and if you've had no luck scrounging for tennis balls at local beaches and parks, Pet Source will sell you a used one for 59 cents. The atmosphere in both locations is laidback, and the Geary location provides a self-service pet wash. For a bit extra, you can turn your dog over to them for flea dipping, nail trimming and de-skunking.

Petcetera

(415) 661-4236
2226 Taraval St
(between 32nd & 33rd sts)
San Francisco, California 94116
Hours: Mon - Fri 10 A.M. - 7 P.M., Sat 9:30 A.M. - 6:30 P.M.,
Sun 11 A.M. - 6 P.M.
Payment: Credit Cards, Checks
Price Range: $$

Formerly Sunset Pet Supply, Petcetera is under new ownership, and dog owners should be pleased with the changes. Sanford and Kimberly are phasing out lower-quality items and focusing on super-premium foods, holistic solutions, raw foods and organic ingredients. Operating Petcetera doesn't cut into Sanford and Kimberly's dog walking and boarding business: As established, 11-year veteran dog walkers, they are both popular within San Francisco's dog community and have a full schedule of one-hour walks and family-style boarding at Sanford's house.

Petco

www.petco.com
Payment: Credit Cards, Checks
Price Range: $$

Parkside Location
(415) 665-3700
1591 Sloat Blvd
(between 34th and 35th aves)
San Francisco, California 94132
Hours: Mon - Fri 9 A.M. - 9 P.M., Sat 9 A.M. - 8 P.M.
Sun 10 A.M. - 7 P.M.

Potrero Hill Location
(415) 863-1840
1685 Bryant St
(@ 16th St)
San Francisco, California 94103
Hours: Mon - Sat 9 A.M. - 9 P.M., Sun 10 A.M. - 7 P.M.
For one-stop shopping it's hard to beat the convenience and
value of this superstore with locations all over the country.
Petco makes it their mission to provide customers with the
food, supplements and products they want for their animals.
Their bed selection runs the gamut, from orthopedic mattresses
along with sheets and throws to chaises that would do an
interior decorator proud. Get a P.A.L.S. (Petco Animal Lovers
Save) card to take advantage of discounts; you may also want
to check out their Top Dog program, which offers even greater
savings to their most loyal customers. Check the contact information for each store for hours and specific service offerings.

Pets Unlimited
(415) 563-6700
2343 Fillmore St
(@ Washington St)
San Francisco, California 94115
www.petsunlimited.org
Hours: Mon - Thu 8 A.M. - 8 P.M., Fri 8 A.M. - 7 P.M.,
Sat - Sun 9 A.M. - 4 P.M.

Emergency Hours: Every Day 24 Hours
Payment: Credit Cards, Checks
Price Range: $$

This unique nonprofit resource offers the city's animal community just about everything they need. Services run the gamut from owner education and shelter/rescue adoption assistance, to animal-emergency care—and for cats only: grooming and boarding. In addition, staff vet Cynthia Easton employs home-opathic treatments. Income from the 24-hour-a-day veterinary hospital helps fund the organization's other efforts, which include providing shelter and medical care for abandoned animals until they are placed in loving homes.

Petraiture

(415) 861-1516
www.kerrymansfield.com
Hours: By Appt
Payment: Checks
Price Range: $$$

Before photographer Kerry Mansfield even takes out her camera, she likes to spend a little time studying your pet's personality. It's clear from her pictures that by the end of the shoot, most of her subjects are studying her. She prefers to have owners out of the picture—literally and figuratively—as she establishes a working relationship with her models. Check out her website, where she places dogs into one of two categories: "woofs" and "yips." She also does kitties, bunnies and horses.

Pooch Coach

(415) 643-3333
www.poochcoach.com
Hours: By Appt
Payment: Checks
Price Range: $$

Just as one size never truly fits all, one method does not train all dogs, according to Beverly Ulbrich, a proponent of one-on-one dog training. She's tested that philosophy by getting some of the city's more downtrodden dogs back in the game in her work at SF ACC, Pets Unlimited, PAWS, the East Bay SPCA and other rescue organizations. In addition to being a whiz with behavioral problems, Ulbrich is also amply qualified to take on basic training issues and more advanced obedience.

Pooches' Playtime
(415) 824-3743
2350 Jerrold Ave
(between Barneveld & Napoleon sts)
San Francisco, California 94124
www.poochesplaytime.com
Hours: Mon - Fri 7 A.M. - 7 P.M., Sat - Sun By Appt
Payment: Credit Cards, Checks
Price Range: $$$

Pooches' Playtime is primarily a doggie day-care spot, but owners Molly and Jen—who live upstairs—will board regulars overnight. They shy away from keeping their guests in kennels and crates, opting instead to let the pups run free at both their facility and during off-leash walks at local parks. They are equipped to handle handicapped dogs and will fetch your playgroup-bound pup if you live in Noe Valley, Bernal Hill, Forest Hills, Woodside, Glen Park, Upper Mission or Portola. A portion of their profits is set aside to support rescue dogs.

Presidio of San Francisco, The
(415) 561-4323
(entrances on Arguello Blvd, Lombard St, Presidio Blvd
& Park Presidio)
San Francisco, California 94129
www.nps.gov/prsf

Part pristine urban oasis, part ex-military base, the Presidio of San Francisco offers almost 1,500 acres of historic buildings, coastal defense fortifications, a national cemetery, a pet cemetery, a historic airfield, a saltwater marsh, native plant habitats, coastal bluffs and some of the most spectacular views in the world. You and your pooch will enjoy exploring—albeit on leash—the miles of hiking trails that wind through eucalyptus and cypress groves, beaches and meadows. For specific destinations, check out the entries for Baker Beach, Land's End/ Lincoln Park, Ocean Beach and Crissy Field.

PuppyCat

(415) 621-5911
289 Divisadero St
(@ Page St)
San Francisco, California 94117
Hours: Mon - Fri 10 A.M. - 8 P.M., Sat - Sun 10 A.M. - 6 P.M.
Payment: Credit Cards, Checks
Price Range: $$

Although it's only been open for 18 months, PuppyCat is already scoring big points; *SF Weekly* named it the Best Specialty Pet Store of 2003. Friendly and knowledgeable, owner Deanndra stocks only natural and prepared foods like Nature's Variety and Primal, and she won't carry or order any-thing that she wouldn't give to her own dog. Though it looks high end, PuppyCat's prices are actually very reasonable, and Deanndra will give you the scoop on her favorite groomers, dog walkers and pet-sitters.

puppyDog

(415) 675-5885
www.sfpuppydog.com
Hours: By Appt
Payment: Checks
Price Range: $

Victoria Robinson has been wrangling dogs for seven years. First as owner of North Beach Pet Sitter (NBPS), and now with puppyDog, a day-care and mobile pet-services company that extends care to dogs of all ages, including those with special needs. Robinson offers off-leash play groups, puppy care, groomer drop-off and pick-up, convalescent care and pet-sitting in her home or yours. Off-leash playgroups guarantee a minimum of 45 minutes of romping for your pup, and puppy care includes basic training. Victoria serves North Beach, Telegraph Hill, Russian Hill, Marina, Cow Hollow and Pacific Heights.

Reigning Dogs & Cats

(415) 431-3647
1766 Mission St
(between Duboce & 14th sts)
San Francisco, California 94103
www.reigningdogsandcats.qpg.com
Hours: Mon - Fri 7 A.M. - 7 P.M., Sat 9 A.M. - 5 P.M.,
Sun 10 A.M. - 2 P.M.
Payment: Credit Cards, Checks
Price Range: $$

Although you might have many options for boarding your pup, Reigning Dogs & Cats is one of the select facilities that allows free roaming, with pooches returning to their private quarters only for meals and bedtime. Dogs are urged to play with toys, with specialized equipment and with one another, as the trained staff supervises them. Reigning Dogs & Cats suggests pet owners bring their dogs' favorite beds and blankets with them, and they keep a separate area for very small or young dogs. In addition to day-care and boarding services, they provide grooming and offer discounts for long-term guests or multiple pets from the same household.

Rocket Dog Rescue

(415) 642-4786
P.O. Box 460826
San Francisco, California 94146
www.rocketdogrescue.org
Payment: Credit Cards, Checks
Price Range: $

Staffed completely with volunteers, Rocket Dog Rescue "saves dogs at the speed of light." Accepting non-aggressive dogs of all breeds, Rocket Dog places its rescues in foster homes for socialization and behavior modification, and then actively seeks permanent homes for each dog. Honored with a 2001 Points of Light Award for outstanding volunteerism, founder Pali Boucher ensures each companion animal is spayed or neutered before adoption into a rigorously screened home. Potential parents can view adoptable pups on the organization's website. Interested volunteers can find information about fostering, mobile adoptions, dog walking and rescue transport here as well.

RUFF 'N READY

(415) 831-2651
871 38th Ave
San Francisco, California 94121
www.ruffnready.biz
Hours: Mon - Sat 10 A.M. - 6 P.M.
Payment: Credit Cards, Checks
Price Range: $$

RUFF 'N READY provides playgroups and boarding for its RUFF Riders. Playgroups take place only in city-designated, fenced-in dog parks and pups get picked up in a state-of-the-art, climate-controlled van. They are strong proponents of communication, sending clients e-mail news updates and a monthly newsletter. Boarding clients receive pictures via e-mail every other day so they can keep up on their dog while they are away. Ruff serves the Richmond district, Noe Valley, Bernal Heights, the Castro, the Haight, Cole and Hayes valleys and Potrero Hill.

Ruffhouse Dogs

(415) 552-7833
www.ruffhousedogs.com
Hours: By Appt
Payment: Checks
Price Range: $$

Small play groups of fewer than six dogs and varied destinations throughout San Francisco make Ruffhouse Dogs an appealing doggie day-care option. In addition to daily 45-minute outings (not including transportation time), Peter and Rich offer a variety of canine catering services: If you're out of town, they'll take care of your pooch and your home; if you run out of food, they will deliver some kibble; and if your car's in the shop, they will chauffeur your pup to the vet or groomer.

Russian Hill Dog Groomers

(415) 776-9529
1929 Hyde St
(between Union & Green sts)
San Francisco, California 94109
Hours: Tue - Sat 8 A.M. - 5 P.M.
Payment: Credit Cards, Checks
Price Range: $$$

Nationally certified master groomer and 10-year veteran Leonard Montgomery is the man to see if you're looking for a fancy cut for your precious pooch. The relative calm of the shop belies the number of dogs they handle in a day. Dogs are bathed and hand dried in the back and then led to one of two grooming stations in the front room so you can watch the master at work. Some clients have complained about the attitude, but others consider it part of the charm of this haute dog stylist.

San Francisco Dog Owners Group
(415) 339-7461
www.sfdog.org
Payment: Checks
Price Range: $

Revived in 1997 after 20 years of dormancy, SFDOG is an advocacy group promoting responsible dog ownership and working to preserve off-leash access to city, state and federal park lands. SFDOG is central in the effort to repeal leash laws in such Golden Gate National Recreation Area hotspots as Crissy Field and Fort Funston. The organization is supported entirely by volunteers so your $10 dues go a long way toward helping their cause. Their website contains updates, a calendar of events, links to recommended resources and their latest newsletters.

San Francisco SPCA
(415) 554-3000
2500 16th St
(between Bryant & Harrison)
San Francisco, California 94103
www.sfspca.org
Payment: Checks
Price Range: $

This revered Bay Area institution is an exemplary animal-welfare organization that inspires animal-rights activists around the country. Founded in 1868, the SF SPCA became an official no-kill shelter in 1984—and promptly lost all government funding. In 1994 the SF SPCA signed an adoption pact with SF ACC, making San Francisco the first major city not to euthanize rehabilitatable animals. Its standout programs include the Academy for Dog Trainers as well as dog training; Maddie's Adoption Center; the SF SPCA Spay/Neuter Clinic; SF SPCA Animal Hospital; and their hearing dog and animal-assisted-therapy programs. Between fostering and volunteering, there are plenty of opportunities for you to get involved. You should definitely check out their adoptable animals.

San Francisco Pet Grooming

(415) 861-0111
209A Sanchez St
(@ Market St)
San Francisco, California 94114
Hours: Tue - Sat 10 A.M. - 5:30 P.M.
Payment: Cash Only
Price Range: $$

Owner Tomo has been grooming dogs for five years, although she has been at this location only a few months. All breeds are welcome in her brightly painted shop, where dogs run free while waiting their turn. An elaborate gate system prevents escape. Tomo will air, towel, hand and cage dry, depending on the season and the dog. All cage drying is supervised. Pick up one of her frequent-grooming cards, 10 visits earn a free gift.

San Francisco Raw Feeders Co-op

(415) 518-9575
1867 Jefferson St
(@ Divisadero St)
San Francisco, California 94123
www.sfraw.com
Hours: See website
Payment: Credit Cards
Price Range: $$

If your dog is on a veterinarian-approved raw diet, join San Francisco Raw Feeders Co-op and buy in bulk to take advantage of their good prices and quality raw food from hormone and steroid-free, organic and ethically treated animals. After joining the co-op, you place a monthly order between the 13th and 21st of every month, then you pick up your order on the third Thursday of the following month. Pick-ups are scheduled in San Francisco's Marina district. Check their website for delivery specifics and a comprehensive list of local vets and kennels advocating and supporting raw-food diets.

SF Barking Station

(415) 756-7535
646 35th Ave
(@ Balboa St)
San Francisco, California 94121
Hours: By Appt
Payment: Checks
Price Range: $$$

If you've had it with sterile dog kennels, try SF Barking Station, where dogs are treated as members of the family. Owner Alex will even take on puppies and dogs with special needs and administer medication when necessary. Your pup will enjoy specialized, personal care: Seven pups are the limit, with a two-dog maximum for large dogs. Although the Barking Station is primarily for boarding, doggie day care is also available, with enjoyable outings to the beach and Land's End.

SF Hound Lounge

(415) 255-1170
2825 Mariposa St
(between Alabama & Florida sts)
San Francisco, California 94110
www.sfhoundlounge.com
Hours: Mon - Fri 7 A.M. - 7 P.M.
Payment: Credit Cards, Checks
Price Range: $$$

If your pooch is bored, lonely or restless during weekday business hours, take him to SF Hound Lounge. This 5,000-square-foot facility is within a couple of blocks of the SF SPCA, whose associates helped create SF Hound Lounge. Because the Lounge accepts all breeds, sizes and ages of canines, staff members are trained to monitor moods and to help socialize your dog. After passing an initial interview where you demonstrate your dog's friendly and nonaggressive behavior, your pup can relish a full day of romping with pals at the lounge.

Silver Poodle Pet Grooming

(415) 752-7167
938 Clement St
(between 10th & 11th aves)
San Francisco, California 94118
Hours: Tue - Sat 8 A.M. - 5 P.M.
Payment: Checks
Price Range: $$

New owner Christine has some big grooming shoes to fill.
She hopes to maintain the shop's excellent grooming standards
while updating the interior of the 42-year-old shop. She's also
adding additional retail items to the store's current scant sup-
plies. The Silver Poodle takes on all breeds but doesn't do
show cuts. They use a variety of drying methods, including air,
hand and cage drying.

Smilin Dogs

(415) 699-9337
San Francisco, California
www.smilindogs.com
Hours: By Appt
Payment: Checks
Price Range: $$$

If your idea of a happy dog is a tired dog, then sign her up with
Smilin Dogs. Dogs spend their days hiking on a 1,500-acre San
Mateo County coast cattle ranch, swimming, and lounging at
the "dog shed." Boarding is also offered for day-care dogs.
Smilin Dogs is all about convenience with the price of admis-
sion including door-to-door service and monthly billing.

Stenstrom, Elizabeth

(415) 661-8141
Hours: By Appt
Payment: Checks
Price Range: $

Dog walker and sitter Elizabeth Stenstrom provides her services to dogs out in the avenues. Her walks are for leashed dogs only, and her limit is four dogs per walk. A fan of retractable leashes, she is in the process of marketing her own 53-foot leash for dogs who can't quite handle complete freedom. She will also administer medication as needed. Areas covered: outer Sunset and outer Richmond.

Stern Grove

(415) 831-2700
19th Ave
(@ Sloat Blvd)
San Francisco, California 94116

Stern Grove, home of the city's outdoor music concerts, is a dog walking favorite with owners and walkers alike. Situated in a valley near the zoo, Stern Grove is buffered from busy traffic. The official off-leash area is Wawona Street between 21st and 22nd avenues, but you'd never know that from the pups happily roaming and wrestling throughout the park.

Upper Douglass Park

(415) 695-5017
(between Douglass & 26th sts)
San Francisco, California 94114

Dogs have been running free at Upper Douglass Park for years, but the city just sanctioned it as an official off-leash dog park in 2003. Although some view the upper-tier dog park—distinguished from lower Douglass Park, where you'll find kids and the playground—as a victory for canine companions, others point out that the field is a glorified swamp and that surrounding cliffs make the park dangerous. However, you can't argue with the dogs, who are perfectly content to roll in the mud with their buddies.

Upper Noe Recreation Center

(415) 695-5011
Day St
(@ Sanchez St)
San Francisco, California 94131
Hours: Mon - Fri 9 A.M. - 10 P.M., Sat 9 P.M. - 5 P.M.,
Sun 12 P.M. - 5 P.M.
Although the Upper Noe Recreation Center off-leash dog area, adjacent to the ball field, is little more than an L-shaped, fenced-in patch of dirt, the dogs enjoy the freedom and the company. The park—including the dog area—is slated for renovation and expansion in 2005, but don't hold your breath: Its off-leash status is currently up in the air pending city review.

Urban Pet, The

(415) 673-7708
3429 Sacramento St
(between Walnut & Laurel sts)
San Francisco, California 94118
www.theurbanpet.com
Hours: Mon - Thu 10 A.M. - 1:30 P.M., 2 P.M. - 6 P.M.,
Fri - Sat 10 A.M. - 1:30 P.M., 2 P.M. - 5 P.M.
Payment: Credit Cards, Checks
Price Range: $$$
This swanky boutique stocks traditional pet foods and canine crowd pleasers like the Humunga Tongue and the Babble Ball (it talks and giggles), but the store's bread and butter is couture pet clothing and $500 dog beds. Leather leashes and collars—as well as limited-edition cloth collars made from the finest Parisian material—share shelf space with pet travel bags and

wrought-iron dog-bowl stands. If you'd like memorabilia beautiful enough to hang on your wall, co-owner Rive Nester is a skilled pet portraitist; for somewhere between $800 to $1,200, she'll create an oil painting from a favorite photo.

Urbanhound
(415) 378-3015
Hours: By Appt
Payment: Checks
Price Range: $$
Dog walker Michael Moore prefers to give his charges a run for their money, letting them loose at one of the city's fenceless off-leash areas. Generally restricting his pack to six, Michael keeps things under control through positive reinforcement (a.k.a. treats). It goes without saying that dogs must be under voice control and well behaved. Walks are an hour, not including traveling time. Michael covers Pacific Heights, Lake Street and Inner Richmond.

VIP Grooming
(415) 282-1393
4299 24th St
(@ Douglass St)
San Francisco, California 94114
Hours: Tue - Sat 8 A.M. - 5 P.M.
Payment: Credit Cards, Checks
Price Range: $
Owner Lancy Woo has been grooming dogs for more than 20 years, and her popularity speaks to her expertise. Even with a team of groomers and bathers working for her, she still books a few weeks out, so plan ahead. They handle most breeds and give special attention to elderly dogs, but Lancy recommends going elsewhere for "foo-foo" cuts. Shampoos are all-natural and groomers use a variety of drying techniques, including supervised cage drying.

Wags

(415) 409-2472
1840 Polk St
(@ Jackson St)
San Francisco, California 94109
www.sfwags.com
Hours: Tue - Fri 10 A.M. - 7 P.M., Sat 9 A.M. - 6 P.M.,
Sun 10 A.M. - 6 P.M.
Payment: Credit Cards, Checks
Price Range: $$$

On an otherwise nondescript block, Wags stands out for its white-picket fence and the legions of loyal dog owners who flock to the store. In addition to high-end supplies and premium food, the store provides grooming, dog walking and pet-sitting. Owners Tyler and Johnny will pet-sit at your house, or they will take your pup to their home. Groomer Jerico, who has 25 years of experience that includes show cuts, will wash and style your dog or you can always utilize the self-grooming service. Their dog walks would be more aptly named adventure walks; two hours of exercise is the norm.

Washington Square

Filbert and Stockton sts
(@ Columbus Ave)
San Francisco, California 94133

Although dogs are not allowed off leash at this neighborhood park, there is an active dog community here, especially during pre- and post-work hours. The community is diverse—bring your dog for some socializing, and you may find yourself in the company of a local tattoo artist or the president of the North Beach Chamber of Commerce. The small park is bordered by busy streets and has a vocal homeless population, so it's not always peaceful. There's no drinking water here: be sure to bring some for you and your dog.

North Bay

EMERGENCY PET TRANSPORT

AMERS Animal Ambulance
(877) 426-3771 (emergency)
(925) 261-9111 (office)
www.animalmedics.com
Hours: Every Day 24 Hours
Payment: Credit Cards, Checks
Emergency Fee: $175

Pet Taxi
(415) 386-2534
Hours: Every Day 7 A.M. – 7 P.M.
Emergency Hours: Every Day 24 Hours
Payment: Checks
Price Range: $$/$$$

ANIMAL EMERGENCY FACILITIES

Animal Care Center
(707) 584-4343
6470 Redwood Dr
Rohnert Park, CA 94928
www.accsonoma.com
Hours: Every Day 24 Hours
Payment: Credit Cards, Checks
Price Range: $$

Animal Kingdom Veterinary Services

(707) 254-0500
3164 Dry Creek Rd
Napa, California 94558
Hours: Every Day 24 Hours
Payment: Credit Cards
Emergency Fee: $54

Pet Care Emergency Hospital

(707) 579-5900
1370 Fulton Rd
Santa Rosa, California 95401
Hours: Every Day 24 Hours
Payment: Credit Cards, Checks
Price Range: $$

Pet Emergency and Specialty Center of Marin

(415) 456-7372
901 E Francisco Blvd
San Rafael, California
Hours: Mon – Fri 5:30 P.M. – 8 A.M., Sat - Sun 24 Hours
Payment: Credit Cards, Checks
Price Range: $$

Silverado Veterinary Hospital

(707) 224-7953
2035 Silverado Trl
Napa, California 94558
Hours: Every Day 24 Hours
Payment: Credit Cards, Checks
Price Range: $$

Solano Pet Emergency Clinic

(707) 864-1444
4437 Central Pl, Ste B3
Cordelia, California 94585
Hours: Mon – Fri 6 P.M. – 8 A.M., Sat - Sun 24 Hours
Payment: Credit Cards, Checks
Price Range: $$

ANIMAL POISON HOTLINE

ASPCA Animal Poison Control Center
(888) 4ANI-HELP
Hours: Every Day 24 Hours
Payment: Credit Cards
Consultation Fee: $45

ADOPTION

Benicia *Pet Food Express*
Novato *Marin Humane Society, The*
Rohnert Park *Petsmart*
San Rafael *Give Your Dog a Bone*
Willits *Milo Foundation*

ALTERNATIVE PRODUCTS/SERVICES

Corte Madera *Pet Club*
San Anselmo *Pet Food Cottage*
Sonoma *Brighthaven—A Nonprofit, Holistic Animal Retreat*
• *Sonoma Dog Camp*
Vallejo *Powell Bros. Feed & Pet Supply*

DOG BOARDING

Corte Madera *Camp K-9 of Marin*
Napa *Bonny Doone Kennel*
Novato *Postmore Kennels* • *Romar Kennels*
San Rafael *Planet Canine*
Sebastopol *Tappen Hill*
Sonoma *Maranda Ranch Kennels*

DOG DAY CARE

Corte Madera *Camp K-9 of Marin*
Novato *Postmore Kennels*
San Rafael *Planet Canine*
Sonoma *Maranda Ranch Kennels* • *Sonoma Dog Camp*

DOG GROOMING

Mobile *Wizard of Paws Mobile Grooming*
Eureka *Petco*
Mill Valley *Doggie Styles* • *Kennel Club, The*
Napa *Petco*
Novato *Petco* • *Postmore Kennels*
Petaluma *Dawg Groomer*
Rohnert Park *Petsmart*
San Anselmo *Boulevard Dogs*
San Rafael *Gay's Doggie Salon* • *Pet Agree* • *Petco*
Santa Rosa *Petco*
Sonoma *Maranda Ranch Kennels* • *Show Time*
Tiburon *Creature Comforts Pet Grooming*
Vacaville *Petco*
Vallejo *Petco* • *Powell Bros. Feed & Pet Supply*

DOG GROOMING—SELF-SERVE

Novato *Pet Food Express*
Petaluma *Dawg Groomer*
San Rafael *Pet Agree*

DOG HIKES & SOCIALS

San Rafael *McInnis County Park*

DOG PARKS—OFF LEASH

Mill Valley *Bayfront Park*
Napa *Alston Dog Park*
Novato *Dogbone Meadow*
San Rafael *Field of Dogs* • *McInnis County Park*
Sonoma *Elizabeth Anne Perrone Dog Park*

DOG TRAINING

Eureka *Petco*
Benicia *Pet Food Express*
Corte Madera *Camp K-9 of Marin* • *Take the Lead*
Napa *Petco*
Novato *Marin Humane Society, The*
Petaluma *Unleashed!*
Rohnert Park *Petsmart*
San Rafael *Petco*
Santa Rosa *Petco*
Sebastopol *Tappen Hill*
Vacaville *Petco*
Vallejo *Petco*

DOG WALKING/PET-SITTING

Napa *Wheeler Pet Care*
Novato *Dog-Gone Walkin'*
San Rafael *Dog-Gone Walkin'*

PET-SUPPLY STORES

Benicia *Pet Food Express*
Corte Madera *Pet Club*
Eureka *Petco*
Healdsburg *Fideaux*
Mill Valley *Alpha Dog* • *Critterland Pets*
Napa *Petco* • *Wilson's Feed & Supply*
Novato *Marin Humane Society, The* • *Pet Food Express*
• *Petco*
Petaluma *Our Best Friend* • *Rivertown Feed and
Pet Country Store*
Rohnert Park *Petsmart*
San Anselmo *Pet Food Cottage* • *Red Hill Pet Center*
San Rafael *Give Your Dog a Bone* • *Pet Agree* • *Petco*
Santa Rosa *Petco*
Sonoma *Brocco's Old Barn* • *Granary Feed and Pet Supply,
The* • *Show Time* • *Sonoma Dog Camp*
St. Helena *Fideaux*
Vacaville *Petco*
Vallejo *Petco* • *Powell Bros. Feed & Pet Supply*

VACCINATIONS—LOW-COST

Benicia *Pet Food Express*
Corte Madera *Pet Club*
Eureka *Petco*
Mill Valley *Critterland Pets*
Napa *Petco*
Novato *Marin Humane Society, The* • *Pet Food Express*
• *Petco*
Petaluma *Rivertown Feed and Pet Country Store*
Rohnert Park *Petsmart*
San Rafael *Petco*
Santa Rosa *Petco*
St Helena *We Care Animal Rescue*
Vacaville *Petco*
Vallejo *Petco* • *Powell Bros. Feed & Pet Supply*

CITY DOG PICKS

Corte Madera *Camp K-9 of Marin*
Novato *Dogbone Meadow* • *Marin Humane Society, The*
San Rafael *Planet Canine*
Sebastopol *Tappen Hill*
Sonoma *Brighthaven—A Nonprofit, Holistic Animal Retreat*
• *Sonoma Dog Camp*
St Helena *We Care Animal Rescue*

General Listings

Alpha Dog
(415) 389-6500
6 Miller Ave
(@ Throckmorton Ave)
Mill Valley, California 94941
www.alphadog.com
Hours: Mon - Sat 10 A.M. - 7 P.M., Sun 11 A.M. - 6 P.M.
Payment: Credit Cards, Checks
Price Range: $$$
Kelly has successfully resisted stuffing this Mill Valley boutique
with all the high-end dog merchandise of the moment.
Instead, she stocks her store with products that fit her ideas
about what makes dogs happy and healthy and what keeps
their owners amused. Two custom dog artists are represented
on the walls, there's one type of raw dog food in the freezer
and one brand of quality kibble on the shelf. The treat collection
is characterized by unique goodies like Dig The Earth. There's a
sophisticated collection of collars, beds, bowls and nutritional
supplements, a small line of people tags, a sweet little kitty
corner and a do-it-yourself tag engraver.

Alston Dog Park
Dry Creek Rd @ Trower Ave
Napa, California
Hours: Dawn to Dusk
In a county with very few off-leash options, this open-space
park functions as the main social scene for Napa County dogs.
The fenced-in area next to the parking lot looks like a big sub-
urban backyard with newly planted trees, a canvas cabana
and plenty of lawn furniture scattered over several tidy, wood
chip-covered acres. At peak evening hours, people might be
engaged in wine tasting while the dogs play. There's a separate
small-dog area, and a substantial open space designated for
off-leash adventures on grass-rimmed trails.

Bayfront Park

(415) 383-1370
Sycamore Ave
(@ Camino Alto)
Mill Valley, California 94941
www.cityofmillvalley.org/parks-bayfront-main.html
Hours: Dawn to Dusk

Enjoy Bayfront Park's killer views as you parade your pup along the long and partially fenced popular dog promenade. On leash, you can explore the park's multi-use areas and the wilder marsh area. The estuary is a draw for waterdogs, but the mud they bring home may prove a little too enduring—perhaps due to the park's former life as a dump and sewage-treatment site.

Bonny Doone Kennel

(707) 226-1200
1003 Los Carneros Ave.
Napa, California 94559
(off Hwy 12 west of Napa, right before Domaine Chandon)
Hours: Mon - Fri 8 A.M. - 12 P.M., 2 P.M. - 7 P.M.
Sat 8 A.M. - 12 P.M., 2 P.M. - 6 P.M., Sun 4 P.M. - 6 P.M.
Payment: Checks
Price Range: $$

Local vets and trainers all seem to think that this cheery, farm-like kennel is the best place in the Napa Valley to board your pet. Rhonda's magic formula is meticulous maintenance, comfortable quarters, plenty of outdoor recreation and lots of face time. Dogs get to play with other guests—and the resident sheep and ducks—through the wire fences of their adjoining runs. Safety is the top priority here, so there's no group play unless it's prearranged.

Boulevard Dogs

(415) 485-1636
749 Sir Francis Drake Blvd
(west of the Red Hill Ave junction)
San Anselmo, California 94960
Hours: Tue – Sat 9 A.M. – Last Dog
Payment: Checks
Price Range: $$

Cindy's tiny salon and jam-packed appointment book make it difficult for her to take more pups. But if your dog can get in, Cindy's one of the rare groomers who'll clip anything from an Alaskan husky to a Shih-Tzu. In this bare-bones shop, washing is done in back in a little closet. She uses a variety of shampoos and drying methods but doesn't believe in cage dryers.

Brighthaven—A Nonprofit, Holistic Animal Retreat

(707) 578-4800
19229 Sonoma Hwy
(south of Maxell Farms Regional Park)
Sonoma, California 95476
www.brighthaven.org
Hours: By Appt
Payment: Credit Cards, Checks
Price Range: $$$

Retirement homes could learn a thing or two from this cage-free haven for elderly and disabled animals. Brighthaven isn't just for dogs and cats. They also welcome everything from ducks to horses. The animals—most of whom are rescues or orphans—eat a natural diet and enjoy the benefits of holistic medical treatment. Volunteers are encouraged to visit and spend quality time with the animals or to help the staff with the daily chores. The website is filled with pictures of Brighthaven's residents as well as information on holistic animal wellness.

Brocco's Old Barn

(707) 938-2291
19660 Arnold Dr
(southwest of town @ Orange Ave)
Sonoma, California 95476
Hours: Mon - Fri 8:30 A.M. - 5:30 P.M., Sat 8:30 A.M. - 5 P.M.
Payment: Credit Cards, Checks
Price Range: $$

In case you hadn't already figured it out, the grapevines in the fields outside the Old Barn will let you know you're in Sonoma's old wine country. Inside Brocco's you can scoop rawhide chews and dog biscuits out of ancient wooden bins and choose from a respectable selection of quality brands of kibble and basic dog supplies. And they sell the HyperDog Tennis Ball Launcher—a godsend for entertaining the dog that never seems to tire. You'll also find a comprehensive arsenal for removing unwanted wild critters.

Camp K-9 of Marin

(415) 924-2267
5810 Paradise Dr
(3 blocks south of Tamalpais Dr)
Corte Madera, California 94925
www.campk-9ofmarin.com
Hours: Mon - Fri 7 A.M. - 11 A.M., 1 P.M. - 7 P.M.,
Sat - Sun 9 A.M. - 11 A.M., 4 P.M. - 6 P.M.
Payment: Credit Cards, Checks
Price Range: $$$

In Marin, it's truly a dog's life. Camp K-9's luxurious facility includes 6,000 square feet of padded indoor space and eight outdoor yards, each with shade and a wading pool. Dogs are sorted by size, age and temperament; unaltered or aggressive dogs chill out in "private camp." Walkie-talkies allow counselors to keep track of their canine charges, and owners can spy on their little campers via a 24-hour webcam.

Creature Comforts Pet Grooming

(415) 435-3630

80 Main St, Ste C

(@ Tiburon Blvd)

Tiburon, California 94920

Hours: Tue - Fri 9:30 A.M. - 5 P.M. – Last Dog

Payment: Credit Cards, Checks

Price Range: $$$

Susan runs a one-woman/one-parrot show and has been grooming all breeds of dog and cat for more than 20 years. "The Bird Lady," as she's known locally, never crates her charges, preferring a more open environment. The schedule fluctuates at her small but super-friendly shop and she's usually booked at least a week out, so be sure to call ahead.

Critterland Pets

(415) 383-7387

336 Miller Ave

(between Locust Ave & Willow St)

Mill Valley, California 94941

Hours: Mon - Sat 9:30 A.M. - 6 P.M.

Payment: Credit Cards, Checks

Price Range: $

Critterland is jammed to the gills with supplies and small pets of the rodent, fish, and bird variety. Most of the collars, toys and knickknacks are in plain view, but you'll have to walk behind the counter to reach the food section. The store is pleasantly laid back, and owner Mark Fong, a Mill Valley native, has run it for over 20 years. Family members pitch in to help make the place a local favorite.

Dawg Groomer

(707) 763-2144
225 2nd St
(@ D St)
Petaluma, California 94952
www.dawggroomer.com
Hours: Tue - Sat 8 A.M. - 4 P.M.
Payment: Credit Cards, Checks
Price Range: $$

This Dog Row grooming salon was originally a historic livery
stable. Owner Denise retrofitted the huge space in a dramatic
style best described as industrial-chic. She outfitted the salon
with plenty of modern amenities, including built-in stairs for
your pup's convenience, the HydroSurge bathing system and
high-powered blow dryers for both self-serve and full-service
customers. Shampoos are all natural and organic, and you can
even get organic flea products. The two groomers give profes-
sional cuts on canines of any breed.

Dogbone Meadow

(415) 897-4323
Novato Blvd
(½ mile west of Sutro Ave)
Novato, California 94947
www.ci.novato.ca.us/parks/parks.cfm
Hours: Every Day 6 A.M. – 10 P.M.

An agility course, picnic benches, water station, tiny shelter
and biodegradable Mutt Mitts make this one of the most
accommodating dog runs around. It's all thanks to the park's
tireless activists, who call themselves Dog Owners Group
Bettering Our Novato Community, or DOGBONE. With an
acronym like that, it should come as no surprise that this park
is, in fact, shaped like a dog bone. The elongated plot allows
dogs to run for a tennis ball without smashing into a fence.
Wood chips and turf are soft on the paws, and when the oak
saplings come of age, they should offer some nice shade.

Doggie Styles

(415) 647-9873

401 Miller Ave, Ste E

(@ La Goma St)

Mill Valley, California 94941

Hours: Tue - Sat 8:30 A.M. - 5 P.M.

Payment: Credit Cards, Checks

Price Range: $$$

In spite of the address, Doggie Styles is nearly a block off Miller Avenue across from Old Mill Creek. Twin sisters Janine and Melinda, who grew up in Mill Valley, have owned it for more than eight years and employ four longtime helpers in their well-run, cheery shop. They try to groom most dogs on leash in open booths, but the occasional aggressive groomee will get caged. Drop-off for baths and minor trims is from 8:30 A.M. to noon, but you need to book four to six weeks ahead for a full cut.

Dog-Gone Walkin'

(415) 497-5002 (San Rafael)

(415) 725-3352 (Novato)

www.doggonewalkin.com

Hours: By Appt

Payment: Checks

Price Range: $$

Dog-Gone Walkin's owners and operators Molly and Laura Gregg are all about customer service and communication. The two regularly update dog owners about what's transpired under their watch. Dog walks last about 30 to 40 minutes. Pet-sitting visits (two a day) last from 30 to 110 minutes. The Greggs ask that you choose the 110-minute option when you're out of town, so your pup will get plenty of attention. They will also take care of mail and plants during their visits.

Elizabeth Anne Perrone Dog Park

13630 Sonoma Hwy
in Sonoma Valley Regional Park
(southeast of Glen Ellen @ Hwy 12)
Hours: Dawn to Dusk
The shade and relaxing rustle of the tall cottonwoods make
this park one of the most pleasant anywhere around the Bay.
You'll find the grass-topped one-acre park a bit sandy, but no
one seems to mind, as the area is kept up well. Both people
and dogs are friendly—if you happen to be a newcomer you'll
feel welcome from the start. Bring baggies, water is provided.

Fideaux

Healdsburg Location
(707) 433-9935
43 North St
(@ Healdsburg Ave)
Healdsburg, California 95448

St. Helena Location
(707) 967-9935
1312 Main St
St. Helena, California 94574

Hours: Every Day 9:30 A.M. - 5:30 P.M.
Payment: Credit Cards, Checks
Price Range: $$$
This fabulous shop with two locations offers a wide array of
uniquely styled collars, leashes and all-weather apparel, plus
jewelry, books, cards and decor items. But your dog's practical
needs are met as well. Jennifer stocks her store with a discrete
selection of high-quality foods, supplements and grooming
products. If you don't see the product you want on the
shelves, she is happy to special order it for you.

Field of Dogs

P.O. Box 4088
Civic Center Dr
(across from the Marin County Civic Center)
San Rafael, California 94913
www.fieldofdogs.org
Hours: Dawn to Dusk

The Marin County Civic Center, a spectacular structure designed by Frank Lloyd Wright, shields this popular dog park from the Highway 101. With the help of the Marin Humane Society and a devoted community of volunteers (check out their Yahoo! group), this six-year-old park boasts an airlock entry, water for dogs and people, benches, pooper scoopers, baggies and tree-studded landscaping. Although the park is open from dawn to dusk, you'll find the most action in the evenings. Warning: The small-dog area is really small, so if your petite pooch wants social interaction, he'd better be comfortable with bigger dogs.

Gay's Doggie Salon

(415) 456-6050
511 4th St
(between Irwin St & Grand Ave)
San Rafael, California 94901
Hours: Tue - Sat 8:30 A.M. - 6 P.M.
Payment: Credit Cards, Checks
Price Range: $$

There's nothing frou-frou about Gay's: Dogs have been getting groomed here for decades. It's a friendly place with a dependable reputation, and Lisa, the owner for the past five years, has 25 years of grooming experience. Gay's is famous for undercoat removal, and they claim to be the only salon in Marin that doesn't require an appointment. Dogs are worked on in open stalls. You can drop off your dog between 8:30 A.M. and 10 A.M.

Give Your Dog a Bone

(415) 499-0364
2180 Northgate Mall
(Macy's—Ollini entrance, across from Rite Aid)
San Rafael, California 94903
Hours: Mon - Sat 10 A.M. - 9 P.M., Sun 11 A.M. - 6 P.M.
Payment: Credit Cards, Checks
Price Range: $$

Yes, you can buy your dog a bone here, but you can also pick her up a pair of angel wings, a sailor hat, a feather bed or a fainting couch. The bright, attractive store stocks unusual toys—try a lingual dog translator to discover what your pal is really saying—clothes and pet gear as well as a small selection of pet foods. Give Your Dog a Bone is active in adoption and on Saturdays, they extend space to Second Chance Rescue.

Good Dog Portraits by Lyn Dillin

(707) 829-6933
375 Taft St
Sebastopol, California 95472
www.dillindesign.com
Hours: By Appt
Payment: Checks
Price Range: $$

Frequenters of Petaluma's Dog Row might have noticed all the impressionistic dog portraits. They are the work of Lyn Dillin, a graphic artist, illustrator and calligrapher who was drawn to pup portraiture by her desire to immortalize the unique spirits of dogs. She works from photographs, but likes to meet the dog as well. Don't expect to see preliminary drafts because she prefers to let her paintings reveal themselves without too much outside direction.

Granary Feed and Pet Supply, The

(707) 938-8011
19626 8th St E
Sonoma, California 95476
Hours: Mon - Fri 9 A.M. - 5 P.M., Sat 9 A.M. - 3 P.M.
Payment: Credit Cards, Checks
Price Range: $$

Stop by the Granary in the spring and you might get to see three-day-old chicks, ducklings, goslings and pullets. Inside the big warehouse, you can browse through the store's 12,000 items, including collars, treats, high-quality dog food and all-natural grooming products. In case you start to wonder about the chirping you hear while sifting through the brass bull leaders and hoof knives, it's boxes of crickets. They serve as food for the fledgling feathered bunch.

Guide Dogs for the Blind

(415) 499-4000
350 Los Ranchitos Rd
(south of Northgate Mall in Terra Linda)
San Rafael, California 94903
www.guidedogs.com
Hours: Mon - Fri 8 A.M. - 5 P.M.,
Drop-in Tours: Mon – Sat 10:30 A.M. and 2 P.M.
Payment: Credit Cards, Checks
Price Range: $$

A Bay Area institution since 1942, Guide Dogs for the Blind has provided service companions for more than 10,000 visually impaired people. In addition to training service dogs, the school works with future service-dog owners to ensure they will be speaking the same language as their canine companions. Visitors are always welcome to take the organized tour or to visit during a graduation ceremony, held once a month on Saturdays. In addition to volunteering at the vet or boarding facilities, you can also opt to foster, housebreak and socialize a young guide-dog-to-be.

Kennel Club, The

(415) 381-2275
322 Miller Ave
(@ Willow St)
Mill Valley, California 94941
Hours: Tues - Fri: 9:30 A.M. – Last Dog
Payment: Credit Cards, Checks
Price Range: $$

This small, sparkling grooming business is run by a former vet-tech. As if to mirror the shop's diminutive size, her canine clients are mostly small breeds. (However, Lab and Bouvier-type customers have been spotted here). It's possible to book a bath for the same day, but call well in advance for more elaborate treatments. Cage dryers are used here, but only at a low temperature and under strict supervision.

Maranda Ranch Kennels

(707) 996-9472
3350 Westlach Way
(on Hwy 121, enter via Ramal Rd)
Sonoma, California 95476
www.marandaranch.com
Hours: Sat 8 A.M. - 12 P.M., Sun 4 P.M. - 6 P.M.,
Mon - Fri 8 A.M. – 12 P.M., 4P.M. – 6 P.M.
Payment: Credit Cards, Checks
Price Range: $$

Budget-conscious owners should like this affordable facility, where dogs stay in a veritable Garden of Eden, complete with Christian broadcasts in the background. Owners Dave and Maribeth, who met while working at Guide Dogs for the Blind, renovated this old kennel which now boasts abundant greenery, group play areas, a small-dog motel and clean, spacious runs. Dogs are given plenty of personal attention, and water and food intake is carefully monitored. If you want your dog spruced up for your return, Maranda Ranch can also give your pup a bath.

Marin Humane Society, The

(415) 883-4621
171 Bel Marin Keys Blvd
(east of Hwy 101, Bel Marin Keys/Ignacio exit)
Novato, California 94949
www.marinhumanesociety.org
Hours: Tue 10 A.M. - 5:30 P.M., Wed 10 A.M. - 7 P.M.,
Thu - Sun 10 A.M. - 5:30 P.M.
Payment: Checks
Price Range: $

In addition to affordable pet adoptions, the Marin Humane
Society offers a phenomenal roster of classes and workshops.
Behavior and training director Trish King designed a program
that covers everything from basic puppy and family dog classes
to trail manners, street smarts, leash-free training, agility and
tricks. There are specific classes for small dogs, difficult dogs
and bull breeds, as well as workshops to teach people how to
understand dog body language.

McInnis County Park

(415) 499-6387
Smith Ranch Rd
(1 mile east of Hwy 101)
San Rafael, California 94903
www.co.marin.ca.us
Hours: Spring/Summer Every Day 7 A.M. – 11 P.M.,
Fall/Winter Every Day 9 A.M. – 5 P.M.

A large group of dog enthusiasts made such a good impression
on this park's administration that dogs won the right to enjoy
their favorite off-leash activities in the area adjacent to the
playing fields. The dog scene has ebbed since then, but as long
as you carry your leash, clean up after your dog and maintain
voice control, your pup can roll around on some of the greenest
groomed grass in the county.

Our Best Friend

(707) 763-6560
301 2nd St
(off D St & Petaluma Blvd)
Petaluma, California 94952
Hours: Mon - Fri 10 A.M. - 5:30 P.M., Sat 10 A.M. - 5 P.M.,
Sun 12 P.M. - 4 P.M.
Payment: Credit Cards, Checks
Price Range: $$

Our Best Friend opened for business long before the chic dog boutiques came into vogue. You'll find plenty of breed-specific gear in addition to Wysong food, organic treats, specialty pet-care items and raised feeding stations—which are made on-site. The store also carries gift items—including jewelry, Limoge boxes, games, books, toys and dog clothes. Local therapy dogs stop by to get dolled up before visiting the hospital.

Pet Agree

(415) 453-8210
1920 4th St
(@ 2nd St)
San Rafael, California 94901
Hours: Mon - Sat 8 A.M. - 7 P.M., Sun 10 A.M. - 4:30 P.M.
Payment: Credit Cards, Checks
Price Range: $$

For over 20 years, Pet Agree's cozy style has made it the perfect place to bring a shaggy pet in need of a haircut. Pet Agree uses all-natural bath products like Earthbath and Magic Coat and offers hand scissoring, towel drying, and forced-air and regular hand drying. Cage drying is only done in the fall and winter. Nutritional advice is also on the salon's menu. The store stocks the all-natural line, Front River Ranch.

Pet Club

(415) 927-2862
508 Tamalpais Dr
Corte Madera, California 94925
www.petclubstores.com
Hours: Mon - Fri 9 A.M. - 8 P.M., Sat 9 A.M. - 7 P.M.,
Sun 10 A.M. - 7 P.M.
Payment: Checks
Price Range: $

Think Costco for pets, and you'll understand the concept of this no-frills, warehouse-style pet emporium. You'll find a wide range of traditional and holistic pet supplies. When you see the rock-bottom prices you may not care that the sales clerks are little more than cashiers. Don't bother bringing your credit card: Pet Club accepts only checks, cash or ATM cards.

Pet Food Cottage

(415) 485-1158
326 San Anselmo Ave
(between Ross & Mariposa aves)
San Anselmo, California 94960
Hours: Mon - Sat 10 A.M. - 6 P.M.
Payment: Credit Cards, Checks
Price Range: $$

If you think that raw food is a newfangled food fad, think again. When the Pet Food Cottage opened its doors in 1939, people came to the store to buy fresh raw meat for their dogs and cats. A few years ago, owners Sandy and Gay decided to return their business to its roots. Now customers flock here from all over and many are referred here by their holistic vets. Ask a nutrition or health question, and you can expect a detailed answer that might include mention of some of the many holistic products on the shelves. But they're not product pushers; they give you the science to support their claims.

Pet Food Express
www.petfoodexpress.com

Benicia Location
(707) 748-4477
838 Southampton Rd
(across from Raleys)
Benicia, California 94510
www.petfoodexpress.com
Hours: Mon - Fri 9:30 A.M. - 8 P.M., Sat 9 A.M. - 7 P.M.,
Sun 10 A.M. - 6 P.M.
Payment: Credit Cards, Checks
Price Range: $$

Novato Location
(415) 878-0111
912 Diablo Ave
(across from Safeway)
Novato, California 94947
Hours: Mon - Fri 9:30 A.M. - 8 P.M., Sat 9 A.M. - 8 P.M.,
Sun 10 A.M. - 6 P.M.
Payment: Credit Cards, Checks
Price Range: $$

Pet Food Express is a pet-supply chain with numerous franchises throughout the Bay Area. They sell a variety of pet supplies, including specialty items like the safety light dog collar and the Cider Mill dog trolley. Brands such as Avo Derm and Pinnacle are on the shelves, and Pet Express staff is friendly and helpful. Dog training classes and low-cost vaccinations are available. The store's My Mutt program promotes adoption of the mighty mixed breed.

Petco
www.petco.com
Payment: Credit Cards, Checks
Price Range: $$

Eureka Location
(707) 445-1256
3300 Broadway St
Eureka, California 95501
Hours: Mon - Sat 9 A.M. - 9 P.M., Sun 10 A.M. - 7 P.M.

Napa Location
(707) 224-7662
3284 Jefferson St
(between Trancas St & Claremont Way)
Napa, California 94558
Hours: Mon - Sat 8 A.M. - 9 P.M., Sun 10 A.M. - 8 P.M.

Novato Location
(415) 898-9416
208 Vintage Way
(@ Rowland Blvd)
Novato, California 94945
Hours: Mon - Sat 9 A.M. - 9 P.M., Sun 9 A.M. - 7 P.M.

San Rafael Location
(415) 457-5262
375 3rd St
(between Mary & Union sts)
San Rafael, California 94901
Hours: Mon - Sat 9 A.M. - 9 P.M., Sun 10 A.M. - 7 P.M.

Santa Rosa Location
(707) 566-7900
2765 Santa Rosa Ave
(between Yolanda Ave & Burt St)
Santa Rosa, California 95407
Hours: Mon - Fri 9 A.M. - 9 P.M., Sat 9 A.M. - 8 P.M.,
Sun 9 A.M. - 7 P.M.

Vacaville Location
(707) 448-2020
210 Nut Tree Pkwy
(southwest of Harbison Dr)
Vacaville, California 95687
Hours: Mon - Sat 9 A.M. - 9 P.M., Sun 9 A.M. - 7 P.M.

Vallejo Location
(707) 649-8081
161 Plaza Dr
(between Admiral Callaghan Ln & Turner Pky)
Vallejo, California 94591
Hours: Mon - Sat 9 A.M. - 9 P.M., Sun 10 A.M. - 8 P.M.

For one-stop shopping it's hard to beat the convenience and value of this superstore with locations all over the country. Petco makes it their mission to provide customers with the food, supplements and products they want for their animals. Their bed selection runs the gamut, from orthopedic mattresses along with sheets and throws to chaises that would do an interior decorator proud. Get a P.A.L.S. (Petco Animal Lovers Save) card to take advantage of discounts; you may also want to check out their Top Dog program, which offers even greater savings to their most loyal customers. Check the contact information for each store for hours and specific service offerings.

Petsmart

(707) 586-1891
575 Rohnert Park Expressway
(@ Labath Ave)
Rohnert Park, California 94928
www.petsmart.com
Hours: Mon - Sun 9 A.M. - 9 P.M.
Payment: Credit Cards, Checks
Price Range: $$

This standout superstore is to pet owners what Home Depot is to homeowners. PetSmart stocks an unbelievably wide range of products that will meet almost any budget. They carry the better dog food brands—including Bil-Jac. And whenever possible, they offer all-natural options in their selection of treats, supplements and skin products. A viewing window allows see-for-yourself grooming so you don't have to worry about what happens behind closed doors. They get major points for promoting their adoptions all the time. And they have a staff that's always available to advise you and to help you find what you need. It's places like PetSmart that give superstores a good name.

Planet Canine

(415) 459-6130
1123 Francisco Blvd E
(@ Bellam Blvd)
San Rafael, California 94901
www.planetcanine.com
Hours: Mon - Fri 7 A.M. - 7 P.M., Sat - Sun 8 A.M. - 6 P.M.,
Closed: Mon - Fri 11:30 A.M. - 2:30 P.M.,
Sat - Sun 10 A.M. - 4 P.M.
Payment: Credit Cards, Checks
Price Range: $$

Kate, Planet Canine's owner and operator, designed her pleasant day-care and boarding facility around some of her unique observations on the nature of dogs. They have been entertaining themselves for centuries; they sleep an average of 18 hours a day; and their brains are surprisingly small. She only takes about 26 dogs at a time—moving them around, inside and out, to create the happiest and safest groupings. Noting that dogs tend to tear their beds apart when they are away from home, Kate supplies washable bathroom rugs for bedding.

Postmore Kennels

(415) 897-5892
753 McClay Rd
(1½ blocks southwest of Center Rd)
Novato, California 94947
Hours: Mon - Sat 8:30 A.M. - 5:30 P.M.
Payment: Credit Cards, Checks
Price Range: $$

Unlike the many day cares located in industrial zones, Postmore is located in an upscale neighborhood. Robbie and his staff have stayed in the neighbors' good graces by running a clean and quiet operation hidden behind fencing and greenery. Small dogs mingle in the groom room by day—watching a steady stream of dogs get washed and expertly styled. The big dogs, who hang out in climate-controlled runs, enjoy twice-daily romps in a huge, clean, wood chip-covered yard that comes complete with weeping willows. Day care is available for half the price of boarding.

Powell Bros. Feed & Pet Supply

(707) 644-3333
1895 Broadway
(1 block south of Marine World Pkwy)
Vallejo, California 94589
Hours: Mon - Sun 9 A.M. - 7 P.M.,
Grooming Thu - Tue 9 A.M. - 5 P.M.
Payment: Credit Cards, Checks
Price Range: $$

This old feed store is still the best spot to pick up some laying mash, turkey starter, chicken scratch or a bale of hay, along with all-natural dog products. Owners Pen and Vincent stock many of the holistic dog kibble brands, as well as all-natural shampoos. Your leashed dog can shop with you and make the acquaintance of exotic birds, goldfish, baby chicks and rabbits, among other critters. Powell Bros. also provides grooming services, and will handle all breeds—unless your giant breed is a handful. They use clippers or a clipper vac. All of their dryers—cage, hand and stand-up—are thermostat controlled, and cage drying is supervised.

Red Hill Pet Center

(415) 457-0927
906 Sir Francis Drake
(in Red Hill Shopping Center)
San Anselmo, California 94960
Hours: Mon - Sat 10 A.M. - 7 P.M., Sun 11 A.M. - 6 P.M.
Payment: Credit Cards, Checks
Price Range: $$

After 25 years in the same spot, owner Elvis just swapped his small space for a larger one in the same center. Now he has sufficient room to stock his impressive selection of high-quality dog foods, which includes several raw varieties. There are plenty of other dog supplies, plus everything you need if you keep birds, bunnies or freshwater fish. You can even pick up one of the aforementioned animals while you're here, but there are no puppies or kittens for sale—just plenty of assistance with making your pup a happy one.

Rivertown Feed and Pet Country Store

(707) 762-4505
200 1st St
Petaluma, California 94952
Hours: Mon - Sat 8 A.M. - 5:30 P.M., Sun 10 A.M. - 2 P.M.
Payment: Credit Cards, Checks
Price Range: $$

You can pick up cowboy boots, hay bales and rubbers for slopping the hogs, but the real draw here is the premium dog food brands and several raw-food choices. You'd be hard-pressed to find a better selection of basic nylon dog collars anywhere in the Bay Area: They even carry the now-rare tennis ball collar, de rigeur with fetch fanatics. Another favorite item is the rubber chicken. But think twice about letting your dog parade past the local chicken farmers with one in his mouth.

Romar Kennels

(415) 892-3868
402 Indian Springs Rd
(off S Novato Blvd)
Novato, California 94947
www.romarkennels.com
Hours: Mon - Fri 9 A.M.–12 P.M., 2 P.M.– 6 P.M.,
Sat 9 A.M. - 1 P.M., Sun 2 P.M. – 6 P.M.
Payment: Checks
Price Range: $

Jan, who watches over the dogs at Romar, believes that dogs are like people: Some like cocktail parties and some don't. Romar is a good place for those who prefer peace and quiet, fresh air and open views of the northern Marin farm-lands. Accommodations are clean in an old, wooden barn—heated in the winter and cooled by a swamp cooler in the summer. Dogs here don't miss out on any playtime: There's a large play area where dogs enjoy daily romping.

Show Time

(707) 939-0117
529 Broadway
(½ block from the town square)
Sonoma, California 95476
Hours: Tue - Sat 9 A.M. - 5:30 P.M.
Payment: Credit Cards, Checks
Price Range: $$

This new shop offers a full view of the grooming tables from outside or inside the salon. Pam, the owner, has an affinity for bichons, but she'll do anything from a basic mutt cut to a fancy poodle 'do in her environmentally friendly shop. And if your dog's breath needs a little sprucing up, she even brushes teeth. Your dog's comfort is paramount at Show Time. Ramps and lifts ease dogs onto and off of the tables, and the unique clipper-vac system is cooled. They also offer the Prima bathing system and all-natural shampoos.

Sonoma Dog Camp

(707) 935-3645
1061 Broadway (2 blocks south of MacArthur, across from Sonoma Valley High School)
Sonoma, California 95476
www.sonomadogcamp.com
Hours: Mon - Fri 6:30 A.M. - 6:30 P.M., Sat 10 A.M. - 4 P.M.
Store Hours: Mon - Fri 10 A.M. - 6:30 P.M.
Payment: Credit Cards, Checks
Price Range: $$

You'll find eco-hip hemp collars, organic treats, all-natural shampoos and high-tech toys in this country home-style dog camp. Vintage dog accouterments are scattered among impressive antique furnishings. The facility's stunning art and book gallery serves as a gathering place for animal shelter benefits. In the day-care areas, dogs enjoy clean, climate-controlled play-rooms with comfy furniture and ample outdoor space. All potential campers are carefully screened, but there's a vet tech on staff in case a problem should arise.

Take the Lead

(707) 546-5959
www.taketheleadtraining.com
Hours: By Appt
Payment: Checks
Price Range: $$

Dana Pearlman takes the lead among Sonoma and Napa dog trainers, offering one-on-one work in basic obedience, off-leash training, trick training, aggression management, behavior modification and puppy issues. She puts her background in psychology to work in understanding the dynamics of how dogs operate in our households. She'll show you how to teach your dog exactly what it is you want him to do rather than focusing on the things you don't want him to do. Dana works in Sonoma and Napa counties.

Tappen Hill
(707) 824-9100
4801 Llano Rd
(off Hwy 116, north of Petaluma Ave)
Sebastopol, California 95472
www.tappenhill.com
Hours: Every Day 8 A.M. - 12 P.M., 2 P.M. - 6 P.M.
Payment: Credit Cards, Checks
Price Range: $$$

You may have an easier time gaining entry into a certain Bay Area all-male club—as a woman—than getting your dog accepted into Tappen Hill. The major difference, of course, is that this canine retreat is absolutely worth the effort. All new guests are assigned to a group to spend their days and nights with. Outdoor recreation includes swimming in two beautiful pools as well as frolicking on play structures. The large staff meticulously attends to every need and whim of their guests. Owners Annie and Christopher, who come from an impressive background of service-dog training, live on-site and oversee all dog care and training.

Unleashed!
(707) 763-9882
225-B 2nd St
(next to Dawg Groomer)
Petaluma, California 94952
Hours: By Appt
Payment: Checks
Price Range: $$

Unleashed! trainers Laurel, Mandy and Charlie have put together
a comprehensive dog-training program. They hold group classes
in Rivertown Feed's big storage barn, where everyone but allergy
sufferers should appreciate the distinctive aroma of alfalfa. The
curriculum includes Puppy Play School, Smart Starts, Look Who's
Walking and Downtown Dogs. If your dog makes it through the
rigorous program, you can rest assured he'll make a positive
impression on the people of Petaluma.

We Care Animal Rescue

(707) 963-7044
1345 Charter Oak Ave
(Hwy 29)
St Helena, California 94574
www.wecareanimalrescue.org
Hours: Tues - Sat 12 P.M. - 5 P.M. (Call First)
Payment: Checks
Price Range: $

This no-kill rescue organization, which was created in 1982,
provides nurturing care for up to 75 homeless cats and dogs
in the Napa Valley area. This means animals will be taken care
of for as long as it takes to find them a loving home. Facilities
include three cat rooms where felines roam free and a large
play yard for dogs. They also have a public-education program
that teaches children about the responsibilities of pet ownership. Like any nonprofit, We Care is privately funded and
always appreciates donations of money, time and materials.

Wheeler Pet Care

(707) 253-0173
4870 Dry Creek Rd
Napa, California 94558
Hours: By Appt
Payment: Credit Cards, Checks

Price Range: $

Debby usually pet-sits for dogs, cats, goldfish, hamsters and bunnies. However, she was raised around dairy farms, so she is also qualified to feed and water cows, horses, pigs, goats, chickens or other animals you may have. Dog walks last 30 minutes, but she's happy to go longer if you ask. If you're planning to spend the afternoon in the vineyards, she will come to your dog-friendly hotel and watch your pet while you're out.

Wilson's Feed & Supply

(707) 252-0316
1700 Yajome St
(@ Yount St)
Napa, California 94559
Hours: Mon - Fri 8 A.M. - 5:30 P.M., Sat 8 A.M. - 4 P.M.
Payment: Credit Cards, Checks
Price Range: $$

You can choose between 52 different kinds of dog food at Jim Wilson's big old barn, or pick up feed for your horse, cow, sheep, goat, pig, chicken, duck, llama or emu—just as local farm folks have been doing here for the past 30 years. They have a smaller selection of other dog supplies, some handsome leather collars and leashes plus plenty of breed books.

Wizard of Paws Mobile Grooming

(707) 869-9966
www.wizard-grooming.com
Hours: By Appt
Payment: Checks
Price Range: $$

Certified master groomer Leslie Craig earned her reputation during her 20-year stint at Novato's Who Does Your Dog, but now she's gone mobile with a pristine, state-of-the-art grooming van. She has an extensive knowledge of breed styling and an abiding concern for your pet's welfare and unique sensitivities. To put your dog at ease, Leslie plays soothing music and uses aromatherapy oils. All of this has earned her the seal of approval from Marin dog pros, as well as raves from many other local dog professionals. Areas covered include Guerneville to San Rafael and farther north.

East Bay

EMERGENCY PET TRANSPORT

AMERS Animal Ambulance
(877) 426-3771 (emergency)
(925) 261-9111 (office)
www.animalmedics.com
Hours: Every Day 24 Hours
Payment: Credit Cards, Checks
Emergency Fee: $175

Pet Taxi
(415) 386-2534
Hours: Every Day 7 A.M. – 7 P.M.
Emergency Hours: Every Day 24 Hours
Payment: Checks
Price Range: $$/$$$

ANIMAL EMERGENCY FACILITIES

American Animal Hospital
(510) 791-0464
37177 Freemont Blvd
Freemont, California 94536
Hours: Every Day 24 Hours
Payment: Credit Cards, Checks
Price Range: $$

Bay Area Veterinary Emergency Clinic
(510) 352-6080
14790 Washington Ave
Oakland, California 94607
Hours: Every Day 24 Hours
Payment: Credit Cards, Checks
Price Range: $$

Berkeley Dog & Cat Hospital
(510) 848-5150 (specialists and 24-hour emergency)
2426 Haste St
(between Shattuck Ave & Fulton St)
Berkeley, CA 94704
www.berkeleydogandcat.com
www.specialvetservices.com
Emergency Hours: Mon – Fri 6 P.M. – 8 A.M.,
Weekends & Holidays 24 Hours
Payment: Credit Cards, Checks
Price Range: $/$$/$$$

Contra Costa Veterinary Emergency Clinic
(925) 798-2900
1410 Monument Blvd
Concord, California 94520
Hours: Mon – Fri 6 P.M. – 8 A.M.
Weekends & Holidays 24 Hours
Payment: Credit Cards, Checks
Price Range: $$

Ohlone Veterinary Emergency
(510) 657-6620
1618 Washington Blvd
Fremont, California 94539
Hours: Mon – Fri: 5:30 P.M. – 8 A.M. Sat – Sun 24 Hours
Payment: Credit Cards, Checks
Price Range: $$

Pet Emergency Services

(510) 548-6684
1048 University Ave
Berkeley, California 94710
Hours: Mon – Fri 6 P.M. – 8 A.M.
Weekends & Holidays 24 Hours
Payment: Credit Cards, Checks
Price Range: $$

University Veterinary Hospital

(510) 841-4415
810 University Ave
Berkeley, California 94710
www.uvhberkeley.com
Hours: Every Day 24 Hours
Payment: Credit Cards, Checks
Price Range: $$

Veterinary Hospital

(510) 797-7387
5245 Central Ave
Fremont, California 94536
Hours: Every Day 24 Hours
Payment: Credit Cards, Checks
Price Range: $$

ANIMAL POISON HOTLINE

ASPCA Animal Poison Control Center

(888) 4ANI-HELP
Hours: Every Day 24 Hours
Payment: Credit Cards
Consultation Fee: $45

ADOPTION

Berkeley *Berkeley East Bay Humane Society*
Concord *Petsmart*
Dublin *Petsmart*
Fremont *Bogie's Discount Pet Supply and Dog Wash*
● *Furry Friends Rescue*
Lafayette *Nitro Dog*
Newark *Petsmart*
Oakland *East Bay SPCA* ● *Hopalong Animal Rescue* ● *Pet Food Express* ● *Pet Vet/Pet Food* ● *Redhound* ● *Smiley Dog Rescue*
Pittsburg *Petsmart*
Richmond *Petsmart*
San Leandro *Petsmart*
Walnut Creek *Arf*

ALTERNATIVE PRODUCTS/SERVICES

Albany *Alpha Pet Supply and Wild Bird's Nest* ● *Dog's Best Friend & The Cat's Meow*
Berkeley *George* ● *Holistic Hound*
Emeryville *Pet Club*
Fremont *Fremont BARF Co-op*
North Oakland *Brill, Glenn*
Oakland *Creature Comfort* ● *Pet Vet/Pet Food* ● *SOL Companion*
San Ramon *Pet Care Depot at Bishop Ranch Veterinary Center*

ANESTHESIA-FREE TEETH CLEANING

Albany *Alpha Pet Supply and Wild Bird's Nest*
Berkeley *Holistic Hound*
Fremont *Bogie's Discount Pet Supply and Dog Wash*
Oakland *Creature Comfort* ● *Pet Vet/Pet Food* ● *Redhound*
San Ramon *ShamPooches*

DOG BOARDING

Mobile *Apronstrings Pet Sitting* **(S)** ● *Gentle Persuasion, LLC*

Castro Valley *Club K-9* **(S)**
Danville *Breton's School for Dogs and Cats*
Emeryville *Every Dog Has its Daycare, Inc.*
Hayward *Hayward Pet Complex*
Lafayette *Waiterock Kennels*
Oakland *Citizen Canine* • *East Bay Pet Sitters Association*
• *Happy Hound Play & Daycare/Bed & Bone Hound Hotel* **(S)**
San Ramon *Pet Care Depot at Bishop Ranch Veterinary Center*
• *Puppy Playland*
Sunol *Happiness Country Kennels*
Walnut Creek *North Main Pet Lodge*

DOG DAY CARE

Mobile *Apronstrings Pet Sitting* **(S)**
Castro Valley *Club K-9* **(S)**
Concord *All Breed Pet Daycare* • *Kathleen Huston's All Breed Grooming*
Emeryville *Every Dog Has its Daycare, Inc.*
Oakland *Broadway Pet Grooming* • *Citizen Canine* • *East Bay Pet Sitters Association* • *Happy Hound Play & Daycare/Bed & Bone Hound Hotel* **(S)**
Pleasant Hill *Pam Miller, Pet Nanny* **(S)**
San Ramon *Puppy Playland*

DOG GROOMING

Alameda *Petco*
Alamo *Dog and Cat Laundromat*
Albany *Dog's Best Friend & The Cat's Meow*
Berkeley *Kutz For Mutz* • *PAWS* **(S)** • *Wizard of Paws*
Castro Valley *Club K-9* **(S)** • *Petco*
Concord *All Breed Pet Daycare* • *Kathleen Huston's All Breed Grooming* • *Launder Mutt* • *Regina's Pet Grooming* • *Petco* • *Petsmart*
Dublin *Petsmart*
Danville *Blackhawk Grooming Salon, Inc.*
El Cerrito *Petco*
El Sobrante *Waggs & Whiskers*
Emeryville *Every Dog Has its Daycare, Inc.*
Fremont *Bogie's Discount Pet Supply and Dog Wash* • *Petco*
Hayward *Hayward Pet Complex*
Lafayette *Clip Joint, The* • *Waiterock Kennels*

Oakland *Broadway Pet Grooming* ●*Citizen Canine* ● *East Bay Pet Sitters Association* ● *Happy Hound Play & Daycare/Bed & Bone Hound Hotel* **(S)**
Newart *Petsmart*
Pittsburg *Petsmart*
Richmond *Dogs by Dianne* **(S)** ● *Mudpuppy's Tub & Scrub* ● *Petsmart*
San Leandro *Kaycee's Pet & Groom* ● *Petsmart*
San Ramon *Pet Care Depot at Bishop Ranch Veterinary Center* ●*Petco* ● *Puppy Playland* ●*ShamPooches*
Sunol *Happiness Country Kennels*
Union City *Petco*
Walnut Creek *North Main Pet Lodge* ● *Petco*

DOG GROOMING—SELF-SERVE
Albany *Dog's Best Friend & The Cat's Meow*
Concord *Launder Mutt*
Lafayette *Clip Joint, The*
Oakland *Pet Food Express*
Richmond *Mudpuppy's Tub & Scrub*
San Ramon *ShamPooches*
Walnut Creek *Petco*

DOG HIKES & SOCIALS
Berkeley *Caesar Chavez Park* ●*Pawsitively Pampered Pet, The* **(S)**
Castro Valley *Club K-9* **(S)**
Concord *Paw Patch, The*
Oakland *Bright Eyes Animal Care*
Pleasant Hill *Dog Park at Paso Nogal Park*
Richmond *Point Isabel Regional Park*

DOG PARKS—OFF LEASH
Benicia *Phenix Dog Park*
Berkeley *Caesar Chavez Park* ● *Ohlone Dog Park*
Castro Valley *Earl Warren Park*
Concord *Paw Patch, The*

Fremont *Drigon Dog Park*
Oakland *Hardy Dog Park*
Piedmont *Dracena Park* • *Linda Park* • *Piedmont Park*
Pleasant Hill *Dog Park at Paso Nogal Park*
Pleasanton *Muirwood Dog Park*
San Ramon *Alta Mesa Memorial Park* • *Del Mar Dog Park*
Sausalito *Remington Dog Park*

DOG TRAINING

Mobile *Canine Communications* • *Canine Culture* • *Canines & Kids Family Dog Training* • *Gentle Persuasion, LLC* • *Pawsitive Steps Dog Training*
Alameda *Petco*
Alamo *Pawsitive Experience* **(S)**
Berkeley *Berkeley East Bay Humane Society*
Castro Valley *Club K-9* **(S)** • *Petco*
Concord *Petco* • *Petsmart*
Danville *Breton's School for Dogs and Cats*
Dublin *Laura For Dog* • *Petco* • *Petsmart*
El Cerrito *Petco*
El Sobrante *EZTrain Dog Training*
Emeryville *Every Dog Has its Daycare, Inc.*
Fremont *Bogie's Discount Pet Supply and Dog Wash* • *Petco*
Hayward *Hayward Pet Complex*
Martinez *Petco*
Oakland *Citizen Canine* • *East Bay Pet Sitters Association* • *East Bay SPCA* • *Happy Hound Play & Daycare/Bed & Bone Hound Hotel* **(S)** • *Pet Food Express*
Newark *Petsmart*
Pittsburg *Petsmart*
Richmond *Petsmart*
San Leandro *Mike's Feed & Pets* • *Petsmart*
San Ramon *Pet Care Depot at Bishop Ranch Veterinary Center* • *Petco* • *Puppy Playland*
Sunol *Happiness Country Kennels*
Union City *Petco*
Walnut Creek *Arf* • *Laura For Dog* • *Petco*

DOG WALKING/PET-SITTING

Mobile *Apronstrings Pet Sitting* **(S)** • *Tooth & Nail* **(S)**
Alamo *Pawsitive Experience* **(S)**
Berkeley *PAWS* **(S)**
El Cerrito *Safe Hands*
Oakland *Bright Eyes Animal Care* • *Dogspeed* • *East Bay Pet Sitters Association*
Pleasant Hill *Pam Miller, Pet Nanny* **(S)**
San Leandro *Run With The Big Dog* **(S)**

PET-SUPPLY STORES

Alameda *Dog Bone Alley* • *Petco*
Alamo *Alamo Hay & Grain Company*
Albany *Alpha Pet Supply and Wild Bird's Nest* • *Dog's Best Friend & The Cat's Meow*
Berkeley *Alan's Petzeria* • *Animal Farm* • *George* • *Holistic Hound* • *Lucky Dog, The*
Castro Valley *Club K-9* **(S)** • *Petco*
Concord *All Breed Pet Daycare* • *Kathleen Huston's All Breed Grooming* • *Petco* • *Petsmart*
Danville *Blackhawk Grooming Salon, Inc.* • *Breton's School for Dogs and Cats* • *Molly's Pup-purr-ee*
Dublin *Petco* • *Petsmart*
El Cerrito *Petco*
Emeryville *Every Dog Has its Daycare, Inc.* • *Pet Club*
Fremont *Bogie's Discount Pet Supply and Dog Wash* • *Fremont BARF Co-op* • *Petco*
Lafayette *Nitro Dog* • *Petco*
Martinez *Petco*
Oakland *Citizen Canine* • *Creature Comfort* • *Pet Food Express* • *Pet Vet/Pet Food* • *Redhound*
Newark *Petsmart*
Pleasanton *Petway*
Pittsburg *Petsmart*
Richmond *Mudpuppy's Tub & Scrub* • *Petsmart*
San Leandro *Mike's Feed & Pets* • *Petsmart*
San Ramon *Pet Care Depot at Bishop Ranch Veterinary Center* • *Petco* • *Puppy Playland*
Sunol *Happiness Country Kennels*
Union City *Petco*
Walnut Creek *Petco*

VACCINATIONS—LOW-COST

Alameda *Petco*
Berkeley *Berkeley East Bay Humane Society*
Castro Valley *Petco*
Concord *Petco • Petsmart*
Dublin *Petco • Petsmart*
El Cerrito *Petco*
Emeryville *Pet Club*
Fremont *Bogie's Discount Pet Supply and Dog Wash • Petco*
Lafayette *Petco*
Martinez *Petco*
Oakland *East Bay SPCA • Pet Food Express • Pet Vet/Pet Food • Redhound*
Newark *Petsmart*
Pittsburg *Petsmart*
San Leandro *Mike's Feed & Pets • Petsmart*
Union City *Petco*
Walnut Creek *Petco*

CITY DOG PICKS

Albany *Alpha Pet Supply and Wild Bird's Nest*
Berkeley *Alan's Petzeria • Wizard of Paws*
Fremont *Fremont BARF Co-op*
Oakland *Dogspeed • East Bay Pet Sitters Association*
Pleasant Hill *Dog Park at Paso Nogal Park*
Sausalito *Remington Dog Park*
Walnut Creek *Apronstrings Pet Sitting • North Main Pet Lodge*

General Listings

Alamo Hay & Grain Company

(925) 837-4994
3196 Danville Blvd
(@ Stone Valley Rd)
Alamo, California 94507
Hours: Mon - Sat 8 A.M. - 6 P.M.
Payment: Credit Cards, Checks
Price Range: $$

This old-fashioned feed store takes you back a few decades, and comes complete with cranky employees, a drive-through metal hangar that smells like a stable and piles of hay stacked in the back yard. Come by to purchase extra-large bags of dog food while picking up some adorable baby chicks, ducklings or bunnies for the country farm.

Alan's Petzeria

(510) 528-2155
843-B Gilman St
(@ 6th St next to the Royal Robbins Outlet)
Berkeley, California 94710
Hours: Mon - Fri 10 A.M. - 6:30 P.M., Sat 9:30 A.M. - 6 P.M.,
Sun 10 A.M. - 5 P.M.
Payment: Credit Cards, Checks
Price Range: $$

Alan's may not serve your pup pepperoni pizza, but gourmet treats include carob-dipped squirrel cookies, doggie lattes and Chinese dogstickers. Raw food fiends will be pleased with the Petzeria's freezer case. And in addition to the wide variety of pup chow, the shop is brimming with supplies for all kinds of pets. Take heed of the sign warning that dogs are not allowed on the stairs leading to the wild-bird loft.

All Breed Pet Daycare

(925) 680-7800
4311 Treat Blvd
(south of Clayton Rd near Turtle Creek Rd)
Concord, California 94521
Hours: Tue - Fri 8 A.M. - 6 P.M.
Payment: Checks
Price Range: $$

This day-care facility is all things to all breeds, offering older dogs leisurely, canal-side walks and for the more energetic types, an off-leash play area at the nearby Paw Patch. The decor is day-care chic: Leopard print couches fill the cottage. The outdoor run is covered in wood chips, which means less dirt to wipe off your dog. And All Breed fills up the pool in the summertime, so dogs can take a dip to cool off.

Alpha Pet Supply and Wild Bird's Nest

(510) 525-7361
960 San Pablo Ave
(in Town Center between Solano & Marin aves)
Albany, California 94706
Hours: Mon - Fri 10 A.M. - 6:30 P.M., Sat 10 A.M. - 5 P.M.,
Sun 10 A.M. - 5 P.M.
Payment: Credit Cards, Checks
Price Range: $$

You'll know you're near Berkeley when you spot the selection of shade-grown fair-trade coffee. But Alpha goes far beyond PC coffee beans, making it tops for products with an all-natural and holistic bent. Owners Vicky and Tina have carefully packed their tiny mall space with an excellent selection of holistic foods, treats, supplements, medicines and accessories. If you need a laugh, check out the selection of humorous pet toys, including political effigies that will warm any lefty's heart.

Alta Mesa Memorial Park
(925) 973-2500
Bollinger Canyon Rd
(west of San Ramon Valley Blvd)
San Ramon, California 94583
Hours: Dawn to Dusk
Everyone complains about the sand surface and lack of trees here, but the large, pristine space and wide, open views reel in valley dogs who seem perfectly content despite the dust. The park is consistently packed with pooches racing around or pan-handling for ear-scratches and treats. The fire hydrants are fake, but there are enough to go around, including the small dog area where pups under 20 pounds run the roost.

Animal Farm
(510) 526-2993
1531 San Pablo Ave
(@ Cedar St)
Berkeley, California 94702
Hours: Mon - Sun 9 A.M. - 7 P.M.
Payment: Credit Cards, Checks
Price Range: $$
Forget the images its Orwellian name may summon. Animal Farm is a cheerful, neighborhood pet store with old wooden floors and a good selection of edible, wearable and chaseable products. It's a lot bigger than it looks from out front; it's large enough to house nearly every Kong product known to dog. Be sure to seek out the large back area and the annex full of wild-bird supplies.

Apronstrings Pet Sitting

(925) 798-7621

www.apronstringsonline.com

Hours: By Appt

Payment: Credit Cards, Checks

Price Range: $$

Apronstrings owner Kim Tank is not only a registered veterinary technician, but she is also the Pet Sitters International ambassador for the state of California. If she can't go to your home herself, she'll send one of her team members, who will tend to your pets, give meds, make your house look lived in, scoop the litter box and the yard, and exercise your dog. And above all, Apronstrings will give your dog plenty of TLC. She serves central Contra Costa County.

ARF (Animal Rescue Foundation)

(925) 256-1273

2890 Mitchell Dr

Walnut Creek, California 94598

www.arf.net

Hours: See Website

A stray cat wandered onto the field during an Oakland A's game. Tony La Russa lured the kitty into the dugout and rescued her only to later find out she would be euthanized at a local shelter. After Tony and his wife Elaine found the kitty a home, they founded ARF. Well over a decade and two thousand animal adoptions later, ARF is a pioneer in community-service programs. Through their Teaching Loving Care program, girls in the Chris Adams Center (a mental health/probation facility) learn the value of interpersonal relationships by caring for resident cats and visiting dogs. Check ARF's website to see adoptable dogs, and to learn about their volunteer and foster programs.

Berkeley East Bay Humane Society

(510) 845-7735
2700 9th St
(@ Carlton St)
Berkeley, California 94710
www.berkeleyhumane.org
Hours: Tue - Sat 11 A.M. - 7 P.M., Sun 11 A.M. - 5 P.M.
Payment: Credit Cards, Checks
Price Range: $

Housed in an older building in a semi-industrial part of town, this well-run shelter is fairly mellow, thanks to the volunteers who hand-feed the dogs, walk them three times a day and housebreak them in preparation for their new homes. There's a strong emphasis on rescuing animals slated for euthanasia at other facilities. Rescued dogs are temperament-tested prior to arrival, and potential adopters are screened by application to find suitable matches. Fees are $125 per dog and $100 per cat, and include spay/neuter, vaccinations, basic obedience training, microchipping and a Kong toy to take home. All profits from the full-service, on-site veterinary clinic support the shelter, which also offers obedience and socialization classes.

Blackhawk Grooming Salon, Inc.

(925) 736-5900
9000-X Crow Canyon Rd
(@ Center St)
Danville, California 94596
www.blackhawkgrooming.com
Hours: Mon - Thu 8 A.M. - 6 P.M., Sat 9 A.M. - 5 P.M.
Payment: Credit Cards, Checks
Price Range: $$

After learning to groom his schnauzer, owner Jonathan honed his skills in grooming school and now runs this sprawling, chic shop with top-notch show groomer, Leslie, working beside him. The friendly pair takes gentle care of many older dogs and can coordinate visits to the vet, which is only a door away. You can count on all-natural products, hand drying, and pampering that promises to make your pet the envy of unkempt dogs. Also available is an eclectic collection of home-baked treats, toys and gifts for both people and dogs. They groom feline friends too. You can get groomed yourself at the skin-care salon next door.

Bogie's Discount Pet Supply and Dog Wash

(510) 795-6000
37030 Post St
(@ Thornton Ave)
Fremont, California 94536
www.bogiespet.com
Hours: Mon 10 A.M. - 8 P.M., Tue - Wed 10 A.M. - 9 P.M.,
Thu - Fri 10 A.M. - 8 P.M.
Sat 8:30 A.M. - 7 P.M., Sun 10 A.M. - 6 P.M.
Payment: Credit Cards, Checks
Price Range: $$

Fremont's mom-and-pop pet supply store is named for the resident rescue dog, but cats, fish, birds and horses are like-wise honored on the big mural in the parking lot. There's a wide variety of products, with an emphasis on Innova and California Natural foods and the full C-Derm line of shampoos and skin-care products. Bogie's offers obedience classes, including puppy and conformation. And there's a full-service grooming salon next door.

Breton's School for Dogs and Cats

(925) 736-6231
1455 Lawrence Rd
(about 1 mile south of Camino Tassajara)
Danville, California 94526
Hours: Mon - Tue 8 A.M. - 6 P.M., Thu 8 A.M. - 6 P.M.,
Sat 8 A.M. - 2 P.M.
Payment: Credit Cards, Checks
Price Range: $$

Breton's School is a clean, safe and comfortable place to spend a few nights under the experienced care of Ann Breton and her extended family. Dogs don't mingle, so there's no admissions exam to pass. Base prices are very reasonable, but outdoor play costs extra. Also available are group and private lessons in obedience and agility with expert trainer Alan Levens. Dogs attend this school from far and wide, and Ann will coordinate transportation from anywhere around the globe. All dogs go home freshly bathed, which invariably gets an A from their owners.

Bright Eyes Animal Care

(510) 533-0930

www.brighteyesanimalcare.com

Hours: By Appt

Payment: Checks

Price Range: $$

Beth Murray leads a small group of dogs on hikes in the East Bay Regional Parks. Her groups are reserved for dogs who play well with others. She also does neighborhood walks, makes home visits and will even look in on a bird or reptile. As an animal homeopath-in-training and an intern at Creature Comforts Veterinary Center, she likes to introduce clients to the world of holistic animal medicine. Bright Eyes serves Oakland.

Brill, Glenn

(510) 654-3135

Hours: By Appt

Payment: Checks

Price Range: $$$

For people obsessed with dogs and fine art, both worlds collide will apprreciate the work of Glenn Brill. Glenn's fascination with dog portraiture emerged while he used photos of his dogs for monoprint technique to teach students at local colleges. He found himself capturing the essence of his dogs' lives, an experience that quickly turned into a business creat ing commission work for dog owners and art patrons. If you can afford it, commissioned art presents the perfect way to immortalize your pet. Glenn has also written and illustrated his own dog book.

Broadway Pet Grooming

(510) 444-1159
1104 Jefferson St
(@ 10th St)
Oakland, California 94607
www.groomingclinic.com
Hours: Tue - Sat 9 A.M. - 5 P.M.
Payment: Credit Cards, Checks
Price Range: $

Don't expect anything fancy at this tiny place in downtown Oakland; the front door might well be locked and the reception area filled with excited day-care dogs. The Brazilian groomer uses all-natural products on his clients, and he is adept at dealing with skin problems and advising people about canine nutrition. He'll pretty up your pet, whether it be a dog, cat, rabbit or bird, and his prices won't break the piggy bank.

Caesar Chavez Park

(510) 981-6700
Marina Blvd
(@ Berkeley Marina)
Berkeley, California
www.ci.berkeley.ca.us/Parks/parkspages/CesarChavez.html
Hours: Mon - Sun 6 A.M. - 10 P.M.

Dog people who like to stroll, but don't like the pandemonium at Point Isabel, make Cesar Chavez a daily ritual. The off-leash area takes up 17 of the highest acres in this 90-acre park and offers the best views of the bay, the bridges and the San Francisco skyline. But dogs have to be on leash for quite a distance before you get to the designated and unfenced, off-leash meadow. Also, this section isn't irrigated, so in summertime you really need to watch out for foxtails.

Canine Communications

(925) 676-2154
Hours: By Appt
Payment: Checks
Price Range: $$

As a kid, Rachelle amused herself by making her dogs sit and stay in the cornfield. She got serious when she learned the Sirius method of positive reinforcement training and saw how it opened the door to canine communication. Rachelle's focus is on making your dog comfortable in real-life situations. Younger dogs will benefit from puppy classes in Concord and Walnut Creek, while budding athletes train in Freilance Dog Sports classes in Martinez. Rachelle is the go-to trainer of renowned master groomer Kathleen Huston.

Canine Culture

(510) 261-3386
www.canineculture.net
Hours: By Appt
Payment: Checks
Price Range: $$

Alison is the pick of the pack with many local dog professionals as the go-to trainer when a dog bites or has problems with aggression. She teaches behavior modification through positive reinforcement—one-on-one at clients' homes (for aggressive dogs) or in classes, offered at various locations. Dogs ready to move on from puppy school can take Basic Manners 1 and 2, held indoors, and then graduate to Basic 3: a class that helps your dog navigate the urban landscape. Alison's website has valuable articles on training issues. One of her points to ponder: Dogs learn things all the time, and we should be aware of what they take in.

Canines & Kids Family Dog Training

(510) 869-3799

Hours: By Appt

Payment: Checks

Price Range: $$

On many afternoons Jane Rosenblum, CTC, can be found in an East Bay park with a small group of very well-behaved dogs. Their good manners, she'll explain, are the result of clear communication about what's expected of a dog out on a walk. She draws on her background in psychiatric nursing for to work with families at resolving problems between dogs and young children. She emphasizes positive methods that are fun and effective for both dog and owner. Canines & Kids serves Berkeley, Oakland, El Cerrito and Richmond.

Citizen Canine

(510) 562-1750

420 Hegenberger Rd

(1 block west of Hwy 880)

Oakland, California 94621

www.citizencanine.net

Hours: Mon - Fri 7 A.M. - 7 P.M., Sat - Sun 7 A.M. - 6 P.M.

Payment: Credit Cards, Checks

Price Range: $$$

A swankier boarding facility would be hard to come by. Citizen Canine's 50 plush rooms were designed for maximum comfort; three play yards let guests mingle with well-matched buddies. Although California Natural is the house brand, owners are welcome to leave a supply of their regular food. At the end of their stay, dogs are issued a report card identifying troublesome health or behavioral issues.

Clip Joint, The

(925) 283-1001
3322 Mt Diablo Blvd
(@ Carol Ln)
Lafayette, California 94549
Hours: Tue - Sat 8 A.M. - 5 P.M., Mon By Appt
Payment: Credit Cards, Checks
Price Range: $$

These highly regarded groomers will tackle anything from thick-haired Portuguese water dogs, to Airedales whose wiry coats require hand-stripping to maintain their color. The Clip Joint uses non-toxic shampoos, and they specialize in hard-to-handle and geriatric dogs. Self-serve dog washing is available here, but if you want full-service grooming, be sure to call at least two weeks in advance.

Club K-9

(510) 247-9600
10671 Crow Canyon Rd
(between Norris Canyon Rd & I-680)
Castro Valley, California 94552
www.clubk9inc.com
Hours: Mon - Sun 8 A.M. - 8 P.M.
Payment: Credit Cards, Checks
Price Range: $$

There are no poolside cocktails or bikinis at Club K-9, but on a hot day, dogs can lounge beneath colorful beach umbrellas in one of nine play yards on this 20-acre ranch. High-energy dogs run wild, while canine senior citizens and toy breeds enjoy distinguished miniature societies of their own. There are also spaces for dogs who want to be alone. Three trainers make the rounds all day to lead fun activities and ensure safety. (They're also available for private lessons and agility training.) Dogs who get dirty can receive a bath or an all-out grooming session before heading home.

Creature Comfort

(510) 530-1373
2501 MacArthur Blvd
(@ Boston Ave, 2 blocks east of Fruitvale Ave)
Oakland, California 94602
www.creaturecomfort.com
Hours: Mon - Fri 9 A.M. - 6 P.M., Sat 9 A.M. - 5 P.M.
Payment: Credit Cards, Checks
Price Range: $$$

An ounce of prevention definitely seems to be the approach at Creature Comfort, where Doctors Taylor and Reed prefer to address deeper health issues rather than simply treat acute symptoms. Chinese medicine, homeopathy, herbal therapies, chiropractic and several types of massage are all offered as gentle means to treat and prevent illness. Their ultimate goal is to keep your dog out of their office by encouraging a proper diet and a healthy lifestyle.

Del Mar Dog Park

(925) 973-3200
Del Mar Dr
(north of Pine Valley Rd)
San Ramon, California
Hours: Mon - Fri 7 A.M. to Dusk, Sat - Sun 8 A.M. to Dusk

If you can imagine the buzzing power lines here are cicadas, you might think you're on a Nebraska prairie. This fenced-in dog park dots a deserted area. It's covered with clean wood chips and long enough to lob a tennis ball a respectable distance. A few newly planted trees promise future shade, but for the time being, you and your pooch will have to camp out under the small shelter to escape the sun. Better yet, come by in the cool morning or evening hours. That's the only time you'll see anyone else.

Dog Bone Alley

(510) 521-5800
1342 Park St
(between Central & Encinal aves)
Alameda, California 94501
www.dogbonealley.com
Hours: Sun - Thu 10 A.M. - 7 P.M., Fri - Sat 10 A.M. - 8 P.M.
Payment: Credit Cards, Checks
Price Range: $$
You'll definitely find something to take home from the
adorably modern Dog Bone Alley. The store is well lit and well
stocked. A large selection of all-natural, holistic foods is
stacked high on the black-and-white shelves that line the bou-
tique. You can also stock up on collars, leashes, beds and car-
riers. The selection may be small, but you can find durable
classics that will last years. If your pup is the type to want to
select her own toys and treats, go ahead and bring her with
you: Pets are always welcome.

Dog and Cat Laundromat

(925) 837-7912
120 Alamo Plaza, Ste D
Alamo, California 94507
Hours: Mon 9 A.M. - 6 P.M., Tue - Sat 7:30 A.M. - 6 P.M.
Payment: Credit Cards, Checks
Price Range: $$
Owner Jane Riley takes pet washing seriously at this busy shop,
and the handsome dogs parading out the door are living proof.
Medium-sized pooches can be groomed for $45 to $100. The
place is simple, reliable and smells pleasantly of clean, wet
dog. Be sure to call for an appointment, especially because
they're planning to change locations in the near future.

Dog Park at Paso Nogal Park

Paso Nogal Ave
(between Morello Ave & Pleasant Hill Rd)
Pleasant Hill, California 94523
Hours: Mon, Wed - Fri Dawn to Dusk, Tue 12 P.M. to Dusk,
Sat 9 A.M. to Dusk
On weekday evenings, you can find 60 or more dogs gathered
at this enormous, fenced-in, off-leash park. The dogs love to
romp through the big, grassy meadow and lap from water
buckets, while people tend to cluster to chat or recline in the
shade with a good book. A grove of gorgeous old oaks along
the southern perimeter provides the perfect spot for a leisurely
stroll with older dogs looking to escape the hectic activity of
the meadow.

Dog's Best Friend & The Cat's Meow

(510) 526-7762
525 San Pablo Ave
(3 blocks north of Solano)
Albany, California 94706
www.dogsbestfriendcatsmeow.com
Hours: Tue - Sat 8:30 A.M. - 6 P.M.
Payment: Credit Cards, Checks
Price Range: $$
This tidy shop with grooming awards adorning the walls boasts
four groomers, two bathers and a knowledgeable receptionist.
Owner Nancy encourages her groomers to continue their
grooming, handling and animal-health education. She also
offers grooming workshops for her clients at the shop. The
retail area offers a few grooming products, as well as Flint River
Ranch pet food, supplements, flower-based remedies, various
toys and some dog accessories. Appointments are preferred.

Dogs by Dianne

(510) 236-0588
6511 Arlington Blvd
(about 3 blocks north of Barrett Ave)
Richmond, California 94805
Hours: Tue - Sat 8 A.M. - 6 P.M. – Last Dog
Payment: Credit Cards, Checks
Price Range: $$

Inside this quiet little grooming shack in a Richmond hilltop neighborhood you'll find Dianne and her son Ben offering pet clips for all breeds using basic equipment (including some cage dryers) and vet-recommended products. Their calm and assuring manner is what earns them referrals from other groomers, who send over seniors and first-timers that require a little extra care. Dianne grew up helping to raise and train setters, and now in her spare time, she shows her favorite breed: boxers. Ask about dog pick-up and drop-off.

Dogspeed

(510) 333-6750
P.O. Box 19231
Oakland, California 94619
www.dogspeed.net
Hours: By Appt
Payment: Checks
Price Range: $$

Heidi Zawelevsky will care for any type of pet, but where she really stands out is with special-needs animals. Her 15 years of experience as a veterinary nurse—seven were in specialty surgical practice—give her the skills to provide intensive post-op home care and administer medications and fluids. But she's also happy simply to drop by to fill food and water bowls and take your dog for a walk. Dogspeed is fully licensed and insured. Her service area includes Oakland and South Berkeley. For special cases, she will make arrangements for pets outside her service area.

Dracena Park

(510) 420-3006
(west of Highland Ave, north of Oakland Ave @ Blair Ave)
Piedmont, California 94611
www.ci.piedmont.ca.us/welcome.htm
Hours: Dawn to Dusk

If you're in need of a respite from urban life, Dracena Park offers a gorgeous wooded area for a little hike with your dog. Just be careful when you let your dog off leash: The street is within close proximity to the off-leash area. And be aware that technically you are supposed to have a city-issued permit to let your dog run free. Bags and trash cans are ample and a picnic table at the lower end of the off-leash area offers a nice spot to rest.

Drigon Dog Park

(@ 7th St, 1 block west of Mission)
Hours: Every Day 6 A.M. - 10 P.M.

The concrete-cast fake fire hydrants, big bone signs and spiffy agility course proclaim to anyone driving by that this city-run park is a hot spot for doted-on dogs. The fenced-in acre has a trim, prim look, just like the surrounding subdivision, and you won't suffer from lack of shade, water or a nearby garbage can. Small dogs have their own area. People form relaxed, friendly groups as they watch the dogs run about. Park on the street and keep your dog on-leash until you enter the outer gate.

Earl Warren Park

(510) 881-6700
4660 Crow Canyon Rd
(behind Creekside Middle School)
Castro Valley, California 94546
Hours: Dawn to Dusk

For dogs who love to locate lost tennis balls and track squirrels, this densely green dog park is a little piece of paradise. Like any established dog community, Earl Warren's people (and its dogs) have their social groups, but they're usually friendly to newcomers. Since the small-dog area is almost entirely unused, little dogs must come over to the big dog area if they want company. No bags are provided, so come prepared.

East Bay Pet Sitters Association
(510) 530-0207
P.O. Box 27251
Oakland, California 94602
www.ebpsa.com
Hours: By Appt
Payment: No Charge
From its humble beginnings as a coffee klatch, the East Bay Pet Sitters Association has grown into a well-organized nonprofit with the admirable goal of making Alameda and Contra Costa counties a great place for pets and their people. Before they'll extend an invitation to join their group, current members thoroughly research and vote on qualified applicants. Once accepted, members must pay dues, adhere to the group's code of ethics and participate in the group's community-based endeavors. Potential clients can browse a user-friendly database of pet-sitters and dog walkers, coded according to territory and services provided. EBPSA serves Alameda and Contra Costa counties.

East Bay SPCA
(510) 569-0702
8323 Baldwin St
Oakland, California 94621
www.eastbayspca.org
Hours: Tue - Wed 10 A.M. - 8 P.M.,
Thu - Sat 10 A.M. - 6:30 P.M., Sun 10 A.M. - 4:30 P.M.
Payment: Credit Cards
Price Range: $

It's not as well known as its San Francisco counterpart, but the East Bay SPCA, which has been in business for 130 years, is one of the city's most active animal rescue organizations. Before their animals—most of whom have been pulled from local shelters—are offered for adoption, they go through through socialization classes. Mobile adoption units and a website with online photo listings give the public even greater access to adoptable pets. Affordable veterinary and spay/neuter services are available at the Oakland and Dublin centers.

Every Dog Has its Daycare, Inc.

(510) 655-7832
1450 63rd St
(@ Hollis St)
Emeryville, California 94608
www.everydog.com
Hours: Mon - Fri 7 A.M. - 7 P.M., Sat 9 A.M. - 10 P.M.,
Drop-off: 7 A.M. - 9 A.M.
Pick-up: 4 P.M - 7 P.M.
Payment: Credit Cards, Checks
Price Range: $$

One of the first Bay Area day cares, Every Dog is still one of the largest and most comprehensive. Most people know them for their superb nutrition counseling, but they offer so much more. Their list of services seems endless: boarding, day care, grooming, transportation, training and a recently added in-house veterinary facility. Dogs play by day in Big Dog Land, Small Dog Land or Puppy Playland and spend their nights in the Dog Hotel. They do their best to accommodate most special requests. A webcam helps ease people's worries by letting them catch a glimpse of their pup at play. Enrollment is on a membership basis.

EZTrain Dog Training

(800) down-boy

www.eztrainonline.com

Hours: By Appt

Payment: Credit Cards, Checks

Price Range: $$

In addition to his popular, two-week board and train classes, master trainer Kirk Turner offers disease and cancer-detection training for eligible dogs, enabling them to participate in a three-year controlled study at the Pine Street Clinic in San Anselmo. Dogs that make the cut can use their astounding olfactory sensitivity, intelligence and compassion to benefit potential cancer victims, all the while leading happy lives as well-trained family dogs.

Fremont BARF Co-op

(510) 791-6419

www.fremontbarfcoop.com

Hours: See website

Payment: Credit Cards, Checks

Price Range: $

If you're thinking of putting your pooch on a raw-food diet, and you live anywhere near Fremont, you might want to join the Fremont BARF Co-op (never fear, BARF stands for Biologically Appropriate Raw Food, or Bones and Raw Food). Twice a month, members place wholesale orders for everything from human-grade whole carcasses to muscle meats, meaty bones and organ meats from nearby suppliers. The Co-op also offers bulk quantities of vegetables, locally made dog treats, various herb blends, healthy powders and omega 3 oils that are important staples in the BARF diet.

Full Circle Dog Training

(510) 452-4745

Hours: By Appt

Payment: Checks

Price Range: $$

If your dog is having a little trouble coming out of his shell, Amy Cook could be the trainer you need. She works with shy dogs by maintaining a respectful distance, staying below their fear threshold as she steadily builds their trust. Her one-on-one lessons start in your home, although her ultimate goal is to take your dog out into the real world as soon as he is ready. She charges by the session, but doesn't designate any time limit. She doesn't like to stop until she's seen a positive change. Amy covers the Oakland area and does private lessons only.

Furry Friends Rescue

(510) 794-4703

P.O. Box 7270

Fremont, California 94537

www.furryfriendsrescue.org

Payment: Checks

Price Range: $$

This nonprofit rescue organization relies completely on volunteers, donations and foster parents to save the lives of hundreds of homeless pets. Each animal is treated by a veterinarian (exam, immunization, spay/neuter) before being placed in a loving home. Pictures of adoptable dogs and cats, along with plenty of pertinent information, are featured on their website. You'll also find happy adoption stories. Adoption locations change periodically, so call or check the website for the latest information.

Gentle Persuasion, LLC

(510) 336-1740

www.gentlepersuasion.com

Hours: By Appt

Payment: Checks

Price Range: $$

"Consistent, gentle persuasion," says Kathy, is the key to an obedient, well-mannered canine companion. She helps clients develop the communication skills, respect and compassion necessary for a gratifying dog-human relationship. Consultation and one-on-one sessions can be held at your home or anywhere else you like. She also offers boarding and leads several group classes, including the popular Total Recall class at Dog Tec, which teaches dogs to respond immediately to their owners' call. Kathy offers group and private lessons and will also board dogs while she trains them.

George

(510) 644-1033

1844 4th St

(@ Hearst St)

Berkeley, California 94710

www.georgesf.com

Hours: Mon - Sat 10 A.M. - 6 P.M.,

Sun 11 A.M. - 6 P.M.

Payment: Credit Cards, Checks

Price Range: $$$

When George opened its doors more than 12 years ago, it instantly became the prototype for posh pet boutiques. The store has a loyal following that can't get enough of the perennially hip, quality products. George's two Bay Area locations are styled like classic general stores, filled with homemade treats, toys and highbrow dog fashions. If you can't get to either of the stores, browse their website or check your local pet boutique for genuine George accessories.

Happiness Country Kennels

(925) 862-1900
5815 Mission Rd
(Andrade Rd exit, off I-680)
Sunol, California 94586
www.topnotchtraining.com
Hours: Mon - Fri 8 A.M. - 6 P.M., Sat 9 A.M. - 2 P.M.
Payment: Credit Cards, Checks
Price Range: $$

Aptly named, Happiness is a full-service kennel located next to a palm-studded golf course. Canine clients are offered daily exercise and playtime in the kiddie pool. Grooming is available, as are evening classes with trainer and kennel manager Karen Ten Eyck. Once dogs make it through basic obedience, they're eligible for the far more entertaining and challenging—classes in agility and competitive obedience.

Happy Hound Play & Daycare/Bed & Bone Hound Hotel

(510) 547-DOGS
1695 34th St
(between Mandela Pkwy & Wood St)
Oakland, California 94608
www.happyhound.com
Hours: Mon - Fri 7 A.M. - 7 P.M.
Payment: Credit Cards, Checks
Price Range: $$$

This gigantic, 6,800-square-foot warehouse gone eco-friendly day-care and boarding facility offers dogs plenty of space to roam, including a sundeck for cage-free play and restful nights. Other offerings include shuttle service, grooming and dog training. Owner Suzanne brings 30 years of experience with animals to Happy Hound, and she has also completed numerous dog behavior classes.

Hardy Dog Park

491 Hardy St
Oakland, California 94618
Hours: Dawn to Dusk

It's easy to find fault with this tiny patch of dirt, gravel and asphalt that crouches in the perennial shadow of a freeway overpass. But Hardy Park is Oakland's only official off-leash dog park and the people who battled the anti-off-leash forces to get it don't want to hear the bashing. Hardy Park is heavily and successfully used, proving that well-socialized dogs can up the value of a neighborhood. In fact, the derelicts who once loitered here have been replaced by families, and the surrounding park has been redesigned into an exemplary public space. Parking is easy, and amenities include a high fence, water and a few chairs.

Hate to Doo

(925) 787-3176
P.O. Box 2095
Martinez, California 94553
www.hatetodoo.com
Hours: Mon - Fri 8 A.M. - 5 P.M.
Payment: Checks
Price Range: $$

Like their name says, these folks will do what you hate to do. They'll come by, pick up your dog's waste and put it in your garbage bin or dumpster. Pet sitting is offered as well, and includes twice-daily visits for feeding, walking and playtime. Other services, such as full housecleaning and security maintenance while you're away, are also available. Service is limited to the Walnut Creek, Martinez and Concord areas. To get a quick estimate, fill out the online application. Seniors and those with disabilities are eligible for discounts.

Hayward Pet Complex

(510) 886-1522
619 Greely Ct
(off Mission, north of Industrial Blvd)
Hayward, California 94544
www.mastergroomer.com
Hours: Tue - Sat 8 A.M. - 5 P.M.
Payment: Checks
Price Range: $$

This small, cheerful pet-styling salon is home to master groomer Paula Lafferty, who has been bringing out the best in show dogs and family pets for over 20 years. The Pet Complex's list of services includes both basic and custom grooming. Bring your dog in for a hot-oil treatment, full scissor cut or an all-natural flea bath using Bubble Neem's eucalyptus and cedar dip. Boarding is also available in a tidy kennel of 11 runs, and a trainer is available by appointment only.

Holistic Hound

(510) 843-2133
1510 Walnut St in Walnut Square
(around the corner from Peet's Coffee & Chez Panisse)
Berkeley, California 94709
www.theholistichound.com
Hours: Tue - Wed 10 A.M. - 6 P.M., Thu 10 A.M. - 7 P.M.,
Fri - Sat 10 A.M. - 6 P.M., Sun 11 A.M. - 5 P.M.
Payment: Credit Cards, Checks
Price Range: $$

This space, which used to be home to the Elephant Pharmacy, has been transformed into the Holistic Hound, and it's a perfect fit in Berkeley's Gourmet Ghetto. You will find Great Life holistic kibble with raw-food coating, natural flea-repellent systems, homeopathic and aromatic remedies and completely washable beds filled with scraps from the fleece-clothing industry. The educational center offers in-house seminars as well as a bookshelf that's unrivaled in the subjects of dog health and behavior.

Hopalong Animal Rescue

(510) 267-1915
P.O. Box 27507
Oakland, California 94602
www.hopalong.org
Hours: By Appt
Payment: Checks
Price Range: $$

Hopalong Animal Rescue, inspired by a 1993 newspaper article highlighting an injured cat of the same name, was voted Best Place to Find a Pet in the *East Bay Express* in 2004. Dedicated animal volunteer Helen Hill single-handedly started the organization, which works with the Oakland Animal Shelter, and has placed thousands of pets through mobile adoptions and community outreach. All animals are spayed or neutered before adoption. Check the website for photos and descriptions of the many available animals. The Adoption fee is $150.

Kathleen Huston's All Breed Grooming

(925) 676-8888
4311 Treat Blvd
(south of Clayton Rd near Turtle Creek Rd)
Concord, California 94521
Hours: Wed - Sat 8:30 A.M. – Last Dog
Payment: Checks
Price Range: $$

Counted among Kathleen's long list of regulars are numerous bichons and Yorkies, including one who arrives by limo from Carmel. Customers get bathed with all-natural or prescription shampoos and are groomed by a master. Kathleen has trained and certified 3,500 other groomers and been a judge at many shows. Under no circumstances does Kathleen cage dry. While waiting their turn, dogs roam freely through her bright, clean shop or go out to visit friends at the adjacent All Breed Day Care. Plan as far ahead as possible: She stays booked.

Kaycee's Pet & Groom

(510) 569-1167
710 E 14th St
(1 block northwest of civic center, inside Mike's Feed & Pets)
San Leandro, California 94577
Hours: Tue - Sat 8:30 A.M. - 5 P.M.
Payment: Checks
Price Range: $$

"We do it right or you don't leave," is groomer Janet's motto. The many photos of happily groomed clients that cover her walls support this statement. Groomers are very relaxed and friendly, and the dogs seem equally content. They cut and style a lot of Old English sheepdogs and some show dogs, but they draw the line at cats. You can count on all-natural shampoos and unheated forced-air dryers or the old-fashioned hand-held blow dryer.

Kutz For Mutz

(510) 540-6088
911 University Ave
(between 7th & 8th sts, park at rear of building)
Berkeley, California 94710
Hours: Tue - Sat 8 A.M. - 5 P.M.
Payment: Credit Cards, Checks
Price Range: $$

Don't let the name fool you: Owner Darrell Brewer is more in the business of hand stripping and hand scissoring show terriers and poodles than grooming mutts. All-natural shampoos are used, and drying is always done by hand. Darrell says the 200 birds that are kept in cages lining the walls add a soothing sound to calm the dogs. At the very least, they distract the cats.

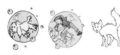

Launder Mutt

(925) 685-1690
2958-C Treat Blvd
(behind Trader Joe's in the Oak Grove Shopping Center)
Concord, California 94518
Hours: Tue - Sun 9 A.M. - 5 P.M.
Payment: Credit Cards, Checks
Price Range: $

Launder Mutt offers everything you need to scrub your pup,
including someone to clean up the mess when you're done.
Or you can take advantage of their very affordable full-service
grooming. Owners Kim and Laurie have years of experience
and are really gentle with their pups. If you go with self-serve,
you have the option of aloe or flea-deterring all-natural shampoos, and you can rest assured that your dog won't be stuck in
a cage dryer.

Laura For Dog

(925) 447-3647
P.O. Box 931
Livermore, California 94551
Hours: By Appt
Payment: Checks
Price Range: $$$

For over 22 years, Laura has been "raising up people to train
the pups," using Dr. Ian Dunbar's Sirius Puppy Training
method. Her goal is to shape puppies into good family pets
and people into good pet families. She runs a tight ship, and
puts an emphasis on safety and establishing proper bound-
aries. Classes are held at her small but air-conditioned store-
front in Dublin or at the JCC in Walnut Creek, where she
keeps groups small. She encourages people to come and
observe before signing up.

Linda Park

(510) 420-3006
Entrances along Linda Ave
(west of Grand Ave, north of Oakland Ave
@ the corner of Oakland & Sunnyside aves)
Piedmont, California 94611
www.ci.piedmont.ca.us
Hours: Dawn to Dusk

Piedmont dog owners love this fenced-in dog park mostly for the social scene. The eastern exposure makes this a nice spot to hang out in the morning. Technically, you are supposed to have a Piedmont police-issued permit to let your dog off leash here. The rest of the rules fall under the common sense/common courtesy category. Only three dogs per person are allowed, and you must carry a leash for each dog and keep your dog(s) in your sight at all times. Trainers and dog walkers are not allowed to use the park while working.

Lucky Dog, The

(510) 843-0633
2154 San Pablo Ave
(between Allston Way & Cowper Ave)
Berkeley, California 94702
Hours: Mon - Sat 10 A.M. - 6 P.M., Sun 11 A.M. - 6 P.M.
Payment: Credit Cards, Checks
Price Range: $$

It may take a few visits, but once the owner and staff of this neighborhood pet store warm up to you, you'll be in for life. The moose head on the wall and the worn wooden floors give the place an old-time feel, and there's a fair selection of alternative products, along with birds, fish, toys and basic supplies. Prices run a bit on the high side, but they are by no means unreasonable.

Mike's Feed & Pets

(510) 638-2005
710 E 14th St
(between Oaks & Begier, 1 block northwest of the civic center)
San Leandro, California 94577
Hours: Mon - Tue 10 A.M. - 7 P.M., Wed 9 A.M. - 7 P.M.,
Sun 10 A.M. - 6 P.M.
Payment: Credit Cards, Checks
Price Range: $$

This gigantic storefront has an old-world quality with high, exposed rafters and a great display of rusty antiques. The tropical fish gallery and assortment of feathered, scaled and furry animals make for an especially fun place to browse. Puppy training takes place in the loft, and Kaycee's Pet & Groom is nestled in the back corner. If you've come to pick up your Innova, California Natural or basic dog supplies, the helpful staff will assist you in your trek to the parking lot.

Molly's Pup-purr-ee

(925) 820-8222
425 Hartz Ave
(1½ blocks south of Diablo Rd)
Danville, California 94526
www.mollyspup.com
Hours: Mon - Fri 10:30 A.M. - 6 P.M., Sat 10 A.M. - 5:30 P.M.
Payment: Credit Cards, Checks
Price Range: $$

"Life's too short to wear boring collars," reads the writing on the wall above an incredible inventory of snazzy collars, harnesses and leashes from all over the globe. You'll find adorably ostentatious miniature dog coats, sweaters, T-shirts, formal wear and gobs of jewelry, sometimes modeled by Molly herself. But since this stylish little Welsh terrier can't wear all the cute outfits at once, Molly-size "dogequins" serve as stand-in displays. The toy, treat and dinnerware selections rival the apparel line, as do the gift options for dog lovers. The gift registry helps canines and people celebrate special events.

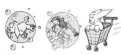

Mudpuppy's Tub & Scrub
(510) 559-8899
Point Isabel Regional Park
1 Isabel St
(@ west end parking lot)
Richmond, California 94804
www.mudpuppys.com
Hours: Mon - Fri 10 A.M. - 5:30 P.M.,
Sat - Sun 9 A.M. - 5:30 P.M.
Payment: Credit Cards, Checks
Price Range: $$

There are a thousand ways for a dog to get dirty at Point Isabel, but with an appointment at Mudpuppy's, you can let your dog party in the mud and still bring her home spotlessly clean. Choose self-serve—which provides all-natural shampoo, combs and brushes—or go for a full-service bath with flea dip, conditioning, blow dry and nail trim as extras. Mudpuppy's new custom-designed bathhouse has expanded to accommodate a shop for toys and treats, as well as the Sit Stay Cafe, a great place to grab a snack while you wait. Consult the handy tide table on their website, and you might be able to avoid the bath all together.

Muirwood Dog Park
(925) 931-5340
Muirwood Community Park
4701 Muirwood Dr
(west of I-680, northwest section of Pleasanton)
Pleasanton, California 94588
www.ci.pleasanton.ca.us
Hours: Dawn to Dusk

If you can imagine that the freeway traffic noise is the surf, this pretty, 20,000-square-foot, wood chip-covered dog run might seem like a perfect place to spend an afternoon. It's an off-leash area, which allows for plenty of ball throwing, chasing and socialization. Big, beautiful trees line the long, winding, fenced-in area, and a real fire hydrant adds to the ambiance.

Crowds gather around 9 A.M. and 5 P.M., but otherwise, you and your dog might have the run to yourselves.

Nitro Dog

(925) 962-BARK
61 Lafayette Cir
(La Fiesta Sq @ Mt Diablo Blvd)
Lafayette, California 94549
www.nitrodog.com
Hours: Mon - Fri 10 A.M. - 6 P.M., Sat 10 A.M. - 5:30 P.M., Sun 11 A.M. - 5 P.M.
Payment: Credit Cards, Checks
Price Range: $$

Go classic, retro or industrial chic with Nitro Dog's items for home, garden, bed and bowl. Owners Len and Leslie set out to create an enjoyable and amusing shopping experience, and they succeeded. They host events in support of Smiley Dog Rescue, Central California Labrador Rescue, Greyhound Friends for Life and Paws With a Cause. This socially minded shop unites dog owners with similar interests, as well as pups looking for new playmates.

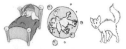

North Main Pet Lodge

(925) 256-0646
2818 N Main
(@ Geary Rd)
Walnut Creek, California 94597
www.petlodge.com
Hours: Mon - Thu 9 A.M. - 5 P.M., Sun 5 P.M. - 7 P.M.
Payment: Credit Cards, Checks
Price Range: $$

People love this place—and not because it's fabulously fancy: It's not. But the owners did their homework, visiting facilities all over the country before building the Pet Lodge. The comfortably large kennels are safe, secure and sanitary. They're kept cool in the summer and cozy in the winter. There's an exercise room that your pup can run around in. The Lodge has an on-site grooming shop. The owners have a long history of caring for animals. They spent the '60s and '70s showing poodles, and they still show Persian cats. But these days they enjoy caring for their guests as much as caring for their own animals.

Ohlone Dog Park

(510) 981-6700
Hearst Ave
(@ Grant St)
Berkeley, California 94703
Hours: Mon - Fri 6 A.M. - 10 P.M., Sat - Sun 9 A.M. - 10 P.M.
Grab your Peet's coffee and plastic bags, pin on your lefty button and settle in on a bench at the nation's first dog park. Ohlone Dog Park was officially established in 1983, a few years after the People's Park advocates annexed the parcel, declaring it a free zone for unleashed recreation. The Ohlone Dog Park Association (ODPA, pronounced "odd paw") keeps the place tidy and safe, but that doesn't deter the neighbors from their perennial efforts to have the park shut down.

Pam Miller, Pet Nanny

(925) 288-9900
155 Fair Oaks Dr
Pleasant Hill, California 94523
Hours: By Appt
Payment: Checks
Price Range: $
Considering that her previous job as director of Pleasant Hill Learning Center involved watching 150 children, taking care of dogs is a piece of cake for Pam Miller. She will take your dog for a walk and offers pet-sitting at your home or hers. She also has experience helping senior citizens with their companion animals, walking their dogs and picking up pet food and supplies when they are unable to do so.

Paula's Penthouse *(See Hayward Pet Complex)*

Paw Patch, The
(925) 671-3270
in Newhall Community Park
@ Turtle Creek Rd
(north from Ygnacio Valley Rd or east from Treat Blvd)
Concord, California 94518
Hours: Every Day Dawn to Dusk
Bird dogs might go berserk over the flocks of ducks and geese
casually strutting along Galindo Creek. If you can keep them
inside the park, they'll be rewarded with lush, green turf to roll
in. There's barely a lick of shade, but there is a spigot and
bucket for heat relief. If you're looking for freedom, this 126-
acre park has plenty of undeveloped, open space to explore.
And after hiking to the top of the hill, both you and your dog
will appreciate the sweeping views of the Carquinez Straits and
Mount Diablo.

PAWS
(510) 464-1011
2700 9th St
Berkeley, California 94710
www.pawseastbay.org
Hours: By Appt
Payment: Checks
Price Range: $
This national nonprofit company PAWS (Pets Are Wonderful
Support) provides pet care only to qualified, low-income pet
owners with chronic illnesses or disabilities. It relies on
volunteers to deliver pet food and do things such as walk,
groom, feed and clean up after clients' dogs. Tax-deductible
donations of time, supplies, veterinary services and

money are very much appreciated. In fact, this organization relies on them, so step up to the plate and give these guys a ring. Or at least check out their website for more information.

Pawsitive Experience

(925) 932-8014
1113 Douglas Ct
San Ramon Valley
Alamo, California 94507
Hours: By Appt
Payment: Checks
Price Range: $$

Walker/sitter/trainer Meredith Gage trained neighborhood strays as a child. Now that she's earned the proper credentials as an adult, she'll look after any pet that needs tending—even snakes. However, her main focus remains on dogs. Whether on an off-leash adventure, a drop-in visit, a taxi ride to the vet, or a vacation weekend on her fenced Alamo acre, dogs can expect plenty of TLC. Meredith offers private instruction in obedience and agility, as well as boarding for small dogs.

Pawsitive Steps Dog Training

(510) 732-7877
www.cvadult.org/dogs.htm
Hours: By Appt
Payment: Checks
Price Range: $$

Lisa Clifton-Bumpass is a pro with the clicker. She studied under the Baileys in Hot Springs, Arkansas. To graduate from school, Lisa had to prove that she could train a chicken, but now she specializes in difficult dogs. She also teaches general puppy and adult dog classes, plus fun subjects like problem-solving, flyball and square dancing. She's a former law enforcement officer and gives great talks and seminars on subjects like dog-to-dog communication, child safety, pet disaster preparedness and first aid. Her service area includes San Leandro, San Lorenzo, Hayward, Casto Valley and the East Bay.

Pawsitively Pampered Pet, The
(510) 336-9861
2625 Alcatraz Ave, P. O. Box 340
Berkeley, California 94705
www.yourpamperedpets.com
Hours: By Appt
Payment: Checks
Price Range: $$
Keeping her business small and her services simple won Heidi Kistler the Pet Sitters International Pet Sitter of the Year award in 1999. She offers house-sitting, home visits and leashed walks, and services are custom tailored to each pet or household. She has a solid list of loyal clients, and new clients usually find her through vet referral. Take a look at the news clippings on her website for a great "when you're away" checklist. Pampered Pet serves the north Oakland area.

Pet Care Depot at Bishop Ranch Veterinary Center
2000 Bishop Dr
San Ramon, California 94583
www.webvets.com
Hours: Mon - Fri 9 A.M. - 7 P.M., Sat 9 A.M. - 5 P.M., Sun 10 A.M. - 4 P.M.
Payment: Checks
Price Range: $$
The vets of Bishop Ranch own this neighboring Pet Care Depot, which means your pet can see the doctor, then walk next door for a treat or a new flea collar. In addition to the vet-prescribed brands, Hills and Royal Canin, the superbly stocked Depot carries Wellness and California Natural, as well as the popular raw food line Primal. You may also spot items you

never knew you needed—a dog step-up stool for an SUV or an urn for the ashes of a departed pet. Training, grooming and boarding are also available.

Pet Club
(510) 595-7955
3535 Hollis St
(East Bay Bridge Shopping Center)
Emeryville, California 94608
www.petclubstores.com
Hours: Mon - Fri 9 A.M. - 8 P.M., Sat 9 A.M. - 7 P.M.,
Sun 10 A.M. - 7 P.M.
Payment: Checks
Price Range: $

Picture Costco for pets and you'll understand the lure of these popular warehouse-style pet supply stores. With seven Bay Area locations, Pet Club prices couldn't be lower. However, the great prices mean no frills and little personalized service. Come stock up on leashes and pet food, but leave your credit card at home; they accept only cash and checks.

Pet Food Express

Oakland-Broadway Location
(510) 654-8888
5144 Broadway
(Broadway @ 51st Ave Rockridge Shopping Center)
Oakland, California 94611
www.petfoodexpress.com
Hours: Mon - Sat 9 A.M. - 8 P.M., Sun 10 A.M. - 7 P.M.

Oakland-Telegraph Ave Location
(510) 923-9500
6398 Telegraph Ave
(@ Alcatraz)
Oakand, California 94609

www.petfoodexpress.com
Hours: Mon - Fri 9:30 A.M. - 8 P.M., Sat 9 A.M. - 7 P.M.,
Sun 10 A.M. - 6 P.M.
Payment: Credit Cards, Checks
Price Range: $$

Pet Food Express is a pet-supply chain with numerous franchises throughout the Bay Area. They sell a variety of pet supplies, including specialty items like the safety light dog collar and the Cider Mill dog trolley. Brands such as Avo Derm and Pinnacle are on the shelves, and Pet Express staff is friendly and helpful. Dog training classes and low-cost vaccinations are available. The store's My Mutt program promotes adoption of the mighty mixed breed.

Pet Vet/Pet Food

(510) 652-9822
4814 Broadway
(@ 51st St)
Oakland, California 94611
Hours: Mon - Fri 9:30 A.M. - 6:30 P.M., Sat 9 A.M. - 6 P.M.,
Sun 10 A.M. - 5 P.M.
Vet Clinic: Sun - Mon 10 A.M. - 4 P.M.
Payment: Credit Cards, Checks
Price Range: $

The brain child of a veterinarian, Pet Vet/Pet Food offers high-quality pet products and expert low-cost veterinary care all under the same roof. Services at the drop-in clinics include vaccinations and basic exams, with no additional fee unless more serious medical conditions are treated. After your pet has seen the doctor, stock up on supplements, all-natural foods like Primal and Nature's Variety, as well as gourmet treats.

Petco

www.petco.com
Payment: Credit Cards, Checks
Price Range: $$

Alameda Location

(510) 864-1844
2310 S Shore Ctr
(between Shoreline and Otis drs)
Alameda, California 94501
Hours: Mon - Fri 9 A.M. - 9 P.M., Sat 9 A.M. - 8 P.M.,
Sun 10 A.M. - 8 P.M.

Castro Valley Location

(510) 886-4466
3735 E Castro Valley Blvd
(between Nugget Canyon Dr & Justco Ln)
Castro Valley, California 94552
Hours: Mon - Fri 9 A.M. - 9 P.M., Sat 9 A.M. - 8 P.M.,
Sun 10 A.M. - 8 P.M.

Concord Location

(925) 827-3338
1825 Salvio St
(between Broadway & Adobe sts)
Concord, California 94520
Hours: Mon - Fri 8 A.M. - 9 P.M., Sat 8 A.M. - 9 P.M.,
Sun 10 A.M. - 8 P.M.

Dublin Location

(925) 803-4045
11976 Dublin Blvd
(@ San Ramon Rd)
Dublin, California 94568
Hours: Mon - Sat 9 A.M. - 9 P.M., Sun 10 A.M. - 8 P.M.

El Cerrito Location

(510) 528-7919
420 El Cerrito Plaza
(between Liberty St & Vista Heights Rd)
El Cerrito, California 94530
Hours: Mon - Sat 9 A.M. - 9 P.M., Sun 10 A.M. - 8 P.M.

Fremont Location

(510) 742-0573
3780 Mowry Ave
(@ Lexington St)
Fremont, California 94538
Hours: Mon - Sat 9 A.M. - 9 P.M., Sun 10 A.M. - 8 P.M.

Lafayette Location

(925) 284-1756
3517 Mt. Diablo Blvd
(between Golden Gate Way & 1st St)
Lafayette, California 94549
Hours: Mon - Fri 9 A.M. - 9 P.M., Sat 9 A.M. - 7 P.M.,
Sun 10 A.M. - 6 P.M.

Martinez Location

(925) 370-6060
1170 Arnold Dr
(between Shadowfalls Dr & Morello Ave)
Martinez, California 94553
Hours: Mon - Sat 9 A.M. - 9 P.M., Sun 10 A.M. - 8 P.M.

San Ramon Location
(925) 275-2111
2005 Crow Canyon Pl
(between 680 Fwy & Camino Ramon)
San Ramon, California 94583
Hours: Mon - Sat 9 A.M. - 9 P.M., Sun 10 A.M. - 8 P.M.

Union City Location
(510) 477-9235
31090 Dyer St
(@ Ratekin Dr)
Union City, California 94587
Hours: Mon - Sat 8 A.M. - 8 P.M., Sun 10 A.M. - 8 P.M.

Walnut Creek Location
(925) 988-9370
1301 S California St
(@ Botelho Dr)
Walnut Creek, California 94596
Hours: Mon - Sat 9 A.M. - 9 P.M., Sun 10 A.M. - 7 P.M.

For one-stop shopping it's hard to beat the convenience and value of this superstore with locations all over the country. Petco makes it their mission to provide customers with the food, supplements and products they want for their animals. Their bed selection runs the gamut, from orthopedic mattresses along with sheets and throws to chaises that would do an interior decorator proud. Get a P.A.L.S. (Petco Animal Lovers Save) card to take advantage of discounts; you may also want to check out their Top Dog program, which offers even greater savings to their most loyal customers. Check the contact information for each store for hours and specific service offerings.

Petsmart

www.petsmart.com
Hours: Mon - Sat 9 A.M. - 9 P.M., Sun 10 A.M. - 6 P.M.
Payment: Credit Cards, Checks
Price Range: $$

Concord Location
(925) 687-7199
1700 Willow Pass Rd
(@ Fry Way)
Concord, California 94520

Dublin Location
(925) 803-8370
6960 Amador Plaza Rd
(@ Dublin Blvd)
Dublin, California 94568

Newark Location
(510) 494-0140
5737 Mowry Ave
(@ Alpenrose Ct)
Newark, California 94560

Pittsburg Location
(925) 706-9975
4655 Century Blvd
(@ Somersville Rd)
Pittsburg, California 94565

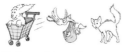

Richmond Location
(510) 758-8990
3700 Klose Way, Bldg 4
(@ Blume Dr)
Richmond, California 94806

San Leandro Location
(510) 317-1880
15555 E 14th St
(@ 156th Ave)
San Leandro, California 94578

This standout superstore is to pet owners what Home Depot is to homeowners. PetSmart stocks an unbelievably wide range of products that will meet almost any budget. They carry the better dog food brands—including Bil-Jac. And whenever possible, they offer all-natural options in their selection of treats, supplements and skin products. A viewing window allows see-for-yourself grooming so you don't have to worry about what happens behind closed doors. They get major points for promoting their adoptions all the time. And they have a staff that's always available to advise you and to help you find what you need. It's places like PetSmart that give superstores a good name.

Petway
(925) 846-3172
5480 Sunol Blvd
(south of Bernal in the Raley's Shopping Center)
Pleasanton, California 94566
Hours: Mon - Fri 10 A.M. - 7 P.M., Sat 9 A.M. - 6 P.M.,
Sun 11 A.M. - 5 P.M.
Payment: Credit Cards, Checks
Price Range: $$
The young guys who run this store take a passionate interest in their products—especially dog food. Quoting the latest

166 • CITY DOG

nutrition news, they can tell you why some of the old standard brands might be harming your dog and what you should expect from any brand that claims to promote your dog's health. You'll find locally made biscuits on the shelves along-side Karma, a pricey new all-organic food. Shoppers who aren't into debating the finer points of dog food science can turn their attention to Athena, the shop's chameleon mascot.

Phenix Dog Park

(707) 746-4285
in Benicia Community Park
Community Park Dr
Benicia, California 94510
Hours: 7 A.M. to Dusk

Benicians had to fight tooth and nail to get permission for their dogs to so much as set foot in a city park, so Phenix holds a special place in their hearts. There are plenty of trees for shade, running water, a large sloped area with wood chips and a grassy patch with picnic benches. You'll find the most action during pre- and post-work hours, when locals let their dogs run free. A double-gated fence makes for easy in and out without any risk of escape. Phenix is located behind Matthew Turner Elementary School. Drive to the rear of the park and walk past the roller hockey rink.

Piedmont Park

(510) 420-3006
711 Highland Ave
(2 blocks southeast of Oakland Ave)
Piedmont, California 94611
www.ci.piedmont.ca.us
Hours: Dawn to Dusk

A great place to watch the sun set over downtown Oakland, Piedmont Park is also quite popular with the dogs. The dense native vegetation makes it one of the best spots for squirrel sightings. An adjacent tennis court supplies flying tennis balls, and the creek flows year-round, pooling up at several water-holes. There's also a great network of winding, paved paths where walkers can get plenty of exercise, while taking in the natural surroundings. The only downside—and it's a really big one—is that the creek gets doused with potentially hazardous lawn chemicals in the summer. Technically, you're supposed to get a city-issued permit to let your dog go off leash in the park.

Point Isabel Regional Park
(510) 562-PARK
Entrances: Isabel St, Rydin Rd
(@ the west end of Central Ave near Costco)
Richmond, California 94530
www.ebparks.org/parks/ptisable.htm
Hours: Mon - Sun 5 A.M. - 10 P.M.
With a stunning view of Angel Island and the Golden Gate and Bay bridges, Point Isabel's 21 acres make it the largest off-leash dog park in the country. An estimated one million dogs visit the park every year to stroll in the grass or race along the Hoffman Channel shoreline. There's also an appealing picnic area alongside dog-washing facilities, appropriately named—Muddy Canines.

Puppy Playland
(925) 725-2300
2556 San Ramon Valley Blvd
(just north of Norris Canyon Rd)
San Ramon, California 94583
www.puppyplayland.com
Hours: Mon - Fri 7 A.M. - 7 P.M.
Payment: Credit Cards, Checks
Price Range: $$
With one caretaker to every 10 dogs and a spacious indoor play area, this full-service center does dog day care right. Canine clients—who must be at least 12 weeks old and have had their DHPP vaccines—are temperament tested before

they're allowed to join the Playland pack. Overnight care—
including weekends—and longterm boarding are available, as
are obedience and agility training. You can also stock up on
supplies here. Playland carries the raw food lines Primal and
Grandads among other brands.

Redhound

(510) 428-2785
5523 College Ave
(between Forest St & Keith Ave)
Oakland, California 94618
www.redhoundpets.com
Hours: Mon - Fri 10 A.M. - 7 P.M., Sat 10 A.M. - 6 P.M.
Sun 11 A.M. - 5 P.M.
Payment: Credit Cards, Checks
Price Range: $$

At this uber-hip, dog-chic boutique, dogs are welcome to put
their paws up on the biscuit bar for a sample of the daily
featured treat. Redhound offers a unique collection of toys,
collars, leashes, beds and hiking gear. It's a great place for
people to learn the latest in all-natural foods and supplements.
In stocking his store, owner David scours reviews from the
Whole Dog Journal to help him find the best new products.
All this, and he matches the prices of Pet Food Express.

Regina's Pet Grooming

(925) 672-8270
5400 Ygnacio Valley Rd, Ste A7
(@ Clayton Rd)
Concord, California 94521
Hours: Tue - Fri 8:30 A.M. - 6 P.M., Sat 7:30 A.M. - 5 P.M.
Payment: Credit Cards, Checks
Price Range: $$

Thirty-some years ago someone named Regina started this
grooming business. But it's the salon's current owner Bonnie
who has made the small, immaculate salon so popular. With
prices ranging from $35-$150, Bonnie is skilled in all types of

cuts and welcomes all dog breeds. She uses natural products like Bio-Groom oatmeal shampoo and Aloe Magic deep cleansers. Bonnie's partial to hand dryers. She'll rarely use a cage dryer, but only in an open and ventilated wire enclosure.

Remington Dog Park

Ebbtide Ave
(@ Bridgeway)
Sausalito, California 94965
Hours: Mon - Fri 6:30 A.M. - 8 P.M., Sat - Sun 8 A.M. - 8 P.M.
Remington may have a Friday night wine and cheese happy hour, but these dog owners aren't just a swirl and sniff kind of crowd. They maintain this city-owned park, and the community's donations have paid for lights, a lawnmower, picnic benches and water fountains. In spite of heavy use, Remington's mostly wood-chip surface still manages to harbor a few grassy/weedy areas. Benches are strategically located under the park's numerous trees. Recycled shopping bags are available. The park is open until 9 P.M. during daylight-saving.

Run With the Big Dog

(510) 568-1875
Hours: By Appt
Payment: Credit Cards, Checks
Price Range: $$
Who's the Big Dog? In this case, it's a German shepherd named Klaus whose owners exercise canine clients in the East Bay regional parks. Besides taking dogs for regular park runs, Pam and Jerry Treber customize exercise programs for individual dogs. You can arrange for private on-leash neighborhood walks or request something a little more vigorous. The Trebers, who also run a pet-transportation service, make home visits for all types of pets, and they're adept at administering medications. The Big Dog serves San Leandro, Alameda, Castro Valley, Oakland and San Lorenzo.

Safe Hands

(510) 710-6700
P.O. Box 2577
El Cerrito, California 94530
www.safehandspetcare.com
Hours: By Appt
Payment: Checks
Price Range: $$

Lee Pang's pet service, based in El Cerrito, offers your pet attentive care while you're working, on vacation or when you simply don't have the time or energy to give your dog the quality time he needs. Safe Hands will visit and care for your pet on their turf or yours—they even e-mail you regular progress reports while you're away. This dedicated company is licensed, insured and bonded. Employees are trained in pet first aid and are kept up to date on current issues and pet-sitting industry practices. In fact, Safe Hands is a member of two pet-sitter organizations.

ShamPooches

(925) 806-0647
3151 I Crow Canyon Pl
(Crow Commons Shopping Center)
San Ramon, California 94583
Hours: Tue, Thu, Fri 8 A.M. - 5 P.M., Wed 7:30 A.M. - 5 P.M.
Payment: Credit Cards, Checks
Price Range: $$

It's truly amazing what's crammed into this tiny mall space. Five days a week you'll find seven veteran groomers giving the face, feet and tail treatment to countless dogs. If you can get an appointment, your pooch will get a bath with hypo-allergenic or flea-treatment shampoo and, if needed, a nice pet cut. The self-service tub is in high demand, so you need an appointment for that as well. Owner Dennis is a canine cop in Oakland, and Linda, the receptionist, offers pet-sitting.

Smiley Dog Rescue

(510) 496-3484
P.O. Box 2728
Oakland, California 94602
www.smileydogrescue.org
Hours: By Appt
Payment: Credit Cards
Price Range: $$

This outstanding Oakland-based organization provides sanctuary for unwanted dogs until the animals can be placed in foster or permanent homes. All dogs are spayed or neutered and kept in good health, and many receive some basic training as well. The adoption fee is $175, and a thorough home visit is required to convince Smiley Dog of a good dog/person fit. Many breeds are in need of adoption, but if you are looking for a specific type of dog and don't see it here, contact them for suggestions. And if you can offer a temporary foster home for one of their dogs, they would greatly appreciate it.

SOL Companion

(510) 832-0929
5299 College Ave, Ste F
(@ Broadway)
Oakland, California 94618
www.solcompanion.com
Hours: Tue - Thu 8 A.M. - 4 P.M., Sat 8 A.M. - 3:30 P.M.
Payment: Credit Cards, Checks
Price Range: $$$

Physical therapists Tammara Moore and Nina Patterson run SOL Companion as a labor of love, doing groundbreaking work in physical rehabilitation for canines. Along with two other therapists, this team of professionals practice on people right next door, bringing a crossover of new techniques to pups who need extra special care. Many dogs trot out of here rejuvenated as their hydrotherapy and home programs have given them years of improved function. SOL also is certified in veterinary acupuncture.

Tooth & Nail

(925) 933-0746

www.tooth-nail.com

Hours: By Appt

Payment: Credit Cards, Checks

Price Range: $$

This dog walking and pet-sitting company serves the cities of
Walnut Creek, Concord, Clayton, Alamo, Danville, Lafayette,
Martinez, Pleasant Hill, Pleasanton and San Ramon. Iris
Giebus and her crew will spend 40 quality minutes with your
pooch, walking, feeding and playing with him. Overnight stays
offer consistency and security for your pet, while one-or two-
hour group hikes let pups socialize. If you're too busy at work
to transport your pup to the veterinarian, Tooth & Nail's pet
taxi service is available, starting at $30 per hour.

Waggs & Whiskers

(510) 222-3375

4344 Appian Way

(@ Santa Rita Rd)

El Sobrante, California 94803

Hours: Every Day 8 A.M. to 5 P.M.

Payment: Credit Cards, Checks

Price Range: $$

Colorful cutout pets walk on the rooftop, bald eagles soar
across an inside mural, and the shop's big front window offers
a great view of the animal show inside. All shapes and sizes of
dogs and cats get bathed and groomed here, and owner
Sharon pampers purebreds and mutts alike. All clients receive
the BioGroom wash and are dried by Mighty Wind heavy-duty
dryers, as well as a nice clip before being sent home with a
sporty bandana around the neck. As an added bonus, the shop
is taking its show on the road with mobile pet grooming!

Waiterock Kennels

(925) 284-4729
18 South Acres Rd
(@ Pine Ln)
Lafayette, California 94549
www.waiterockkennels.com
Hours: Mon - Tue 8:30 A.M. - 5 P.M., Wed 9 A.M. - 12 P.M.,
Thu - Fri 8:30 A.M. - 5 P.M., Sat 9 A.M. - 12 P.M.
Payment: Credit Cards, Checks
Price Range: $$

This highly recommended boarding facility has good grassy
runs and 70 kennels with clean, inside/outside spaces that are
heated in the winter and air-conditioned in the summer. For
those blisteringly hot days, all kennels are equipped with misters.
Dogs receive 30 minutes of playtime a day or an hour of play
for a very reasonable additional $5 fee. Management is strict
about vaccinations, especially for nasal bordetella. Waiterock's
popularity means reservations are a must; for holidays (espe-
cially Christmas) reserve months in advance.

Wizard of Paws

(510) 526-2115
1442 6th St
(between Page & James sts, back alley)
Berkeley, California 94710
Hours: Tue - Sat 8 A.M. - 5 P.M.
Payment: Credit Cards, Checks
Price Range: $$

Wizard of Paws owner Barbara started out as a barber, but 20
years ago she discovered her preference for dog grooming. Pre-
bathing playtime on the grassy patio keeps dogs content. After
they're groomed, dogs are crated so as not to muss up their
locks, but it's a nice, clean, bright and quiet place to hang out.
Her shop uses all-natural scrubs and clips all dogs except over-
sized breeds. Milo and SPCA dogs receive a discount.

South Bay

EMERGENCY PET TRANSPORT

AMERS Animal Ambulance
(877) 426-3771 (emergency)
(925) 261-9111 (office)
www.animalmedics.com
Hours: Every Day 24 Hours
Payment: Credit Cards, Checks
Emergency Fee: $175

Pet Taxi
Bay Area
(415) 386-2534
Hours: Every Day 7 A.M. – 7 P.M.
Emergency Hours: Every Day 24 Hours
Payment: Checks
Price Range: $$/$$$

ANIMAL EMERGENCY FACILITIES

Emergency Animal Clinic of South San Jose
(408) 578-5622
5440 Thornwood Dr
(off Santa Teresa Blvd, just past Blossom Hill Rd)
San Jose, California 95123
Hours: Mon – Fri 6 P.M.– 8 A.M.,
Weekends & Holidays 24 Hours
Payment: Credit Cards, Checks
Emergency Exam Fee: $95

United Emergency Animal Clinic Inc
(408) 371-6252
1657 S Bascom Ave
(corner of Hamilton & Bascom aves)
San Jose, California 95101
Hours: Mon – Fri 6 P.M. – 8 A.M.,
Weekends & Holidays 24 Hours
Payment: Credit Cards
Emergency Exam Fee: $95

ANIMAL POISON HOTLINE

ASPCA Animal Poison Control Center
(888) 4ANI-HELP
Hours: Every Day 24 Hours
Payment: Credit Cards
Consultation Fee: $45

ADOPTION

Campbell *Petsmart*
Los Gatos *Critters Corner* • *Pet Spa, The* **(S)**
Milpitas *Petsmart*
San Jose *Pets and More* • *CARE*
Santa Clara *Humane Society Silicon Valley*

ALTERNATIVE PRODUCTS/SERVICES

Almaden *An-Jan Feed & Pet Supply*
Cupertino *An-Jan Feed & Pet Supply*
Milpitas *An-Jan Feed & Pet Supply*
Mountain View *Country Pet Wash*
San Jose *An-Jan Feed & Pet Supply* • *Grooming Extraordinaire* • *Pets and More*
South San Jose *An-Jan Feed & Pet Supply*
Sunnyvale *For Other Living Things*

ANESTHESIA-FREE TEETH CLEANING

Campbell *Shampoo chez*
Los Gatos *Fluffy Puppy, The* • *Pet Spa, The* **(S)**
Morgan Hill *Pet Station, The*
Santa Clara *Madeline's Pet Grooming Salon and Institute of Pet Grooming* **(S)**

DOG BOARDING

Mountain View *Robalee Kennel*
San Jose *Camp Bow Wow* • *Spots Cageless Boarding* **(S)**
Sunnyvale *Kaluah Kennel* • *Run 'Em Ragged*

DOG DAY CARE

Los Gatos *Fluffy Puppy, The* • *Foxy Hound, The* • *Pet Spa, The* **(S)**
San Jose *Camp Bow Wow* • *Spots Cageless Boarding* **(S)**
Sunnyvale *Run 'Em Ragged*

DOG GROOMING

Campbell *Andrea and Monika's Grooming* • *Petsmart* • *Shampoo chez*
Gilroy *Petco*
Los Gatos *Fluffy Puppy, The* • *Foxy Hound, The* • *Gary's Poodles Unlimited* • *Pet Spa, The*
Milpitas *Petsmart*
Morgan Hill *Pet Station, The*
Mountain View *Critter Clipper* • *Heidi's Dog Grooming*
San Jose *Almaden Pet Salon* • *Grooming Extraordinaire*
Santa Clara *Madeline's Pet Grooming Salon and Institute of Pet Grooming* **(S)** • *Petco*
Sunnyvale *Canine Showcase* • *Run 'Em Ragged* • *Petco*

DOG GROOMING—SELF-SERVE

Campbell *Shampoo chez*
Los Gatos *Pet Spa, The*
Morgan Hill *Pet Station, The*
Mountain View *Country Pet Wash*
San Jose *Pet Food Express • Petco*
Sunnyvale *Petco*

DOG PARKS—OFF LEASH

Mountain View *Mountain View Dog Park*
San Jose *Hellyer County Park • Miyuki Dog Park • Watson Dog Park*
Santa Clara *Santa Clara Dog Park*
Sunnyvale *Las Palmas Dog Park*

DOG TRAINING

Almaden *An-Jan Feed & Pet Supply*
Campbell *Petsmart*
Cupertino *An-Jan Feed & Pet Supply*
Los Gatos *Fluffy Puppy, The • Pet Spa, The • Petco*
Milpitas *An-Jan Feed & Pet Supply • Petsmart*
Morgan Hill *Petco*
San Carlos *Sam's Downtown Feed & Pet Supply*
San Jose *An-Jan Feed & Pet Supply • Pet Food Express • Petco*
• Spots Cageless Boarding **(S)**
Santa Clara *Petco*
South San Jose *An-Jan Feed & Pet Supply*
Sunnyvale *A Dog's Best Friend • Run 'Em Ragged • Petco*

DOG WALKING/PET-SITTING

Los Gatos *Fluffy Puppy, The • Pet Spa, The*
Santa Clara County *Spoil 'em Rotten Pet Sitting Services* **(S)**

PET-SUPPLY STORES

Almaden *An-Jan Feed & Pet Supply*
Campbell *Petsmart • Shampoo chez*
Cupertino *An-Jan Feed & Pet Supply • Petco*
Gilroy *Petco*
Los Gatos *Bow Wowzer • Critters Corner • Pet People • Pet Spa, The • Petco*
Milpitas *An-Jan Feed & Pet Supply • Petsmart*
Morgan Hill *Pet Station, The • Petco*
Mountain View *Country Pet Wash • Critter Clipper • Heidi's Dog Grooming*
San Carlos *Sam's Downtown Feed & Pet Supply*
San Jose *An-Jan Feed & Pet Supply • Gussied Up Dog Boutique • Mutt • Pet Food Express • Pets and More • Petco*
Santa Clara *Madeline's Pet Grooming Salon and Institute of Pet Grooming* **(S)** *• Petco*
South San Jose *An-Jan Feed & Pet Supply*
Sunnyvale *For Other Living Things • Petco*

VACCINATIONS—LOW-COST

Almaden *An-Jan Feed & Pet Supply*
Campbell *Petsmart • Shampoo chez*
Cupertino *An-Jan Feed & Pet Supply • Petco*
Gilroy *Petco*
Los Gatos *Petco*
Milpitas *An-Jan Feed & Pet Supply • Petsmart*
Morgan Hill *Pet Station, The • Petco*
San Carlos *Sam's Downtown Feed & Pet Supply*
San Jose *An-Jan Feed & Pet Supply • Pet Food Express • Petco*
Santa Clara *Petco*
South San Jose *An-Jan Feed & Pet Supply*
Sunnyvale *Petco*

CITY DOG PICKS

Los Gatos *Fluffy Puppy, The • Pet Spa, The*
Morgan Hill *Pet Station, The*
Mountain View *Mountain View Dog Park*
San Jose *Spots Cageless Boarding* **(S)**
Sunnyvale *Las Palmas Dog Park*

General Listings

A Dog's Best Friend
(650) 367-6124
www.martinasdogs.com
Hours: By Appt
Payment: Checks
Price Range: $$$

Trainer Martina Contreras is highly respected in the South Bay dog community for helping people get real about dog socialization. One of her central beliefs is that training should be fun. With a no-nonsense approach, she addresses the need for awareness of other dogs you and your pup will encounter, stressing that your dog should not have to learn self defense at the off-leash park. Among her offerings are puppy kindergarten, basic and advanced obedience, private sessions for behavior and aggression counseling, games and tricks classes, and a kids' workshop on safety around dogs.

Almaden Pet Salon
(408) 927-9166
6055 Meridian Ave, Ste M
San Jose, California 95102
Hours: Tue - Sat 7 A.M. - 6 P.M.
Payment: Credit Cards, Checks
Price Range: $$

Owner Annie has created a quiet, soothing atmosphere at this long-running grooming business. She claims that every dog or cat that comes through the door is treated as one of her own. Three professional groomers keep the pets styled and the place clean. Services range from a simple bath and combing to a full pet cut with hand scissors. A variety of shampoos are used, including all-natural brands, and drying is done with the utmost care and attention.

Andrea and Monika's Grooming

(408) 377-3113
2889 S Bascom Ave
Campbell, California 95008
Hours: Mon - Wed 9 A.M. - 5 P.M., Thu - Fri 9 A.M. - 7 P.M.,
Sat 9 A.M. - 5 P.M.
Payment: Checks
Price Range: $$

This quiet little salon has the air of a doctor's office. You won't be invited beyond the cubbyhole lobby, and you'll have to strain your neck if you want to watch the two master groomers at work. Using mostly client-supplied products, Monika pampers the poodle-types while Andrea, a rescue advocate, takes on the terriers and other breeds. Andrea's book, *What Every Owner Needs to Know About Grooming,* can fill you in on what's going on behind those closed doors.

An-Jan Feed & Pet Supply

www.anjan.com
Payment: Credit Cards, Checks
Price Range: $$

San Jose Location

(408) 293-6232
1633 S 1st St
(@ Monterey Rd)
San Jose, California 95112
Hours: Mon - Fri 9:30 A.M. - 7 P.M., Sat 9 A.M. - 7 P.M.,
Sun 10 A.M. - 5 P.M.

Milpitas Location

(408) 263-1774
111 S Main St
Milpitas, California 95035
Hours: Mon - Fri 9:30 A.M. - 7 P.M., Sat 9 A.M. - 7 P.M.,
Sun 10 A.M. - 5 P.M.

Almaden Location

(408) 269-5551
1109 Branham Ln
(in Long's Drugs Shopping Center)
Almaden, California 95118
Hours: Mon, Wed, Thu, Fri 9:30 A.M. - 7 P.M.,
Tue 9:30 A.M. - 1 P.M., Sat 9:30 A.M. - 7 P.M.,
Sun 10 A.M. - 5 P.M.

South San Jose Location

(408) 578-7790
7128 Santa Teresa Blvd
(@ Bernal Rd)
South San Jose, California 95139
Hours: Mon - Fri 9:30 A.M. - 7 P.M., Sat 9 A.M. - 7 P.M.,
Sun 10 A.M. - 5 P.M.

Cupertino Location

(408) 446-3932
1129 S De Anza Blvd
(@ Blue Hill Dr)
Cupertino, California 95129
Hours: Mon - Fri 9:30 A.M. - 7 P.M., Sat 9 A.M. - 7 P.M.,
Sun 10 A.M. - 5 P.M.

There's more than meets the eye to this basic pet-supply store
stocked with food, treats, toys, shampoos and collars. The
store's name stands for Ann and Jan Rademakers, who, along
with Peter Atkins, founded Natura Pet Products (makers of
Innova), California Natural and now Karma Organics. They
started their good work in 1989, and unleashed a revolution in
dog nutrition. You can also buy the more commercial brands
here. Sign your dog up for the Birthday Club and receive special discounts, as well as updates on classes and events, and a
birthday gift from one of the store's five locations.

Bow Wowzer

(408) 395-2285
100 N Santa Cruz Ave
(@ Bean Ave)
Los Gatos, California 95030

Hours: Mon - Sun 10 A.M. - 6 P.M.
Payment: Credit Cards, Checks
Price Range: $$$

Those in search of that perfect Dalmatian pillow, terrier tile trivet or Great Dane figurine, will probably find it at this specialty boutique that's located on the trendy and upscale North Santa Cruz Avenue in Los Gatos. Bow Wowzer offers everything from pet carriers to water dishes to car seats, along with crystal collars. You'll also find dog magnets, special T-shirts or canine Halloween outfits. After a stop here, your pooch will look great strolling down the dog-friendly strip. This place is for the dog-obsessed only; the cat-obsessed have their own store next door.

Camp Bow Wow
(408) 972-8086
6175A Santa Teresa Blvd
San Jose, California 95123
www.campbowwow.com
Hours: Mon - Fri 7 A.M. - 6 P.M.
Payment: Credit Cards, Checks
Price Range: $$

The owner here calls herself Top Dog, but she's more like a sweet auntie to the 20 lucky dogs who get to spend the day at the charming Camp Bow Wow. The dogs are supervised as they play all day behind the green picket fence, where horse mats on the floor make for low-impact romping. There's a separate enclosure for naps, and dogs that are old, injured or just feeling a little cranky, can come into the office for a snooze. A pooch named Micky does admission evaluations, and all campers learn to use the gravel yard out back to do their business.

Canine Showcase

(408) 738-3782
899 E El Camino Real, Ste 2
Sunnyvale, California 94086
Hours: Mon - Sat 8 A.M. - 6 P.M., Sun 9 A.M. - 4 P.M.
Payment: Checks
Price Range: $$

Owner Linda raises and shows Bengal cats, but she won't have anything to do with grooming kitties. Instead, she concentrates on coiffing canines. All breeds receive a warm welcome and can stay the whole day if necessary. Only hypo-allergenic, all-natural shampoos are used and the drying method is selected to suit the dog. Such personalized attention is par for the course here. Luscious-looking hand-baked treats beckon from the counter, inspired by the tastes of an Airedale client.

CARE

(408) 227-CARE
4190 Piper Dr
San Jose, California 95011
www.carepets.org
Hours: See website
Payment: Checks
Price Range: $$

CARE (The Companion Animal Rescue Effort)—a nonprofit, all-volunteer network that places rescued pets into responsible homes—was founded in 1987 and is based in Santa Clara County. Since CARE has a no-kill philosophy, animals are kept in foster homes until adopted, no matter how long it takes. Other CARE services include referrals to low- or no-cost spay/neuter facilities as well as local groomers and trainers. They also set up information booths at local community fairs and work with other rescue shelters to save as many animals as possible. CARE holds an adoption fair every Saturday from 10:30 A.M. until 2 P.M. Their nonprofit adoption center greatly appreciates volunteers and donations.

Country Pet Wash

(650) 988-9274
1764-B Miramonte Ave
Mountain View, California 94040
Hours: Mon, Wed 10 A.M. - 6:30 P.M., Tue , Thu 11 A.M. - 7
P.M., Fri 10 A.M. - 6:30 P.M.,
Sat, Sun 9 A.M. - 5:30 P.M.
Payment: Checks
Price Range: $$

This do-it-yourself pup scrub has amassed a loyal following.
Give your dog a thorough bath amidst soothing green and
yellow walls covered with charming folk-art pieces that fill
every nook and cranny. While you'll be thankful for the sur-
roundings, your pup will appreciate the fast and easy electric
nail trimmer, the soothing all-natural shampoos, the steps lead-
ing up to the tubs and the treats in the retail corner.

Critter Clipper

(650) 961-4661
1350 Grant Road, Ste 12
Mountain View, California 94040
Hours: Mon - Sat 8 A.M. - 5 P.M.
Payment: Credit Cards, Checks
Price Range: $$$

Your dog can brush up on her Spanish, Russian or Korean as
she gets beautified in this multilingual, 30-year-old salon. The
international staff, which includes two dedicated cat groomers,
uses state-of-the-art equipment such as the HydroSurge
bathing system. Dogs can run free in the large, air-conditioned
workrooms or stay in secure crates. High-tech crates with cir-
culating tepid air provide a perfect drying spot after an all-natural bath. You can continue the haute hygiene at home, since
all-natural shampoos, conditioners and colognes are available
for purchase.

Critters Corner
(408) 402-9660
15545-C Los Gatos Blvd
Los Gatos, California 95032
Hours: Mon - Fri 9 A.M. - 8 P.M., Sat - Sun 10 A.M. - 6 P.M.
Payment: Credit Cards, Checks
Price Range: $$

A trip to this store for quality kibble or basic dog supplies can feel like a safari or a tropical cruise. Join the hoards of enthusiastic kids competing for a chance to hold trophy birds, sacred lizards, sacrificial rats and magic bunnies—most of which are up for adoption. Happily, responsible owners Julie and Annie are as finicky as the SPCA about making sure their exotic friends are going to good homes. Critter Corner also provides exotic pet boarding for vacationing owners.

Fluffy Puppy, The
(408) 354-0078
656A N Santa Cruz Ave
(@ Blossom Hill Rd)
Los Gatos, California 95030
www.fluffypuppy.com
Hours: Tue - Fri 8 A.M. - 6 P.M., Sat 9 A.M. - 5 P.M.
Payment: Checks
Price Range: $$$

Before being admitted into The Fluffy Puppy, dogs must pass a two-hour evaluation. Once they're through the door, they can roam around spacious rooms, playing with other day-trippers. Other offerings include pet-sitting, training classes (owner attendance mandatory) and alternative treatments, such as water therapy, chiropractic adjustments and canine massage. Owner Karyn is trained in physical therapy. Baths are given with aloe vera or oatmeal-based products. Special discounts are available for extended daycare periods. This 10-year-old day-care spot has a long list of loyals.

For Other Living Things

(408) 739-6785
1261 S Mary Ave
Sunnyvale, California 94087
www.forotherlivingthings.com
Hours: Mon 9 A.M. - 7 P.M., Tue - Thu 9 A.M. - 6 P.M., Fri - Sat
9 A.M. - 7 P.M.
Payment: Credit Cards, Checks
Price Range: $$

This Silicon Valley mall shop smacks of downtown Berkeley, boasting shade-grown coffee, hemp dog treats, edible greeting cards, biodegradable poop bags and several different brands of raw dog food. If you're unsure about the latter, snuggle into a sofa and study the back issues of *Whole Dog Journal* to get the scoop. This shop is a model of evolutionary thinking, keeping inventory fresh with new finds for each visit.

Foxy Hound, The

(408) 358-5353
14160 Blossom Hill Rd
(@ Harwood Rd)
Los Gatos, California 95032
www.foxyhound.com
Hours: Tue - Sat 8 A.M. - 6 P.M.
Payment: Credit Cards, Checks
Price Range: $$

Welcome to the canine version of your neighborhood beauty parlor. The Foxy Hound is the oldest salon in town. Grooming prices range from $25 for a Chihuahua to $125 for a Saint Bernard. Looking to splurge on your favorite pooch? Pick up some organic treats and pet supplies from the front counter. Or check out Kit'n K'poodle, the adjacent boutique that carries everything from dog-themed pillows to jewelry and towels.

Gary's Poodles Unlimited

(408) 354-1901

350 Village Ln

(@ Los Gatos Blvd)

Los Gatos, California 95030

Hours: Tue - Sat 8 A.M. - 6 P.M.

Payment: Checks

Price Range: $$$

If you're searching for the best your money can buy, here it is. Gary, a one-man business, is the cream of the well-groomed-dog crop in Los Gatos. This means a two-to four-week waiting list—if he's even taking on new clients. If you and your pet can wait, though, you'll most likely be very happy with the results. Despite the name, Gary grooms all breeds.

Grooming Extraordinaire

(408) 298-6435

347 Lincoln Ave

(1½ blocks south of W San Carlos St)

San Jose, California 95126

Hours: Tue - Fri 6:30 A.M. - 6 P.M., Sat 7:30 A.M. - 6 P.M.

Payment: Credit Cards, Checks

Price Range: $$

Owner and head groomer Mark Collins claims he was born into the dog-grooming trade, and after trying other things, he has returned to his true calling. He shows Bedlingtons, but bichons, Kerry blues, soft-coated wheatens and all three varieties of schnauzers come to his busy shop for the perfect clip. Those may be his speciality, but Mark welcomes all breeds, as well as cats. Boasting a small, holistic apothecary in the shop's lobby, Grooming Extraordinaire uses only mild, all-natural products. Drying is done by hand.

Gussied Up Dog Boutique

(408) 279-2229
1310 Lincoln Ave
(in the Willow Glen district, between Willow St
& Minnesota Ave)
San Jose, California 95125
Hours: Mon - Fri 10 A.M. - 7 P.M., Sat - Sun 9 A.M. - 7 P.M.
Payment: Credit Cards, Checks
Price Range: $$$

Owners Kimberly and Robert gave up the high-tech grind so that Gus, their nine-pound miniature pinscher/Chihuahua rescue, could have his own shop. You'll find fancy beds, cool collars, dapper hats, team sweatshirts and fatigues, nail polish, dog-adoption announcements, birthday invitations, a gumball-machine feeder, dog art, a red fire-hydrant cookie jar and lots of cookies and fancy goodies with which to fill it. With limited space and an eye toward serving only the best, Gussied Up only stocks Wellness brand dog kibble.

Heidi's Dog Grooming

(650) 966-1303
2239 G Old Middlefield Way
(behind the auto repair, 1½ blocks west of Rengstorff)
Mountain View, California 94043
Hours: Tue - Sat 9 A.M. – Last Dog
Payment: Checks
Price Range: $$

The canine traffic coming and going seems unusually calm, most likely thanks to Heidi's relaxed, assured manner with her clients. Private-stock shampoos and conditioners are marked with the names of regulars, but a supply of all-natural products is on hand for new clients. Heidi spares no detail with her careful hand scissoring, and there's not a cage dryer in sight. Heidi will not groom aggressive dogs, but guide dogs get the red-carpet treatment and a hefty discount.

Hellyer County Park

985 Hellyer Ave
San Jose, California 95111
Hours: Every Day 8 A.M. - Dusk
Closed: Wed

Your dog might be more interested in sussing out the wildlife at Hellyer County Park than in sniffing other dogs. The giant old oaks outside the fenced area draw plenty of squirrels. Enough scenery graces the park that you might even forget for a moment that the freeway is just beyond the masonry sound barrier. This spot gets top props for its wild aesthetic, but it's the only dog park around where you have to pay $4 to get in the parking lot. To avoid the fee, park on Tuers Road and walk the half-mile trail to the dog enclosure, which is near the Shadowbluff picnic area.

Humane Society Silicon Valley

(408) 727-3383
2530 Lafayette St
(@ Central Expressway)
Santa Clara, California 95050
www.hssv.org
Hours: Mon - Fri 10:30 A.M. - 7 P.M., Sat - Sun 10 A.M. - 6 P.M.
Payment: Checks
Price Range: $

Visitors to Silicon Valley's Humane Society might get side-tracked by the furry pocket pets up for adoption in the lobby. Kids especially flock to this well-stocked entertainment nook, but follow the paw prints to the back of the facility and you'll find plenty of pups. Once the application process, which is designed to ensure a good match, is completed, your pooch will be spayed or neutered before you take him home. On-site Alpha Pet Supply is the perfect place to pick up all the supplies and toys you'll need for your new life together.

Kaluah Kennel

(408) 245-1234
689 N Mathilda Ave
(across from the Best Western, off Hwy 101)
Sunnyvale, California 94085
Hours: Mon - Tue 9 A.M. - 5 P.M., Wed 9 A.M. - 1 P.M.,
Thu - Fri 9 A.M. - 5 P.M.
Payment: Checks
Price Range: $$

Tom and Debbie might be partial to papillons, but they give
plenty of attention to every dog and cat that comes to stay at
Kaluah Kennel. The owners live on the premises and provide
all the care themselves at this traditional boarding facility. The
food of choice is Pedigree and Eukanuba—be prepared to pay
extra if you choose to bring your own chow. The runs are
impeccable and climate-controlled with heaters, fans and mis-
ters. Cats lounge in rooms decorated with fish tiles, and dogs
are rotated into a play yard throughout the day.

Las Palmas Dog Park

(408) 730-735
850 Russet Dr
(parking at the end of Spinoza, just past Hyde Park)
Sunnyvale, California 94087
Hours: Every Day 8 A.M. - 8 P.M.

The appropriately named Las Palmas dog run is nestled in the
palm trees adjacent to a pleasant picnic area. Inside the fence,
plenty of mature redwood and fruit trees provide shade.
However, because this is one of the South Bay's most accom-
modating and well-used dog parks, you may have to deal
with a few dogs (and people) with anger-management issues.
Parking is available at the dog park gate, but if you arrive dur-
ing prime time, you might have to park farther away.

Madeline's Pet Grooming Salon and Institute of Pet Grooming

(408) 243-1333
820 Kiely Blvd
(@ Homestead Rd)
Santa Clara, California 95051
www.madelinesinstitute.com
Hours: Mon 8 A.M. - 2 P.M., Tue - Fri 7 A.M. - 6 P.M.,
Sat 7:30 A.M. - 6 P.M.
Payment: Credit Cards, Checks
Price Range: $$

For over 40 years, dogs, cats and even a few rabbits have been doing their part to help would-be groomers hone their skills at this prestigious grooming institute. The models don't get a discount, but since the staff is under scrutiny, there's no need to worry about sloppy work, dogs being left unsupervised in cage dryers or less-than-loving care. Students come for a three-month course that's reputed to be fun and fast paced. They leave with all the knowledge and equipment necessary to launch their grooming career. If you're short on time, Madeline's will transport your dog to and from the salon.

Miyuki Dog Park

(408) 277-2811
Miyuki Dr
(@ the north end of Miyuki Dr, off Santa Teresa Blvd)
San Jose, California 95123
www.ci.san-jose.ca.us/prns/parksmiyuki.htm

Unwavering locals—determined to create a doggie destination—turned a deserted site into Miyuki, San Jose's first dog park. The 3/8-acre, gravel-lined, fenced plot has plenty of beautiful trees and is brimming with good vibes—enough to blot out the adjacent freeway and humming power station. There isn't any running water, but regulars bring and leave water jugs and buckets for the dogs. At prime time, usually at least a dozen dogs are romping around or playing with the communal toy collection.

Mountain View Dog Park

(650) 903-6392
Shoreline Park
(North Road @ N Shoreline Blvd)
Mountain View, California 94043
www.mvdp.org

Hours: Every Day 6 A.M. to a half-hour after Dusk

This popular park brings in all types: laid-back folks inter-mixed with cell-phone toting Type-A's. Mountain View is one of the few wheelchair accessible parks in the Bay Area. It offers running water and poop-disposal tools. On sunny days, most dog owners cluster under the only source of shade available, the small shelter. One word of caution: Check the Shoreline Ampitheatre schedule before loading your dog into the car. Around concert time, the traffic in the area is snarled.

Mutt

(408) 249-2345
377 Santana Row, Ste 1065
San Jose, California 95128
www.muttgirls.com

Hours: Mon 10 A.M. - 6 P.M., Tue - Sat 10 A.M. - 9 P.M., Sun 12 A.M. - 6 P.M.

Payment: Credit Cards, Checks

Price Range: $$$

Mutt couture is de rigor for the fabulously frilly red-carpet pups, which include the Osbourne's pack, Paris Hilton's Tinkerbell and the famous Bruiser Woods of *Legally Blond*. *Vogue* and *In Style* have given nods to the products in this stylish store. Mutt carries everything from jeweled collars to designer beds, to organic spa grooming products to raffia totes, as well as all-natural treats and vintage bowls. You'll find excellent customer service, and a knowledgeable staff that sticks by the store's motto: "Pedigree is a state of mind."

Pet Food Express

(408) 239-7777
1787 E Capitol Expressway
(Silver Creek Shopping Center)
San Jose, California 95121
www.petfoodexpress.com
Hours: Mon - Sat 9:30 A.M. - 7:30 P.M., Sun 10 A.M. - 6 P.M.
Payment: Credit Cards, Checks
Price Range: $$$

Pet Food Express is a pet-supply chain with numerous franchises throughout the Bay Area. They sell a variety of pet supplies, including specialty items like the safety light dog collar and the Cider Mill dog trolley. Brands such as Avo Derm and Pinnacle are on the shelves, and Pet Express staff is friendly and helpful. Dog training classes and low-cost vaccinations are available. The store's My Mutt program promotes adoption of the mighty mixed breed.

Pet People

514 N Santa Cruz Ave
(@ Andrews St)
Los Gatos, California 95030
www.epetpeople.com
Hours: Mon - Fri 8:30 A.M. - 7 P.M., Sat 8:30 A.M. - 6 P.M.,
Sun 11 A.M. - 5 P.M.
Payment: Credit Cards, Checks
Price Range: $$

As you walk through the door at Pet People, a neighborhood pet-supply store, a wall of collars greets you. Head out back, and you'll find a showroom brimming with beds and crates. In between are tons of treats and toys, as well as a dozen or so major brands of premium dog food. Although you're in tourist-heavy, shoppe-central Los Gatos, don't expect a high-end boutique attitude. At Pet People, you'll find knowledgeable staff and quality staples, which have kept this mainstay in business, despite the newer Petco down the block.

Pet Spa, The

(408) 379-8911
1516 Pollard Rd
(corner of Pollard Rd & More Ave)
Los Gatos, California 95032
www.spa4pets.com
Hours: Mon - Sat 8 A.M. - 6 P.M.
Payment: Credit Cards, Checks
Price Range: $$$

This popular spa offers plenty of pooch-pampering services, including hypo-allergenic baths, swim and therapy sessions, canine massage and the agility-training workshops. You might also want to check out the many obedience classes: Heeling 101, Tricks, Canine Good Citizenship and Fun & Games. They'll watch your dog either in their nearby day-care facility or visit him at your home. With a long list of "Best of..." awards, this well-run salon comes highly recommended by those in the biz and employs only professionally trained groomers. It's not the cheapest place in town, but it's certainly one of the best.

Pet Station, The

(408) 776-3101
16080 Monterey Rd
(in front of the Precision Tune Auto Care)
Morgan Hill, California 95037
Hours: Mon - Fri 8 A.M. - 6 P.M., Sat 9 A.M. - 6 P.M.,
Sun 10 A.M. - 4 P.M.
Payment: Credit Cards, Checks
Price Range: $$

At The Pet Station, you can treat your dog to a gourmet snack while you get your car tuned up at the adjacent auto shop.

Tina's retro-chic '50s Grooming Bonetique and Bakery features doggie donuts, cinnamon swirls, petit fours and yogurt canoli. There are also self-serve dog-wash facilities as well as full-service grooming. And Tina stocks dog beds, toys and sweaters

Petco

www.petco.com
Payment: Credit Cards, Checks
Price Range: $$

Cupertino Location
(408) 255-2977
10225 S De Anza Blvd
(between Call and Rodrigues aves)
Cupertino, California 95014
Hours: Mon - Fri 9 A.M. - 9 P.M., Sat 9 A.M. - 8 P.M., Sun 10 A.M. - 7 P.M.

Gilroy Location
(408) 846-2844
8767 San Ysidro Ave
(between Las Animas Ave & Leavesley Rd)
Gilroy, California 95020
Hours: Mon - Sat 9 A.M. - 9 P.M., Sun 10 A.M. - 8 P.M.

Los Gatos Location
(408) 354-7670
540 N Santa Cruz Ave, Ste B
(between Ashler Ave & Olive St)
Los Gatos, California 95030
Hours: Mon - Fri 9 A.M. - 9 P.M., Sat 10 A.M. - 7 P.M., Sun 10 A.M. - 6 P.M.

Morgan Hill Location
(408) 778-7838
313 Vineyard Town Center Way
(@ Monterey St)
Morgan Hill, California 95037
Hours: Mon - Fri 9 A.M. - 9 P.M., Sat 9 A.M. - 7:30 P.M.,
Sun 10 A.M. - 7 P.M.

San Jose-Meridian Location
(408) 269-2481
4698 Meridian Ave
(between Branham Ln & Portobelo Dr)
San Jose, California 95118
Hours: Mon - Sat 9 A.M. - 9 P.M., Sun 9 A.M. - 8 P.M.

San Jose-Saratoga Location
(408) 866-7387
500 El Paseo De Saratoga
(between Saratoga Ave & Quito Rd)
San Jose, California 95130
Hours: Mon - Sat 9 A.M. - 9 P.M., Sun 10 A.M. - 8 P.M.

Santa Clara Location
(408) 423-9110
2775 El Camino Real
(@ Bowers Ave)
Santa Clara, California 95051
Hours: Mon - Sat 9 A.M. - 9 P.M., Sun 10 A.M. - 8 P.M.

Sunnyvale Location
(408) 774-0171
160 E El Camino Real
(@ Saratoga Sunnyvale Rd)
Sunnyvale, California 94087

Hours: Mon - Sat 9 A.M. - 9 P.M., Sun 9 A.M. - 8 P.M.
For one-stop shopping it's hard to beat the convenience and value of this superstore with locations all over the country. Petco makes it their mission to provide customers with the food, supplements and products they want for their animals. Their bed selection runs the gamut, from orthopedic mattresses along with sheets and throws to chaises that would do an interior decorator proud. The San Jose-Meridian location offers the latest high-end products, plus Kosher Pets and Halo dog foods in their La Petique section. Get a P.A.L.S. (Petco Animal Lovers Save) card to take advantage of discounts; you may also want to check out their Top Dog program, which offers even greater savings to their most loyal customers. Check the contact information for each store for hours and specific service offerings.

Pets and More
(408) 374-9722
4177 Hamilton Ave
(just east of San Tomas Aquino Rd)
San Jose, California 95130

Hours: Mon - Fri 10 A.M. - 8 P.M., Sat 10 A.M. - 7 P.M., Sun 11 A.M. - 4 P.M.
Payment: Credit Cards, Checks
Price Range: $$
Think twice before bringing your hunting dog into Pets and More, lest he set his sights on the rabbits, rodents, tortoises and snakes the store stocks and brings out for children to

hold—especially during the popular birthday parties. Howard, who left a high-tech career to buy this shop, is an animal-rights and welfare-advocate who believes in giving only the best to our animal companions. Accordingly, he carries raw food and Flint River Ranch; he's currently revamping his stock to so he can offer more nutritious dog foods and treats.

Petsmart
www.petsmart.com
Hours: Mon - Sat 9 A.M. - 9 P.M., Sun 10 A.M. - 6 P.M.
Payment: Credit Cards, Checks
Price Range: $$

Campbell Location
(408) 374-9321
850 W Hamilton Ave
(@ Marathon Dr)
Campbell, California 95008

Milpitas Location
(408) 956-1044
175 Ranch Dr
(@ McCarthy Blvd)
Milpitas, California 95035

This standout superstore is to pet owners what Home Depot is to homeowners. PetSmart stocks an unbelievably wide range of products that will meet almost any budget. They carry the better dog food brands—including Bil-Jac. And whenever possible, they offer all-natural options in their selection of treats, supplements and skin products. A viewing window allows see-for-yourself grooming so you don't have to worry about what happens behind closed doors. They get major points for promoting their adoptions all the time. And they have a staff that's always available to advise you and to help you find what you need. It's places like PetSmart that give superstores a good name.

Robalee Kennel

(650) 965-9425
2254 Wyandotte St
(off Rengstorff, between Middlefield Rd & Hwy 101)
Mountain View, California 94043
www.robalee.com
Hours: Mon - Fri 9 A.M. - 12 P.M.
Payment: Checks
Price Range: $$

Shirlee Roberts has operated the kennel for 30 of the past 70 years that dogs have boarded here. When she and her husband, Gerry, retired from their careers in aerospace, they pursued their love of Irish Setters by breeding and boarding them. They took in any dog or cat looking for a meal and a warm blanket along the way. Accommodations are clean but basic. The house food is Pedigree, and you pay extra for exercise. Shirlee seems a little severe at first, but warms up quickly around dog lovers.

Run 'Em Ragged

(408) 747-1111
1249 Birchwood Dr
(off Tasman Dr near the Lawrence Expressway)
Sunnyvale, California 94089
www.runemragged.com
Hours: Every Day 7 A.M - 7 P.M.
Payment: Credit Cards, Checks
Price Range: $$$

Run Em Ragged is a work in progress. Owner Dyana set up shop in this enormous space, and the business grows into it a bit more each day. You can leave your energetic pup for some quality rough housing under the supervision of the competent staff. And if he's not up to playing, your couch potato can park himself in front of the tube. Health codes preclude visiting the playrooms when the games are in session, but there's a webcam that lets you check up on your pooch.

Sam's Downtown Feed & Pet Supply

(408) 287-9090
759 W San Carlos St
(between Lincoln Ave & S Montgomery Ln)
San Carlos, California 95126
www.samsdowntownfeed.com
Hours: Mon - Fri 8 A.M. - 7 P.M., Sat 8 A.M. - 5 P.M.
Payment: Credit Cards, Checks
Price Range: $$

Local 4-H'ers and Future Farmers of America stock up on hay and grain while hip shoppers fill their baskets with raw food, healthy kibble, homeopathic remedies and gourmet treats. Owners Sam and Lisa provide old-fashioned service with a smile to all comers—dogs included. The shop is in a striking, old brick warehouse and features antique feed signs, a restored 1938 Ford truck and bales of hay stacked sky-high outside. Check out the Henry & Sons vegetarian dog goodies that are baked nearby and sometimes sold warm from the oven.

Santa Clara Dog Park

(408) 615-2260
3450 Brookdale Dr
(between Bing Dr & Curtis Ave)
Santa Clara, California 95051
Hours: Mon - Fri 7 A.M. - a hour after Dusk,
Sat - Sun 9 A.M. - a half-hour after Dusk

With a high prison-yard fence surrounding a rectangle of sand, this park has a forlorn look. However, the end near the street has some beautiful shade trees where you can sit and keep an eye on your pup or ponder the weird wooden Trojan dog who stands guard. A double gate helps facilitate dog entry and exit. A water spigot and clean-up tools make park visits more enjoyable for both dog and owner.

Shampoo chez

(408) 379-9274
523 E Campbell Ave
(between Hwy 17 & the Campbell Civic Center)
Campbell, California 95008
Hours: Tue - Sat 9 A.M. - 5:30 P.M., Sun 11 A.M. - 5 P.M.
Payment: Credit Cards, Checks
Price Range: $$

At Shampoo chez, Carol will clean up your pup, or you can
take on the task yourself. If you plan on bellying up to the
bathtub, you'll need to provide the shampoo, but they have
everything else covered. Carol grooms all breeds of dogs
and cats as well. She uses her own cactus-based shampoo
(available for purchase) and gives dogs a standard cut. She
sometimes cage dries her charges but always under supervi-
sion. Carol stocks a small inventory of high-quality dog and
cat supplies as well as Natura pet food. She also offers referrals
to other dog-related businesses and an informative newsletter.

Spoil 'em Rotten Pet Sitting Services

(408) 559-7297
Santa Clara County, California
Hours: By Appt
Payment: Checks
Price Range: $$

Jamie, who definitely lives up to her company's name, schedules
visits around your needs, allowing your dog to stick to his
daily routine with meals, walks, medications and doses of love
and affection. She can stay overnight at your home, watering
plants, alternating lights and blinds, and taking in
the newspapers and mail at no additional charge. She's trained
in pet first aid and CPR and will gladly take pets to their
appointments with the vet and groomer. Service in the South
Bay includes Campbell, Los Gatos, San Jose and Willow.

Spots Cageless Boarding

(408) 287-7687
561 W Hedding St
(@ Coleman Ave)
San Jose, California 95110
www.spotspets.com
Hours: Every Day 6 A.M. - 9 P.M.
Payment: Credit Cards, Checks
Price Range: $

With five rooms to roam through and 1,800 square feet of outdoor space to sniff, your pup is sure to find a spot that suits him. The bargain prices at this 24-hour dog-care service draw in the crowds, but the staff is small, so your pooch will need to be well socialized. If there's some doubt, you can sign up for any number of training packages, including a 40-day and 40-night training package that even Noah would love. Baths are free with two overnights or a week of day visits.

Watson Dog Park

(408) 277-2757
E Jackson & 22nd
(between E Taylor & E Julian sts)
San Jose, California 95112
www.sjparks.org/Parks/watson.htm
Hours: Dawn to an hour after Dusk

Dog owners are so friendly at Watson Dog Park that you may even find them fighting to pick up your pup's poop for you. They've made such a positive impression on San Jose Parks and Recreation that more dog parks are in the works. Amenities include two picnic benches that are perfectly shaded by a locust tree, a dog fountain and a canvas gazebo donated by one of the regulars. Drive onto the dirt road past Las Milpas Community Garden to find this jewel of a dog park.

Peninsula

EMERGENCY PET TRANSPORT

AMERS Animal Ambulance
(877) 426-3771 (emergency)
(925) 261-9111 (office)
www.animalmedics.com
Hours: Every Day 24 Hours
Payment: Credit Cards, Checks
Emergency Fee: $175

Pet Taxi
(415) 386-2534
Hours: Every Day 7 A.M. – 7 P.M.
Emergency Hours: Every Day 24 Hours
Payment: Checks
Price Range: $$/$$$

ANIMAL EMERGENCY FACILITIES

Adobe Animal Hospital
(650) 948-9661
396 1st St
Los Altos, California 94022
(off the Foothill Expressway, between Lyell & Whitney sts)
www.adobe-animal.com
Hours: Every Day 24 Hours
Payment: Checks, Credit Cards
Emergency Exam Fee: $75 to $92

South Peninsula Veterinary Emergency Clinic

(650) 494-1461
3045 Middlefield Rd
Palo Alto, California 94306
Hours: Mon – Fri 6 P.M. – 8 A.M.,
Weekends & Holidays 24 Hours
Payment: Credit Cards, Checks
Emergency Exam Fee: $85

Veterinary Emergency Clinic Northern Peninsula

(650) 348-2575
277 N Amplett Blvd
San Mateo, California 94401
Hours: Mon – Fri 5:30 P.M.- 8 A.M.,
Weekends & Holidays 24 Hours
Payment: Credit Cards, Checks
Emergency Exam Fee: $75

ANIMAL POISON HOTLINE

ASPCA Animal Poison Control Center

(888) 4ANI-HELP
Hours: Every Day 24 Hours
Payment: Credit Cards
Consultation Fee: $45

ADOPTION

Daly City *Petsmart*
Menlo Park *Pet Place, The*
San Mateo *Peninsula Humane Society and SPCA*

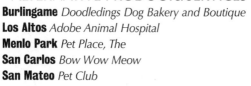

ALTERNATIVE PRODUCTS/SERVICES

Burlingame *Doodledings Dog Bakery and Boutique*
Los Altos *Adobe Animal Hospital*
Menlo Park *Pet Place, The*
San Carlos *Bow Wow Meow*
San Mateo *Pet Club*

ANESTHESIA-FREE TEETH CLEANING

Los Altos *Adobe Animal Hospital*
Redwood City *San Mateo Pet Supply*
South San Francisco *Bark 'n Bubbles*

DOG BOARDING

Pacifica *Pacifica Pet Hospital* • *Shamrock Ranch*
Palo Alto *A Dog's Life*
Redwood City *Affordable Grooming* • *Bark Park, Inc.*
• *Planet Pooch*
San Mateo *Smilin Dogs* **(S)**

DOG DAY CARE

Pacifica *Shamrock Ranch*
Palo Alto *Tracey Lee's Canine Training (TLC Training)*
• *A Dog's Life*
Redwood City *Affordable Grooming* • *Bark Park, Inc.* • *Planet Pooch*
San Mateo *Smilin Dogs* **(S)**

DOG GROOMING

Burlingame *Groomingdales* • *Poochini's*
Daly City *Petsmart*
Los Altos *Barking Lot, The* • *Beaugay's*
Mountain View *Petco*
Pacifica *Coastside Critters*
Palo Alto *Alexander's* • *A Dog's Life*
Redwood City *Affordable Grooming* • *Bark Park, Inc.*
• *Planet Pooch* • *San Mateo Pet Supply* • *Petco*
San Carlos *Bow Wow Meow* • *Fancy Feet Animal Grooming*
San Mateo *Noble Beast* • *Petco* • *Scrub A Pup* • *Super Pups*
South San Francisco *Bark 'n Bubbles*

DOG GROOMING—SELF-SERVE

Burlingame *Pets Are Us*
Daly City *Pet Food Express*
Mountain View *Petco*
Redwood City *San Mateo Pet Supply*
San Mateo *Scrub A Pup*
South San Francisco *Bark 'n Bubbles*

DOG PARKS—OFF LEASH

Belmont *Cipriani Dog Park*
Burlingame *Burlingame Dog Exercise Park*
Palo Alto *Greer Park* • *Hoover Park* • *Mitchell Park Dog Run*
Redwood City *Shore Dogs Park*
San Bruno *San Bruno Dog Park*

DOG TRAINING

Daly City *Pet Food Express* • *Petsmart*
Los Altos *Adobe Animal Hospital*
Menlo Park *Perfect Paws: Menlo Park Location*
Mountain View *Petco*
Pacifica *Shamrock Ranch*
Palo Alto *A Dog's Life* • *Pet Food Depot* • *Tracey Lee's Canine Training (TLC Training)*
Redwood City *Bark Park, Inc.* • *Planet Pooch* • *San Mateo Pet Supply*
San Bruno *Petco*
San Mateo *Peninsula Humane Society and SPCA* • *Petco*

DOG WALKING/PET-SITTING

Mobile *Priceless Pet Care*
Palo Alto *A Dog's Life* • *Tracey Lee's Canine Training (TLC Training)*
Redwood City *4 Runner 4 Your Pets* **(S)** • *Planet Pooch* • *Chris' Critter Care*

PET-SUPPLY STORES

Burlingame *Doodledings Dog Bakery and Boutique* •
Groomingdales • *Pets Are Us* • *Plaza de Paws*
Daly City *Pet Food Express* • *Petsmart*
Los Altos *Barking Lot, The* • *Five Paw Bakery* • *Pet's Delight*
Menlo Park *Menlo Park Pet & Feed Supply* • *Pet Place, The*
Mountain View *Petco*
Pacifica *Coastside Critters* • *Pacifica Pet Hospital*
Palo Alto *A Dog's Life* • *Pet Food Depot*
Redwood City *Petco* • *Planet Pooch* • *San Mateo Pet Supply*
San Bruno *Petco*
San Carlos *Bow Wow Meow* • *Fancy Feet Animal Grooming*
San Mateo *Pet Club* • *Petco* • *Scrub A Pup* • *Togs For Dogs*

VACCINATIONS—LOW-COST

Daly City *Pet Food Express* • *Petsmart*
Los Altos *Adobe Animal Hospital*
Menlo Park *Pet Place, The*
Mountain View *Petco*
Pacifica *Pacifica Pet Hospital*
Palo Alto *Pet Food Depot*
Redwood City *Petco* • *San Mateo Pet Supply*
San Bruno *Petco*
San Mateo *Peninsula Humane Society and SPCA* • *Pet Club*
• *Petco* • *Togs For Dogs*

CITY DOG PICKS

Burlingame *Doodledings Dog Bakery and Boutique*
• *Plaza de Paws*
Los Altos *Five Paw Bakery*
Menlo Park *Pet Place, The*
Palo Alto *A Dog's Life* • *Pet Food Depot*
San Carlos *Fancy Feet Animal Grooming*
San Mateo *Noble Beast*

General Listings

4 Runner 4 Your Pets

(650) 369-3728
P.O. Box 3901
Redwood City, California 94064
Hours: By Appt
Payment: Checks
Price Range: $$

Carole will run out to get special food for your dog, escort him to the vet and take him to the groomer. When she's not shuttling dogs around town, Carole provides dog walking and overnight pet-sitting. Midday you might run into her at Shore Dogs Park, where she regularly runs the extra steam out of a small pack of dogs. Her service area is from Atherton to Belmont.

A Dog's Life

(650) 494-DOGS
885 Commercial St
Palo Alto, California 94303
www.dogslife.biz
Hours: Mon - Fri 7 A.M. - 7 P.M.
Payment: Checks
Price Range: $$$

Let a dog-loving former high-tech recruiter envision the perfect dog day-care establishment and you might end up with A Dog's Life. Armed with training and advice from the SF SPCA, owner Keith outfitted a huge warehouse with soft mats, modular play areas, an air-conditioned nap room, splash pools and enough SF SPCA trainers to ensure an eight-to-one dog-to-trainer ratio. Browse the art gallery for toys and treats while your pup samples from the biscuit-tasting bar. Or head for the lounge where you can sip your morning coffee and check your e-mail while the dogs get acquainted with their playmates for the day.

Adobe Animal Hospital

(650) 948-9661
396 1st St
Los Altos, California 94022
www.adobe-animal.com
Hours: Mon - Fri 7 A.M. - 10 P.M., Sat - Sun 7 A.M. - 6:30 P.M.
Payment: Credit Cards, Checks
Price Range: $$$

Dr. David Roos' revered clinic offers more than just standard and emergency veterinary care. Your pet can get aligned under the chiropractic care of Kelly Thompson, DC CVCP, or turn to the alternative healing of Sara Skiwski, DVM, of Western Dragon. In addition to both Chinese and Western herbal medicine, your pooch can partake in Bach flower-essence remedies and essential oil therapies. The hospital has its own pharmacy, lab, radiology facilities and 24-hour ICU. They also offer on-site puppy classes. If you and/or your dog get separation anxiety, Adobe will not separate you from your dog, whether he's there for a two-minute vaccination or a two-hour surgery.

Affordable Grooming

(650) 365-1594
1744 El Camino Real
(between Roosevelt & Oak aves)
Redwood City, California 94063
Hours: Mon 8 A.M. - 5 P.M., Tue - Sat 7 A.M. - 5 P.M.
Payment: Checks
Price Range: $$

While the decor is minimal, cage-free dogs running through the clippings add a festive air, as do Oliver, the friendly tabby cat, and Trouble, a commentary-providing macaw. Owner Denise's sense of style has evolved during her 20 years in business, and groomers José and Shannon fit right in—pulling off show cuts and hand stripping amid the fun-filled chaos. They use all-natural shampoos and hand dry your pet. The shop will also board your dog and offers four outdoor dog runs with someone onsite around the clock.

Alexander's

(650) 327-6194
2415 Ash St
Palo Alto, California 94306
Hours: Tue - Sat 8 A.M. - 6 P.M.
Payment: Credit Cards, Checks
Price Range: $$$

This elegant salon regularly turns standard poodles into show ring stars with perfect 'dos. Ribboned photos on display show Carole, the owner and a master groomer, with some of her winning dogs. Alexander's welcomes any breed including difficult dogs and only uses all-natural products. Drying is done with unheated, recirculated air. Be sure to call way in advance to make an appointment because they are often backed up with champion pooches in need of a primping.

Bark 'n Bubbles

(650) 589-9274
136 Brentwood Dr
(1½ block off El Camino Real)
South San Francisco, California 94080
www.barknbubbles.com
Hours: Wed - Sat 9 A.M. - 5 P.M.
Payment: Credit Cards, Checks
Price Range: $$

A longtime groomer and former SF SPCA grooming instructor, Gail is a whiz with scissors. She enjoys transforming the more furry breeds like chows, shepherds and samoyeds that many groomers shun. She also offers some special services at the shop, including T-Touch massage and anesthesia-free teeth cleaning, and she is always interested in discussing dog-behavior issues. If you prefer, you can wash your dog yourself. All supplies are provided. When it comes time to settle your bill, hand your dough over to Sadie—the very talented resident toy Poodle—who will deliver it to Gail.

Bark Park, Inc.

(650) 365-6521
840 Sweeney Ave
(Hwy 84, Woodside exit)
Redwood City, California 94064
www.barkparkinc.com

Hours: Mon - Fri 7 A.M. - 7 P.M.
Payment: Credit Cards, Checks
Price Range: $$$

Dogs in this lively, cheerful and popular 10,000-square-foot complex probably don't bother the neighbors, since it's located on a street that's dominated by a busy auto-impounding facility. Behind a secure set of gates, dogs can socialize in one of five indoor playrooms or in the grassy yard. There are multiple kiddie pools for the aquatically inclined and couches for napping. The friendly staff keeps a close eye on the activities.

Barking Lot, The

(650) 949-1870
467 1st St
Los Altos, California 94022

Hours: Tue - Fri 7:30 A.M. - 4:30 P.M., Sat 8 A.M. - 4:30 P.M.
Payment: Checks
Price Range: $$

Wiley Coyote, the nicely coiffed West Highland terrier who suns himself in the tree-lined parking lot of The Barking Lot, is a living advertisement for the groomers' handiwork. Owners Miriam and Alan have been working beside a soothing cloud mural in this peaceful, open-view shop since 1983. The couple does many handsome cuts on purebreds like their own, but they will clip or comb any dog willing to stand for it. They use all-natural, organic products and take careful care of quite a few canine senior citizens. A colorful display of toys, treats, collars and leashes adds a flourish at the entryway.

Beaugay's

(650) 948-4911
385 1st St
Los Altos, California 94022
Hours: Tues - Fri 8 A.M. - 5 P.M., Sat 9 A.M. - 4 P.M.
Payment: Checks
Price Range: $$$

All breeds are welcome at this calm and quiet grooming salon,
but manager Debbie is especially fond of Irish wolfhounds and
terriers. Clients get pampered with all-natural products and are
dried in the fashion that suits them best. Owners are welcome
to watch the beautification process or simply drop their pup off.
When they return, they will find their perfectly groomed pet
awaiting them in one of the kennels.

Bow Wow Meow

(650) 802-2845
737 Laurel St
(between Cherry & Olive sts)
San Carlos, California 94070
Hours: Mon - Thu 10 A.M. - 7 P.M., Fri - Sat 10 A.M. - 7 P.M.,
Sun 10 A.M. - 4 P.M.
Payment: Credit Cards, Checks
Price Range: $$

Both locations of Bow Wow Meow—the wildly popular SF
newcomer and the Peninsula staple—carry high-end food, an
enormous selection of beds and all sorts of little accessories.
Bow Wow also stocks plenty of gift-type items for the animal
lover in your life. Services include full-service grooming, and
their experienced groomers get raves. They bring in trainers for
consultations and specialists like doggie dentists.

Burlingame Dog Exercise Park

Bayside Park
Old Bayshore Freeway
(Anza Blvd & Broadway)
Burlingame, California 94010
www.burlingame.org/p_r/parks/bayside.htm
Hours: Mon - Tue 6 A.M. - 9 P.M., Wed 8 A.M. - 9 P.M.,
Thu - Sun 6 A.M. - 9 P.M.

This is one of the few dog parks with enough room for ball
chasers to actually work up some momentum. The park is also
a hit with dogs that like to chase each other through bushes,
and the winding rim of shrubbery is full of pathways that are
well worn from paw traffic. If your dog needs to simmer
down, the west end has a time-out area. With dogs so well
accommodated, people can enjoy their own socializing on
the well-placed benches.

Chris's Critter Care

(510) 818-9729
Hours: By Appt
Payment: Checks
Price Range: $$

In addition to babysitting your pooch, Chris will gladly take
care of your kitty, snake or rodent. Although she's happy to
perform other tasks, such as shopping, gardening or cleaning
house, being with dogs is her true calling. A dog lover since
the age of nine, Chris began walking the neighborhood dogs
for free, just to be in their company. Today, she's poetry in
motion as she commands her charges, throws tennis balls and
picks up poop—all at the same time. Chris's service area runs
from Burlingame and Hillsborough to Redwood Shores.

Cipriani Dog Park

(650) 595-7441
2525 Buena Vista Ave
(entrances: Monserat Ave parking lot, west side of school)
Belmont, California 94002
Hours: Dawn to Dusk

Cipriani Dog Park requires a bit more of a hike from the car than most other parks, but those extra steps are worth it to gain access to the Belmont Bowser Club. Watch for signs about the club's potlucks, the annual fair and adoption days. The park is fenced in and offers a separate small-dog area. Amenities include a water station, as well as lights for winter evenings and plenty of benches and tables for leisurely summer days.

Coastside Critters

(650) 355-6177
454 Manor Plaza
(off Palmetto Ave @ W Manor Dr)
Pacifica, California 94944
Hours: Mon - Sat 10 A.M. - 7 P.M., Sun 11 A.M. - 4 P.M.
Payment: Credit Cards, Checks
Price Range: $$

It's easy to get distracted by the aquariums at Coastside Critters. But if you came for kibble, talk to Jolynne and Gladys. They specialize in quality dog food and are happy to discuss the merits of the many high-quality brands they stock. A little room in the back is Lisa's grooming domain, where the former accountant offers full-service scrubs and cuts. Lisa hand-scissors and/or clips her pups, depending on the breed and client's wishes. In addition, she recently acquired a clipper-vac. Dogs are hand dried.

Doodledings Dog Bakery and Boutique

(650) 340-7883
1224 Broadway
(between Paloma & Laguna aves)
Burlingame, California 94010
www.doodledings.com
Hours: Tue - Sun 10 A.M. - 5 P.M.
Payment: Credit Cards, Checks
Price Range: $$

Walk through the door of Maritsa and Melanie's unique boutique/bakery, and you might think you've fallen through the rabbit hole. You'll meet Gizmo, Maritsa's rescued Pekingese, who will soon be featured in several children's books. A top San Francisco caterer supplies peanut butter wontons and dog fortune cookies. Bone biscuits and $1 shots of vitamin water are the fare at the monthly Yappy Hour. Watch for the popular Chihuahua trunk show or bring a gang of kids for a Stuff-a-Pup birthday party.

Fancy Feet Animal Grooming

(650) 594-9200
1133 Eaton Ave
(1 block west of El Camino Real)
San Carlos, California 94070
Hours: Tue - Sat 8:30 A.M. - 5 P.M.
Payment: Credit Cards, Checks
Price Range: $$

It's unusual to see such a variety of animals coexisting so peacefully, but that's business as usual at Fancy Feet. A cockatoo and a cat oversee the retail section, while rabbits hop around with the dogs in the grooming area. Jennifer has a soft touch with animals, which has earned her referrals from vets and the Humane Society. She even manages to groom otherwise unmanageable dogs. She uses all-natural shampoos, does hand scissoring as needed, and does all drying by hand.

Five Paw Bakery

(650) 941-5PAW
315 Main St
Los Altos, California 94022
www.fivepaw.com
Hours: Tue - Sat 9 A.M. - 6 P.M., Sun 10 A.M. - 5 P.M.
Payment: Credit Cards, Checks
Price Range: $$$

Follow the herds to this dog bakery where you might find your-self sneaking bites of your pup's pastries. From freshly baked oatmeal softies to carob-dipped biscotti, the goodies here are made with human-grade ingredients and no added salt or sugar. If you can tear yourself away from the pastry case, you'll also find groovy gifts like dog cookie jars, which are filled upon purchase. Pictures of adoptable dogs from the Peninsula Humane Society are projected onto a screen for all to see.

Greer Park

(650) 496-6962
1098 Amarillo Ave
(@ W Bayshore)
Palo Alto, California 94303
www.city.palo-alto.ca.us/parks/greer.html
Hours: Every Day 8 A.M. to Dusk

Greer Park is little more than an empty piece of land with grass and a tiny, fenced-in dog run. It does feature an empty swimming pool, thus attracting a skateboarding crowd that makes the park a little iffy in the evenings, especially for solo females walking their dogs. Locals know they're better off at Mitchell Park, only five minutes away.

Groomingdales

(650) 340-8801
1130 Chula Vista Ave
(½ block off Broadway)
Burlingame, California 94010
Hours: Tue - Sat 9 A.M. - 5 P.M.
Payment: Credit Cards, Checks
Price Range: $$

Wayne may have found his calling in dog grooming, but since his other love is the opera, your Madame Butterfly will be treated like the diva she is. Wayne first trained at the SF SPCA, and then hired Jessa, a master groomer who attracts Schnauzers from as far away as the East Bay. Although they use hypo-allergenic shampoos and will style any dog in the proper manner, they're a little reluctant to take on the giant breeds. While waiting, you can watch them work and shop for a few supplies.

Hoover Park

(650) 496-6962
2901 Cowper St
(between Colorado Ave & Loma Verde)
Palo Alto, California 94306
www.city.palo-alto.ca.us/parks/hoover.html
Hours: Every Day 8 A.M. to Dusk

Hoover Park is popular for sports events, picnics and play-ground fun. However, the long, sandy, fenced-in dog run is seldom used, despite the benches and lovely trees. The only signs of dog use are a few recycled bags tied to the fence and a sign ordering, "Dogs On Leash," and there is neither a trash can nor water near the run. If you and your pooch prefer a quiet dog park, you'll love it here. Otherwise, head for the Foster City dog park.

Menlo Park Pet & Feed Supply

(650) 326-6141
564 Oak Grove Ave
(between El Camino Real & the train tracks)
Menlo Park, California 94025
Hours: Mon - Thu 10 A.M. - 6:30 P.M.,
Fri - Sat 10 A.M. - 5:30 P.M., Sun 11 A.M. - 4 P.M.
Payment: Credit Cards, Checks
Price Range: $$

You can find all the basic dog supplies at this old-fashioned feed store, and you'll love the old, creaky, wooden floors, which take customers at Jeff's feed shop back in time to the days of country stores and lemonade. Popular with families, Menlo Park Pet & Feed Supply attracts packs of kids who love to stare into the fish tanks and oogle the birds, bunnies, geckos, frogs and snakes.

Mitchell Park Dog Run

(650) 496-6962
600 E Meadow Dr
(south of Middlefield Rd)
Palo Alto, California 94306
www.city.palo-alto.ca.us/parks/mitchell.html
Hours: Every Day 8 A.M. to Dusk

This popular dog run is located beside a creek, so it's notoriously muddy in the winter. In summer, you and your pooch can enjoy ample shade, grass at the far end near the creek and the well-placed water station. First-timers should note that the dog run is not very easy to find: It's behind the tennis courts and next to a soccer field that's often used for tournaments. In the evening when school is out, you can park in the school lot, which provides easier access to the dog run.

Noble Beast

(650) 375-1910
267 Baldwin Ave
(San Mateo Dr & N Ellsworth Ave)
San Mateo, California 94401
Hours: Mon - Thu 8 A.M. - 5 P.M., Fri 8 A.M. - 12 P.M.
Payment: Checks
Price Range: $$$

Faux marble walls, fantastic gargoyle sculptures, a moody purple groom room and an antique oak bar reception desk make this one of the most elegant establishments your dog is likely to encounter. Denise and her staff make your pooch look stunning with attentive hand-scissoring and all-natural shampoos. They dry all dogs by hand. A warm welcome is extended to all breeds, and canine clients can linger uncaged all day if necessary.

Pacifica Pet Hospital

(650) 359-3685
4300 Coast Hwy
(Rockaway Beach & Reina Del Mar)
Pacifica, California 94044
www.pacificapet.com
Hours: By Appt
Payment: Credit Cards, Checks
Price Range: $

Some Peninsula folks make the drive to Pacifica just to bring their dog to vet guru Dr. Hurlbut, and many more insist that they wouldn't board their pup anywhere but Pacifica. Boarded dogs get walked at least three times a day and enjoy the doting attention of volunteers and staff. Some volunteers come in just to practice their positive-reinforcement training techniques with the visiting dogs.

Peninsula Humane Society and SPCA

(650) 340-7022
12 Airport Blvd
(west of Hwy 101 next to Coyote Point)
San Mateo, California 94401
www.peninsulahumanesociety.org
Hours: Mon - Fri 11 A.M. - 7 P.M., Sat - Sun 11 A.M. - 6 P.M.
Payment: Checks
Price Range: $

Adopting a friend for life is just $70 at the Peninsula Humane Society and SPCA, and that includes a San Mateo County dog license, a veterinary checkup, initial vaccinations, spay/neuter, microchip ID and counseling to ensure a good match. The facility also offers classes at all levels, and if things aren't going perfectly with your new pup, the behavior helpline is there to guide you. The center also receives and rehabilitates injured and orphaned wild critters.

People Understanding Pets (PUP)

(650) 922-4274
www.peopleunderstandingpets.org
Hours: See website for schedule
Payment: No Charge

A nonprofit group dedicated to improving the quality of life for pets and helping reduce the homeless pet population, People Understanding Pets (PUP) offers community lectures and veterinarian education. They also publish educational materials and produce *Discover Dogs!*, a community TV show that helps people get more out of their relationships with their dogs. Check their website for upcoming lectures and information on dog rescue and training.

Perfect Paws: Menlo Park Location

(415) 647-8000
251 6th St
Menlo Park, California 94025
www.perfectpaws.org
Hours: By Appt
Payment: Credit Cards, Checks
Price Range: $$

This renowned Bay Area institution, which has been around 20-plus years, was one of *San Francisco* magazine's Best of the Bay Area picks in 2002. In addition to puppy and basic-training classes, the organization provides clicker, agility as well as competition training and specific classes to resolve such issues as digging, barking, jumping and the like. Private lessons are available for pups with bigger problems, including aggression, biting and destructive behavior.

Pet Club

(650) 358-0347
1850 S Norfolk St
(north of Hwy 92)
San Mateo, California 94403
www.petclubstores.com
Hours: Mon - Fri 9 A.M. - 8 P.M., Sat 10 A.M. - 7:30 P.M.,
Sun 10 A.M. - 7 P.M.
Payment: Checks
Price Range: $

Picture Costco for pets and you'll understand the lure of these popular warehouse-style pet supply stores. With seven Bay Area locations, Pet Club prices couldn't be lower. But great prices mean no frills, and little personalized service. Come stock up leashes and pet food, but leave your credit card at home; they accept only cash and checks.

Pet Food Depot

(650) 852-1277
3127 El Camino Real
(3 blocks southeast of Page Mill Rd)
Palo Alto, California 94306
Hours: Mon - Fri 9:30 A.M. - 7 P.M., Sat 9 A.M. - 6 P.M.,
Sun 10 A.M. - 6 P.M.
Payment: Credit Cards, Checks
Price Range: $$

Harry's big warehouse-style store not only has low prices and a
huge inventory, but it predates the chains and runs circles
around them with its welcoming atmosphere and knowledge-
able staff. You'll find employees all over the store—hard at work,
but ready to help. There are lots of friendly shoppers too, mak-
ing the Depot something of a community center for pet lovers.
Puppy and obedience classes are available on weekends.

Pet Food Express

(650) 997-3333
6925 Mission St
Daly City, California 94015
www.petfoodexpress.com
Hours: Mon - Sat 9:30 A.M. - 8 P.M., Sun 10 A.M. - 6 P.M.
Payment: Credit Cards, Checks
Price Range: $$

Pet Food Express is a pet-supply chain with numerous franchises throughout the Bay Area. They sell a variety of pet supplies,
including specialty items like the safety light dog collar and
the Cider Mill dog trolley. Brands such as Avo Derm and
Pinnacle are on the shelves, and Pet Express staff is friendly
and helpful. Dog training classes and low-cost vaccinations
are available. The store's My Mutt program promotes adoption
of the mighty mixed breed.

Pet Place, The

(650) 325-7387
777 Santa Cruz Ave
(between Chestnut & Crane)
Menlo Park, California 94025
Hours: Mon - Wed 10 A.M. - 6 P.M., Thu 10 A.M. - 8 P.M.,
Fri 10 A.M. - 6 P.M., Sat 10 A.M. - 5 P.M.
Payment: Credit Cards, Checks
Price Range: $

Locals love this place! And what's not to love? The staff will
research anything having to do with your pet's food, training
or health and then help you track down the solution. The
health-food and supplement choices here are superb, as are
the various aids for convalescent and handicapped pets. Owners
Lynn and Marc Lacey go above and beyond when it comes to
rescuing dogs—and treating rescued dogs—from the pound.
Ask about their adoption program, and definitely check out
their adoptees.

Pet's Delight

(650) 948-0501
390 State St
(between 1st & 2nd sts)
Los Altos, California 94022
Hours: Mon - Fri 10 A.M. - 7 P.M., Sat 9 A.M. - 6 P.M.,
Sun 10 A.M. - 5 P.M.
Payment: Credit Cards, Checks
Price Range: $$

Pet's Delight isn't quite the chic boutique you'd expect from
this trendy Los Altos shopping district, owner Sam's pet-supply
shop carries everything you might need for your dog, cat, fish,
bird or hamster. Browse through a great selection of high-quali-
ty supplies, all-natural grooming products and healthy, premi-
um dog foods. Products are easy to find, and prices are lower
than you would expect from this upscale address.

Petco

www.petco.com
Payment: Credit Cards, Checks
Price Range: $$

Mountain View Location

(650) 966-1233
1919 W El Camino Real
(@ Escala Ave, Clarkwood Shopping Center)
Mountain View, California 94040
Hours: Mon - Sat 9 A.M. - 9 P.M., Sun 10 A.M. - 8 P.M.

Redwood City Location

(650) 364-6077
520 Woodside Rd
(between Ebner St and Hess Rd)
Redwood City, California 94061
Hours: Mon - Sat 9 A.M. - 9 P.M., Sun 10 A.M. - 7 P.M.

San Bruno Location

(650) 952-2025
1282 El Camino Real
(between Citation Ave and Sheath Ln)
San Bruno, California 94066
Hours: Mon - Sat 9 A.M. - 9 P.M., Sun 10 A.M. - 7 P.M.

San Mateo Location

(650) 357-9480
3012 Bridgepointe Pkwy
(across from San Mateo Fashion Mall)
San Mateo, California 94404
Hours: Mon - Sat 9 A.M. - 9 P.M., Sun 10 A.M. - 7 P.M.

For one-stop shopping it's hard to beat the convenience and value of this superstore with locations all over the country. Petco makes it their mission to provide customers with the food, supplements and products they want for their animals. Their bed selection runs the gamut, from orthopedic mattresses along with sheets and throws to chaises that would do an interior decorator proud. Get a P.A.L.S. (Petco Animal Lovers Save) card to take advantage of discounts; you may also want to check out their Top Dog program, which offers even greater savings to their most loyal customers. Check the contact information for each store for hours and specific service offerings.

Pets Are Us

(650) 697-3258
1807 El Camino Real
(@ Trousdale Dr)
Burlingame, California 94010
Hours: Mon - Fri 11 A.M. - 6:30 P.M., Sat 10 A.M. - 6 P.M., Sun 10 A.M. - 5 P.M.
Payment: Credit Cards, Checks
Price Range: $$

This pet store is quite a lively place, with plenty of birds making their presence known. Owner Gary says the feathered chirpers have a hankering for dog biscuits, particularly California Natural, which is the dog food of choice here. The self-serve dog wash is very popular, especially with the sand and surf set, who usually make a point of coming in for a post beach-trip wash. Everything you need is supplied, and while you're leaving with your clean dog, Pets will clean up the mess you've left behind.

Petsmart

(650) 997-0395
315 Gellert Blvd
(@ Serramonte Blvd)
Daly City, California 94015

www.petsmart.com
Hours: Mon - Sat 9 A.M. - 9 P.M., Sun 10 A.M. - 6 P.M.
Payment: Credit Cards, Checks
Price Range: $$

This standout superstore is to pet owners what Home Depot is to homeowners. PetSmart stocks an unbelievably wide range of products that will meet almost any budget. They carry the better dog food brands—including Bil-Jac. And whenever possible, they offer all-natural options in their selection of treats, supplements and skin products. A viewing window allows see-for-yourself grooming so you don't have to worry about what happens behind closed doors. They get major points for promoting their adoptions all the time. And they have a staff that's always available to advise you and to help you find what you need. It's places like PetSmart that give superstores a good name.

Planet Pooch

(650) 364-7792
866 Kaynyne Ave
(west of Bay St)
Redwood City, California 94063
www.planetpooch.com
Hours: Mon - Fri 7 A.M. - 7 P.M., Sat - Sun 8 A.M. - 5 P.M.
Payment: Credit Cards, Checks
Price Range: $$

This new complex with an outer-space theme has a lot of fans, maybe because of its 275-gallon canine swimming pool and the huge space devoted to tennis-ball tossing. Planet Pooch also has 20,000 square feet of indoor/outdoor space for unstructured play, and a couch potato room for dogs who would rather chill than run. Dirty dogs can opt for a cage-free grooming session.

Plaza de Paws

(650) 579-3647
1429 Burlingame Ave
(El Camino Real & Primrose Rd)
Burlingame, California 94010
www.plazadepaws.com
Hours: Mon - Sat 10 A.M. - 6 P.M., Sun 12 P.M. - 5 P.M.
Payment: Credit Cards, Checks
Price Range: $$

Lori has a menagerie of rescued pets, some of whom hang out in her very elegant boutique that's painted to look like an Italian piazza. You might find a dog or kitty guarding the holistic foods and pet pastries, testing out one of the velvet beds, rubbing up against the Muckster Pet Lover's Shoes or contemplating a leap onto a shelf full of vintage knickknacks. The food-bowl collection is especially impressive, and includes a few antiques.

Poochini's

(650) 342-4712
1427 Broadway
(½ block south of El Camino Real)
Burlingame, California 94010
Hours: Tue - Sat 9 A.M. - 5 P.M.
Payment: Credit Cards, Checks
Price Range: $$

Evelyn is an experienced and easygoing groomer whose forte is Bouviers and Wheatons. She'll paint your Poodle's nails, if you like, and she has even given a Schnauzer a Mohawk. The salon offers a wide range of shampoos, including all-natural varieties and a Mighty Wind dryer to hand dry your dog. Evelyn does her magic behind closed doors, although that does mean your newly groomed pooch will be able to make a grand entrance.

Priceless Pet Care

(650) 703-1792
Hours: By Appt
Payment: Checks
Price Range: $$

After spending her days working at A Dog's Life dog day care, Dianna brings the same high standard of pet care to her own business. She provides drop-in visits or overnight care—whatever suits your pooch's needs while you're out of town. In addition to basic home security and maintenance duties, she'll handle light grooming and take your dog for on-leash walks around the neighborhood. She covers San Francisco to Palo Alto.

San Bruno Dog Park

(650) 616-7195
Evergreen Dr
(@ Maywood Dr)
San Bruno, California 94066

You have a view of it all from this fenced-in, off-leash dog park—from the San Bruno Mountains to the Peninsula to the East Bay. Lots of trees make this a cool spot in the summer, especially with the stiff breeze blowing off the bay. In the rainy months, however, the place can get muddy. You don't have to worry about coming unprepared—the park has plenty of baggies and water.

San Mateo Pet Supply

(650) 365-6738
346 El Camino Real
(@ Claremont Ave)
Redwood City, California 94062
Hours: Every Day 9 A.M. - 7 P.M.

Payment: Credit Cards, Checks
Price Range: $$

Despite the name, San Mateo Pet Supply is conveniently located in Redwood City, and the name doesn't do much to hint at the large inventory of farm-animal feed. Besides high-quality dog kibble and a full line of dog supplies, you can scoop your own chicken feed or buy salt-lick bricks in this huge, barn-like store. A big, old-fashioned scale and the sweet smell of hay add to the rustic feel.

Scrub A Pup

(650) 577-9665
119 W 25th Ave
(1½ block west of El Camino Real)
San Mateo, California 94403
Hours: Tue 9:30 A.M. - 5:30 P.M., Wed 9:30 A.M. - 8 P.M.,
Thu - Fri 9:30 A.M. - 5:30 P.M., Sat 9 A.M. - 5 P.M.,
Sun 10 A.M. - 4 P.M.
Payment: Credit Cards, Checks
Price Range: $

If you feel challenged in the dog-washing department, you'll be relieved to find a cheat sheet with instructions over each of Scrub A Pup's self-service tubs. You can pay an extra $8 and get Chrissie and her staff to administer the dreaded nail trim. It might even be worth forking over $22 to $45 to get them to do the whole cleaning, although that doesn't include a clip. Choose from all-natural and medicated shampoos and either a hand blow dry or a good old-fashioned shake-and-go.

Shamrock Ranch

(650) 359-1627
@ south end of Peralta Rd
(off Hwy 1)
Pacifica, California 94044
Hours: Every Day 9 A.M. - 6 P.M.
Payment: Credit Cards, Checks

Price Range: $$

Chic dog spas are springing up all over Silicon Valley, but time stands still at Shamrock Ranch, a kennel and horse ranch that was established in 1943. Long grass engulfs ancient farm equipment and creeps through abandoned kennels beside the antique, but functioning, barns with their indoor-outdoor dog runs. Dogs get Avoderm and Pedigree food. There's an extra charge if you want to bring your own food, and dog walks come at a premium. The ranch is a charming, rustic spot with celebrity trainer, Lisa Rhodes, and a long tradition of board-and-train-programs.

Shore Dogs Park

(650) 780-7000
@ the end of Radio Rd
(Redwood Shores development along the bay)
Redwood City, California 94065
www.shoredogs.org
Hours: Dawn to Dusk

What do pelicans and wire-haired terriers have in common? The off-leash park on the corner of San Francisco Bay. Long popular with migratory birds, this active park is also known for its devoted dog community. Last year the Redwood City site was spruced up with beautiful new sod and "gold dust" (decomposed gravel). Shore Dogs offers two separate fenced areas, water stations, chairs and a lot of tennis balls.

Smilin Dogs

(650) 592-3997
www.smilindog.com
Hours: By Appt
Payment: Checks
Price Range: $$$

If your idea of a happy dog is a tired dog, then sign her up with Smilin Dogs. Dogs spend their days hiking on a 1,500-acre San Mateo County coast cattle ranch, swimming and

lounging at the "dog shed." Boarding is also offered for day-
care dogs. Smilin Dogs is about convenience, with the price of
admission including door-to-door service and monthly billing.

Super Pups
(650) 349-7877
2230 S El Camino Real
(between 22nd & 23rd aves)
San Mateo, California 94403
Hours: Tue - Sat 8:30 A.M. - 4 P.M.
Payment: Checks
Price Range: $$
Joel likes to call his salon the Nordstrom of the grooming
world. His claim is supported by a large photo gallery of
perfectly coiffed Bichons that he and Suzi have groomed and
hand-scissored over their many years in the business.
Professional reputation aside, the place feels like a family
kitchen. The couple's two ancient Shih-Tzus wander around the
open work area and the astroturf-covered yard. They do pro
bono work for rescue organizations and impress upon their
blue-blooded clients the virtues of rescue, spay and neuter.

Togs For Dogs
(650) 574-5364
24 W 41st St
(@ El Camino Real)
San Mateo, California 94403
Hours: Mon - Fri 10 A.M. - 6 P.M., Sat 9 A.M. - 5 P.M.,
Sun 11 A.M. - 5 P.M.
Payment: Credit Cards, Checks
Price Range: $
In spite of the name, you can't write this shop off as just another
high-brow pet-accessory boutique with nothing but too cute
threads for the precious pooch. This family-run pet-supply shop
has an enormous selection, and owners Ed and Dina can most
likely answer any question you have. People bring in their dogs,

cats and birds so their animals can pick out their own toys and treats from Togs' unique selection. The treats are tucked into odd places all over the store, making the shopping process something of an Easter egg hunt.

Tracey Lee's Canine Training (TLC Training)

(650) 494-DOGS
885 Commercial St
(@ Charleston, near the San Antonio exit from Hwy 101)
Palo Alto, California 94303
www.dogslife.biz
Hours: By Appt
Payment: Credit Cards, Checks
Price Range: $$

When Tracey Lee is not managing A Dog's Life, she is training dogs at the store or in your home. She prefers encouraging dogs to use their brains through positive reinforcement, but she says that what's most important is using an approach that owners will stick with. She's especially interested in obedience—loose-leash walking, sit, stay and puppy issues—leaving behavior modification to trainers who prefer that challenge.

Carmel & Monterey

EMERGENCY PET TRANSPORT

AMERS Animal Ambulance
(877) 426-3771 (emergency)
(925) 261-9111 (office)
www.animalmedics.com
Hours: Every Day 24 Hours
Payment: Credit Cards, Checks
Emergency Fee: $175

Pet Taxi
Bay Area
(415) 386-2534
Hours: Every Day 7 A.M. – 7 P.M.
Emergency Hours: Every Day 24 Hours
Payment: Checks
Price Range: $$/$$$

ANIMAL EMERGENCY FACILITIES

Animal Hospital at the Crossroads
(831) 624-0131
3 The Crossroads
Carmel, California 93923
Hours: Doctor will be paged
Payment: Credit Cards, Checks
Price Range: $$

Monterey Peninsula Emergency Clinic & Critical Care Services

(831) 758-0882
2 Harris Ct
Monterey, California 93940
Hours: Mon – Fri 5:30 P.M. – 8 A.M.,
Weekends & Holidays 24 Hours
Payment: Credit Cards, Checks
Price Range: $$

ANIMAL POISON HOTLINE

ASPCA Animal Poison Control Center

(888) 4ANI-HELP
Hours: Every Day 24 Hours
Payment: Credit Cards
Consultation Fee: $45

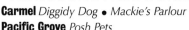

ADOPTION

Carmel Valley *Animal Welfare Information & Assistance, Inc.*
• *Love Your Pet All Creatures Animal Sanctuary*
Monterey *SPCA of Monterey County, The*
Pacific Grove *Animal Friends Rescue Project* • *Posh Pets*

ALTERNATIVE PRODUCTS/SERVICES

Carmel *Diggidy Dog* • *Mackie's Parlour*
Pacific Grove *Posh Pets*

DOG BOARDING

Carmel *Happy Pets*

DOG GROOMING

Carmel *Mid Valley Pet Spa* • *Suds & Scissors*
Monterey *Mobile Pet Grooming* • *Petco*

DOG GROOMING—SELF-SERVE
Carmel *Suds & Scissors*
Monterey *Petco*

DOG HIKES & SOCIALS
Carmel *Carmel River State Beach* • *Garrapata State Park*
• *Happy Pets* • *Mission Trail Park*
Carmel Valley *Garland Ranch Regional Park*
Monterey *Monterey State Beach*
Pacific Grove *Asilomar State Beach*

DOG PARKS—OFF LEASH
Carmel *Carmel City Beach*

DOG TRAINING
Carmel/Monterey *Pam Jackson Dog Training*
Carmel Valley *Love Your Pet All Creatures Animal Sanctuary*
Monterey *Del Monte Kennel Club Obedience Training Classes*
• *Petco* • *SPCA of Monterey County, The*
Watsonville *Monterey Bay Dog Training Club, Inc*

DOG WALKING/PET-SITTING
Carmel *Bored No More* • *Happy Pets*

PET-SUPPLY STORES
Carmel *Diggidy Dog* • *Mackie's Parlour* • *Mid Valley Pet Spa*
• *Petco* • *Total Dog*
Pacific Grove *Posh Pets*
Monterey *Petco*

VACCINATIONS—LOW-COST

Carmel *Petco*
Carmel Valley *Animal Welfare Information & Assistance, Inc.*
Monterey *Petco* • *SPCA of Monterey County, The*
Pacific Grove *Animal Friends Rescue Project* • *Posh Pets*

CITY DOG PICKS

Carmel *Carmel City Beach* • *Diggidy Dog* • *Fountain of Woof* • *Mission Trail Park*
Carmel Valley *Garland Ranch Regional Park*
Monterey *SPCA of Monterey County, The*

General Listings

Animal Friends Rescue Project

(831) 333-0722
P.O. Box 51083
Pacific Grove, California 93950
www.animalfriendsrescue.org
Hours: By Appt
Payment: Credit Cards, Checks
Price Range: $$

Animal Friends Rescue Project is dedicated to finding owners for homeless pets. They rescue pets destined for euthanasia at local shelters and place them in foster care until permanent homes are found. To prevent overpopulation, the project offers spay/neuter vouchers, so local pet owners can get a reduced rate from local vets. Their website lists pets available for adoption. Fees ($125 for an adult dog, $150 for a puppy) cover spay/neuter costs, associated foster care expenses and puppy shots, when applicable. If you are so inclined, they are always looking for volunteers, foster homes, pet supplies and donations.

Animal Welfare Information & Assistance, Inc.

(831) 659-2156
P.O. Box 942
Carmel Valley, California 93924
www.animalwelfare.org
Hours: By Appt
Payment: Checks
Price Range: $

As a nonprofit humane society that relies on the generosity of the public in order to provide its valuable services, Animal Welfare provides shelter services for animals in need, and strives to find adoptive homes for pets. In addition to advocating responsible pet ownership through community education efforts, Animal Welfare offers spay and neuter services, pet-food delivery, animal-emergency assistance and monthly payment plans that make emergency care available to the pets of low-income owners.

Asilomar State Beach

(831) 372-4076
Sunset Dr @ Asilomar Blvd
Pacific Grove, California 93950
This state beach is about a mile long, and offers plenty of sand and rocky coves for you and your dog to explore. However, there will be no games of hide-and-seek for you and your pup—dogs must be on leash at all times. Asilomar means "refuge by the sea." Bring whatever water and beach supplies you need. Despite being on conference grounds in addition to a state beach, it offers no amenities. It's a part of the Pacific Grove Fish Garden Refuge and Monterey Bay National Marine Sanctuary. Your best bet for parking is Sunset Drive.

Bored No More

(831) 620-1581
Carmel, California 93923
Hours: By Appt
Payment: Cash Only
Price Range: $$
Great rates, great references and great enthusiasm make for a great business. For over 10 years, Teah, owner-operator of Bored No More, has been relieving canine boredom with individual and group romps on the beach or hikes through the forest. Teah offers multiple-dog discounts. Clever people recognize the play on words with Bored No More—she takes care of boredom but doesn't board them. Teah also entertains feline friends.

Carmel City Beach

(831) 624-9423
(where Ocean Ave deadends @ beach)
Carmel, California 93923
Located at the end of Ocean Avenue, Carmel City Beach is a
dog institution in Carmel, with a relaxed atmosphere that
belies its prestigious address. Pups get the run of the place—
unemcumbered by those pesky leashes—as long as they're
under voice control. The beach itself is worth the trip: White
sand dunes, cypress trees and an amazing view of Big Sur
make this beach a favorite with locals and tourists alike. And if
that's not enough of a draw, there's plenty of free parking.

Carmel River State Beach

(831) 624-9423
Carmelo St
Carmel, California 93923
Located where the Carmel River meets the Monterey Bay, this
beach is chock-full of waterfowl and songbirds. Your pooch
must remain on leash and isn't allowed in the bird sanctuary,
which is located at the river's delta. Fabulous views from the
trails surrounding this crescent-shaped beach make Carmel
River State Beach a popular hiking spot; although diving is
also popular. Be aware: The surf and undertow are especially
strong at this beach, with people getting carried out to sea
every year, so think twice before diving into the waves with
your dog.

Del Monte Kennel Club Obedience Training Classes

P.O. Box 1022
Watsonville, California 95077
www.montereybaydog.org
Hours: By Appt
Payment: Checks
Price Range: $

The Del Monte Kennel Club offers obedience, agility and conformation classes for pups at all levels of training, whether home, pro or show. With numerous obedience titles and 30 years of experience working with all breeds of dogs, trainer Pluis Davern also trains disaster and search and rescue dogs. A dog-show veteran, Davern spent many years as a professional show handler and is authorized to judge the sporting group.

Diggidy Dog

(831) 625-1585
southwest corner of Mission & Ocean aves
Carmel, California 93921
www.diggidydogcarmel.com
Hours: Mon - Fri 10 A.M. - 6 P.M., Sat - Sun 10 A.M. - 7 P.M.
Payment: Credit Cards
Price Range: $$

Who else but this Carmel boutique offers canine cakes and cannolis in a pink bakery box, and sausages from an in-store butcher shop? Diggidy Dog sells some pet foods like Wellness and Royal Canin, but their real focus is their tasty treats, toys, clothes and accessories. Beach types, can choose from a great selection of T-shirts and scarves.

Garland Ranch Regional Park

(831) 659-4488
Carmel Valley Rd
Carmel Valley, California 93924
www.mprpd.org/parks/garland.html
At this 4,462-acre park, you can take one of the mountain
trails leading up from the valley floor. If your pup has some
bounce in his step, head up the Santa Lucia Mountains for a
spectacular view of the Monterey Peninsula. Dogs must be on
a seven-foot (or shorter) leash or be within view of and under
control of the owner. Most people choose the latter. Some of
the paths will lead you through private property, so stay on
the trail. Remnants of Rumsien Indian sites and former ranch
buildings make this a fun park to explore.

Garrapata State Park

(831) 649-2836
Hwy 1
(6.7 miles south of Rio Rd in Carmel)
Carmel, California 93923
www.parks.ca.gov
Although dogs must be leashed as they romp along this two-
mile stretch of beach, Garrapata State Park is well worth a visit
for its wealth of natural beauty: The absolutely stunning
coastal headlands at Soberanes Point bridge the redwood
groves and the ocean where sea lions, harbor seals and sea
otters often play. In winter months, keep an eye out for migrat-
ing California gray whales. As you and your pup explore the
this 2,800-acre park, make sure you take the short, 50-foot
climb for an amazing view of the Pacific.

Happy Pets

(831) 647-8421
P.O. Box 802
Carmel, California 93921
www.elabhosting.com/design_gallery/happypets
Hours: By Appt
Payment: Checks
Price Range: $$

Owner and dog-sitter extraordinaire Lucinda Andersen will take over for you while you are away, providing meals and meds (at no extra charge), taking your dog on walks, and giving them baths. She will also care for your exotic pets. Home services include giving your house that lived-in look by watering plants, bringing in the mail and taking out the trash. She's not afraid to use her wheels: She'll deliver pet food or take your pup in for a trim or a checkup. She even does airport runs. And she'll come to the rescue if you need last-minute pet-sitting.

Love Your Pet All Creatures Animal Sanctuary

(831) 224-8080
316 Mid Valley Center #109
Carmel, California 93913
www.loveyourpetallcreatures.org
Payment: Checks
Price Range: $$

The nonprofit Love Your Pet All Creatures Sanctuary is run by Allegra Braun, a longtime Carmel Valley resident known for her caring in-home pet-sitting services. Braun is committed to making a difference in the lives of both companion and wild animals by fostering needy pets and providing adoption and rescue services. Her pet-sitting offerings run the gamut from simple walks to overnight and emergency care. Don't worry if your pet is not of the canine variety. She will look after horses, llamas and cats too.

Mackie's Parlour

(831) 626-0600
southeast corner of Ocean Ave & Monte Verde
Carmel, California 93921
www.mackiesparlour.com
Hours: Mon - Sun 10 A.M. - 6 P.M.
Payment: Credit Cards, Checks
Price Range: $$

If you're into canine chic, Mackie's is for you. From jeweled collars and toile fabric donut beds, to pink "croc" travel bags and $150 canine spa baskets, which come with Le Pooch eau de cologne and a terry robe, they've got it all. Mackie's also offers fresh-baked natural treats, made exclusively for the Parlour. Cool with a conscience, Mackie's holds regular fundraising events for the Monterey County SPCA.

Mid Valley Pet Spa

(831) 625-6922
204 Mid Valley Center
(Carmel Valley Rd)
Carmel, California 93923
Hours: Tue - Sat 8:30 A.M. - 5 P.M.
Payment: Checks
Price Range: $$

If your pup has a soft spot for the finer things in life, the Pet Spa may be just the ticket. In addition to a selection of grooming services, the Spa carries premium foods, toys, beds and snazzy collars. The groomers use shampoos appropriate for your pup's particular breed and skin type. And they use both hand and cage dryers. You can watch your dog every step of the way.

Mission Trail Park

(831) 624-3543
Rio Rd
(east of Junipero St across from Carmel Valley Mission)
Carmel, California 93923

A haven for nature junkies and their dogs, the 37-acre Mission Trail Park is also known as a nature preserve. Miles of hiking trails—which offer closeup views of the vegetation and trees: willows, pines and oaks, among others—make this place popular with hikers. Your dog must be under voice command to run free; be sure to keep them on the trail to avoid disrupting the environment. Also, poison oak is in abundance—it won't bother your dog, but if it's on his coat, and you pet him, you can get it! Please be sure to pick up anything your dog leaves behind, bags are available at the entrance. Parking is also offered at the entrance.

Mobile Pet Grooming

(831) 655-5424
Hours: By Appt
Payment: Checks
Price Range: $$

Why leave home, when Linda Milligan, who has more than 20 years of experience grooming, breeding and showing dogs, will come to you. She grooms all breeds and will do show cuts. However, she won't groom show cuts for dogs that are actually headed for the ring. She prefers to leave that work up to the handler. She uses all-natural and organic shampoos and hand dries every dog. Dogs are either hand scissored or clipped, depending on the breed. To be safe, book at least two weeks in advance. Linda works in Carmel, Monterey, Pacific Grove, Marina and parts of Carmel Valley.

Monterey Bay Dog Training Club, Inc

P.O. Box 1022
Watsonville, California 95077
www.montereybaydog.org
Hours: See website for class schedule
Payment: Credit Cards, Checks
Price Range: $$

Offering training classes since 1967, the nonprofit Monterey Bay Training Club, sets the standard for responsible dog ownership. Training categories include puppies, obedience, tracking, agility, conformation, good dogs and canine companions. You can choose from several convenient class locations throughout the Monterey Bay area. Classes begin at $60 for eight weeks. For complete class information visit their website.

Monterey State Beach

(831) 646-3860
(from Warf 2 to Monterey Beach Hotel)
Monterey, California 93940

Two miles long, Monterey State Beach is a favorite among surfers, dogwalkers, kayakers and beachcombers. Because it's a multi-use area, dogs are required to be on leash, which can be a bit of a drag if your pup is an ardent swimmer. If you do choose to let your pooch off leash, keep an eye out for rangers, who regularly patrol the beach. Monterey State Beach also makes a good pit stop if you're hiking the Monterey Recreation Trail.

Pam Jackson Dog Training

(831) 679-2560
Hours: By Appt
Payment: Cash Only
Price Range: $$

Pam has over 27 years of experience and 7,000 dogs under her belt, and plenty of honors to show for it. She has six obedience degrees and six championship degrees; she received her certification from the Dog Training Club of Salinas Valley. Pam provides puppy and confirmation training, and she deals with all behavioral issues. And if your dog has stars in his eyes, Pam can teach him the theatrical tricks of the trade.

Petco

www.petco.com
Payment: Credit Cards, Checks
Price Range: $$

Carmel Location

(831) 625-3109
161 Crossroads Blvd
(off Rio Rd)
Carmel, California 93923
Hours: Mon - Fri 9 A.M. - 7 P.M., Sat 10 A.M. - 6 P.M., Sun 10 A.M. - 6 P.M.

Monterey Location

(831) 373-1310
960 Del Monte Ctr
(off Munras Ave)
Monterey, California 93940
Hours: Mon - Sat 9 A.M. - 9 P.M., Sun 10 A.M. - 7 P.M.

For one-stop shopping it's hard to beat the convenience and value of this superstore with locations all over the country.

Petco makes it their mission to provide customers with the food, supplements and products they want for their animals. Their bed selection runs the gamut, from orthopedic mattresses along with sheets and throws to chaises that would do an interior decorator proud. Get a P.A.L.S. (Petco Animal Lovers Save) card to take advantage of discounts; you may also want to check out their Top Dog program, which offers even greater savings to their most loyal customers. Check the contact information for each store for hours and specific service offerings.

Posh Pets
(831) 375-7387
160 Fountain Ave
(@ Lighthouse Ave)
Pacific Grove, California 93950
Hours: Mon - Fri 10 A.M. - 7 P.M., Sat 10 A.M. - 5:30 P.M., Sun 12 P.M. - 5 P.M.
Payment: Credit Cards, Checks
Price Range: $$
Posh Pets carries a full line of supplies, including high-quality pet food and nutritional supplements. You can also find great gifts here for both pets and people. Owners David and Kelly are tireless in their work to keep pets out of shelters. Posh Pets has on-site pet adoptions with animals from the Animal Friends Rescue Project. They also encourage the purchase of their custom pet ID tags to ensure that lost animals are reconnected with their owners, rather than ending up in a shelter. A low-cost vaccination clinic is held every other Saturday from 12:30 P.M. to 2 P.M.

SPCA of Monterey County, The
(831) 373-2631
1002 Monterey-Salinas Highway
P.O. Box 3058
Monterey, California 93942
www.SPCAmc.org

Adoption Hours: Mon - Fri 11 A.M. - 5 P.M.,
Sat - Sun 11 A.M. - 4 P.M.
Clinic Hours: Mon - Thu 6 A.M. - 12 P.M., 1 P.M. - 4 P.M.
Payment: Credit Cards, Checks
Price Range: $$

The SPCA of Monterey County is a nonprofit organization dedicated to the rescue and shelter of needy animals and to the education of the community. Among the services they offer are animal adoption, training, and a spay and neuter clinic. Their Guardian Angel program allows you to designate a care-taker for your pet in case of death or serious illness. They also rescue and rehabilitate orphaned and injured wild animals, helping more than 2,000 a year. The SPCA is nonprofit and relies on the help of the community to ensure the future of its valuable programs.

Suds & Scissors
(831) 624-4697
223 Crossroads Blvd
(near Carmel Center Pl)
Carmel, California 93923
Hours: Mon - Fri 9 A.M. - 5 P.M., Sat 9 A.M. - 4 P.M.
Payment: Credit Cards, Checks
Price Range: $$

Suds & Scissors, a full-service grooming shop, comes highly recommended by local vets and organizations. Talent and a lot of experience (28 years!) have made the shop's groomer a pro at scissoring, breed-specific cuts and terrier stripping. Grooming services include nail clipping, flea treatments, ear and anal-gland cleaning, and temperature-controlled hand drying. Suds & Scissors welcomes you to poke around their salon before you bring your precious pup in for a cut.

Total Dog
(831) 624-5553
26366 Carmel Rancho Ln
Carmel, California 93923
Hours: Mon - Sat 10:30 A.M. - 5:30 P.M., Sun 12 A.M. - 4 P.M.

Payment: Credit Cards
Price Range: $$

May Carpenter's Total Dog has been for and about pups for 27 years. Her years in the biz have included training, agility, referrals, showing and rescue. Her store is filled with all things dog, including ornaments, cards, pillows, plates and breed-specific Dog Crossing signs. She doesn't push the treats but will hand out lots of free advice.

Cyber Dog

Augie's Doghouse

www.augiesdoghouse.com
Payment: Credit Cards
Price Range: $/$$

If you are willing to sort through the silly stuff, Augie's offers
some great deals. A few of the items are so quirky they're cool.
The snowsuits, fleeces and sweaters aren't exactly fashion for-
ward but are as affordable as you will find. However, dog
lovers may find the Really Bad Dog cat toys to be in really
bad taste.

Babarker

www.babarker.com
Payment: Credit cards
Price Range: $/$$

If knickknacks are your cup of tea, then go no farther. This site has it all. You can search by category or by breed, making this the perfect pit stop for the dog-obsessed shopper. Although babarker.com is geared more toward the dog lover than the dog, it does carry a limited selection of dog items—toys, tags, and the ever-popular edible rawhide greeting cards.

Bark, The

www.thebark.com
Payment: Credit Cards
Price Range: $$

Hailed as the thinking person's dog magazine, this Berkeley-based quarterly magazine is an eloquently outspoken dog-rights advocate. From dog parks—with plenty of on-site tips on how to create and hold on to dog parks—to the horrors of puppy mills, *The Bark* always tells it like it is. And their book reviews are the best. You won't catch them using silly word coinages that are a little too *pawfect*. Check it out at the newsstand or on the Internet. On occasion, they have great online gift-basket subscription incentives.

Bowser Boutique

(866) 382-7171
www.bowserboutique.com
Payment: Credit Cards
Price Range: $$$

Offering fine furnishings for the four-legged set, Bowser Boutique will custom make just about any piece—including chaises, chairs, daybeds and bone-shaped sofas—to your pet's liking. The fabric patterns include dog-print paisley, plaid and the like. Some of their pieces are more stylish than others, and some are just too *too*. If you have to ask, you probably can't afford the furniture, which is as expensive as the human equivalent. But the chic ceramic dishes are definitely worth the added bucks.

Bow Wow Shop

(866) 855-4621
www.bowwowshop.com
Payment: Credit Cards
Price Range: $/$$
This purple-and-yellow no-frills site has some great deals on paw- and leopard-print faux-fur blankets, if that is your sort of thing. The treats seem more strange than sumptuous: low-fat Dixie's banana apple tarts and Dixie's salomon surprise are among the choices. The Outward Hound outdoor/travel supplies hold up, while the dog bowls are cute but not particularly sturdy.

C.A.R.E.

(800) 352-0010
www.canineauto.com
Payment: Credit Cards
Price Range: $/$$/$$$
No more need for soccer-mom arm blocks when you take your dog on the road. C.A.R.E. (Canine Automotive Restraint Equipment) offers seat-belt harnesses as well as barriers to keep dogs safe and secure in the car. Some of the higher-end canine safety systems include The Puppy Package a free puppy-size restraint. They also offer truck restraints, seat covers, ramps and window guards that allow dogs to enjoy fresh air without being able to stick their heads out of the vehicle.

Chic Doggie by Corey

www.chicdog.com
Payment: Credit Cards
Price Range: $$$

This haute dog couture line is created by former investment banker Corey Gelman with the help of her model/muse Bear. The canine cashmere offerings include dog coats, scarves, blankets and pillows, while the silver necklaces look great on you or your pooch. The Hermes-inspired dog carriers make perfect travel accessories; you can finish the look by accessorizing your pet with their little doggie and kitty barrettes. Celebs such as Madonna, Oprah and Aerosmith's Steven Tyler are Chic Doggie clientele.

Colorado Canines

www.coloradocanines.com
Payment: Credit Cards
Price Range: $/$$/$$$

Luckily for the rest of us, this all-natural bakery and boutique is not just for Colorado canines. The bear bells probably won't get much use by anyone outside the Rockies, but the rest of their outdoor equipment—trailblazer packs to go on your dog, car beacons, first-aid kits—are great for outdoor-types anywhere. The treats—including Zuke's Power Bones—are a little more interesting than the dog food, but if all you want is all natural, it's all good.

Decadent Dogs

(866) 4K9-KIDS
www.decadentdogs.com
Payment: Credit Cards
Price Range: $$$

If you are seriously in the market for the decidedly decadent, then the prices are surprisingly reasonable—or at least at the lower end of outrageously expensive. Swarovski crystal collars, fabulous faux-fur coats, hand-painted banquet tables, and sofas, chairs and chaises with fabric choices running from kiwi cool to drab harvest. They cross the line with tiaras and charm tags that are just too *too*, but if you ever need a costume for your pooch, this is the place to get it.

Doctors Foster & Smith

(800) 381-7179

www.drsfostersmith.com

Payment: Credit Cards

Price Range: $/$$/$$$

For one-stop Internet shopping, it is hard to beat this vet-owned shop. The super-durable, hospital-grade orthopedic beds are great for aging dogs, or those with aches and pains. Surprisingly, the colors and patterns for the Orthopedic Beds are infinitely more appealing than the options for the Classic Beds. They also have a great selection of snacks and bones. If your dog is a fast-food fiend, the next time you do drive-through, you might try distracting him with one of their edible bacon-cheeseburger flavored bones that look like the real thing.

Dog Friendly

www.dogfriendly.com

If you're feeling guilty for leaving your dog home alone while you're stuck in the office, this site not only tells you what stores, restaurants and hotels welcome your dog, but also which employers allow dogs in the workplace. This city-specific resource is great for locals and travelers. Every place listed welcomes all sizes and breeds—as long as they are well behaved.

Doggone Good

(800) 660-2665
www.doggonegood.com
Payment: Credit Cards
Price Range: $$

Unless you are an avid agility/show-dog enthusiast, these products may seem more novelty than practical—but the cabana crate is the perfect little tent for any dog in need of a respite. And if you don't mind spending the added dough for human-grade food, Doggone distributes Flint River Ranch's all-natural dog foods.

Doggon' Wheels

www.doggon.com
Payment: Credit Cards
Price Range: $$$

What a lifesaver! These custom-designed wheelchairs are well worth the $200-plus when you think about the freedom and mobility they afford disabled pets. Dogs are their biggest users, but they have also created wheel chairs for cats and bunnies. They also offer support slings, booties and doggie diapers. With their 30-day money-back trial period, you can't lose.

Dog Pals

www.dogpals.com

An affordable alternative to day-care, this community-service site aims to pair up dogs so that they can play while their people are away. With plenty of bulletin boards and chat areas, it's a great idea, but so far there don't seem to be many takers. Let's hope they can hang in until it catches on.

Dogpark.com

www.dogpark.com

Payment: Credit Cards

Price Range: $/$$

Dogpark.com is a no-nonsense, state-by-state reference guide
to the nation's dog parks, with all the specifics and particulars:
location, hours, water options, poop bags, etc. The site is
stocked with borderline gadget items that might seem more
legit with better names: The Chuckit allows you to chuck your
dog's tennis ball without touching it; the Dish-a-go-go is actually a very sensible, portable dog bowl; and the Pupperware
seems the perfect pet-food bag.

Dog Sack

(877) 454-2895

www.dogsack.com

Payment: Credit Cards

Price Range: $$$

The inspiration was a little morbid—a paramedic created the
Dog Sack when he realized he could keep his car clean by
bundling his sandy dog up in a body bag. However, what he
created was a water-resistant bag that keeps your environment
clean, while still allowing your dog full mobility. Needless to
say, your dog's head does not go in the sack. The Dog Sack
looks more like skiwear than a body bag, and with easy-to-fol-
low instructions on the website, suiting up your dog in the
Dog Sack couldn't be simpler.

Dog Toys

(877) DOG-TOYS

www.dogtoys.com

Payment: Credit Cards

Price Range: $/$$/$$$

For the dog that has everything, Dog Toys offers breed-specific suggestions on playthings for your pet. The stuffed toys run the gamut from the basic sock monkey to the frivolous Dog Shews. And with the GoDogGo tennis ball machine, you can save yourself from those endless games of fetch. Treats—biscotti, Alaskan salmon and such—are clearly for the cultivated canine pallet.

Dog Water

www.dogwater.com
Payment: Credit Cards
Price Range: $

It's not Evian but this fluoride-enriched purified water comes in a portable 24-oz. bowl with a lid that doubles as a Frisbee—perfect for play in the park. It sure beats the hassle of makeshift bowls, and it may even save your dog from traumatic trips to the doggie dentist.

Dogz Togz

www.dogztogz.com

If your tastes include wildly embellished polka dot dog coats and sweaters with attached boas, then point your browser at dogztogz.com. The site, offering 17 styles ranging from size XS (7- to 8-inch head to tail) to XL (15- to 16-inch head to tail), clearly caters to more petite pups. If your definition of dressing for success includes coordinating your outfit with your pup's, then you're in luck. The site offers matching purses for each of the featured dog coats.

Duke and Duchess

www.dukeandduchesspetgifts.com

Specializing in products that "make life more luxurious for pets," this site offers such necessities as a lip-shaped dog sofa and cologne for your pooch. And you can outfit yourself in their "Spoiled Bitch" line of caps and tees. Browsing the site is plenty entertaining—although you will quickly find that the selection is rather dissapointing.

Everything but the Pup

(646) 486-5865

www.everythingbutthepup.com

Payment: Credit Cards

Price Range: $$$

Everything but the Pup's Puppy Starter Kit is the perfect gift for first-time parents—supplying all the necessary essentials except the puppy. If you're into one-stop shopping and have plenty of money to spend, go for the Gryphon Deluxe Kit. It's a combination of the Gryphon Sleep, Play, Groom, Train and Mess kits. All they're missing is the first aid kit—and it's a safe guess that they'll have one soon. Thankfully, this site is not only for puppies.

Fetch

www.fetchpets.com

Payment: Credit Cards

Price Range: $$$

Canine chic goes fun and funky at New York's Fetch. The crown-styled beds are fit for the finest pooches—or your canine can go military in the camouflage doghouse. Their top-of-the-line bath supplies will keep dogs sudsy clean and smelling good, and the Good Breath kit is the perfect follow-up to the Poochi Sushi. For a great person/pooch combo gift, go for the snuggly, chic blankets. The often-forgotten kitties no longer have to feel like a fish out of water in the fabulously funky velvet fish beds.

Fido's on Forest
www.fidosonforest.com
Payment: Credit Cards
Price Range: $/$$
The web component of a Laguna Beach Forest Avenue store, fidosonforest.com stocks supplies for your pup and unique items for dog lovers. The site includes gift books, metal dog sculptures and a chess set pitting dogs against cats. The dog gear tends toward the more traditional—Greenies, toys and togs, and a small selection of bowls and beds.

George
(877) 344-5454
www.georgesf.com
Payment: Credit Cards
Price Range: $$/$$$
This effortlessly hip, eclectic store is for those who prefer their pets' stuff cool, not cutesy. The Sock Monkey striped sweater is a standout, along with the Oxford Stripe quilt, with '70s-colored preppy stripes on one side and snuggly sherpa on the other, you may want to keep this one for yourself. The dog beds—definitely more canine cool than shabby-chic—will brighten any room you put them in. Cat offerings include hemp beds, fish chips and organic catnip.

Get Royal Treatment

www.getroyaltreatment.com

Payment: Credit Cards

Price Range: $$/$$$

If you're unwilling to bask in the dogginess of your pooch, order a supply of fresh currant shampoo or papaya and aloe wipes. Prince Lorenzo Borghese, grandson of cosmetics queen Princess Marcella Borghese, developed the Royal Treatment line of all-natural, human-grade pet bath and body products as a reaction to his 11-year-old black Lab "smelling like a dog." In addition, Borghese offers a line of pet treats. The site also carries a limited supply of collars, leashes, clothing, and beds.

Halo, Purely for Pets

(800) 426-4256

www.halopets.com

Payment: Credit Cards

Price Range: $$$

Halo offers comfort food for pets. Spot's Stew—made of slow-cooked chicken and vegetables without any fillers—even looks like people food. You will definitely feel the push for all-natural products from this holistic site, but they also offer supplements for those who can't swallow the financial commitment required for the food. If you're willing to do the cooking, they've even been known to send out their recipe.

Harry Barker

(800) HI-HARRY

www.harrybarker.com

Payment: Credit Cards

Price Range: $$$

Enjoy J. Crew-cool offerings from this community-conscious Georgia-based company. From sweaters to bathrobes, any comfy thing your pet might need for a lazy weekend can be found here. And the porcelain bowls are refreshingly fun, not fussy. Plus, they offer all-natural treats, made by Savannah's Welfare to Work program. Harry's own all-natural shampoos come in handy for home bathing, with the Prickly Pear Cactus a safe alternative to flea repellents. And their eclectic selection of collars is definitely more funky than preppy.

J-B Wholesale Pet Supplies, Inc.

(800) 526-0388
www.jbpet.com
Payment: Credit Cards
Price Range: $/$$/$$
Luckily for the rest of us, this site is no longer just for New Yorkers. All of their items are reasonably priced, and people that don't mind dressing their dog in last season's styles, can get unbelievable bargains on their closeout items. Those that like to dress their canine for the Christmas holiday, will appreciate their seasonal costumes, which are appropriately festive and silly. Tired pooches can get human-grade rest on their Simmons Orthocare beds. All products come with a seven-day guarantee.

K-9 Top Coat

(888) 833-K9K9
www.K9topcoat.com
Payment: Credit Cards
Price Range: $$$
A scuba suit for dogs, these waterproof Lycra bodysuits can be used to protect your dog from your environment, your environment from your dog, or your dog from himself. The snug-fitting suit doesn't hamper activity at all, and it's great for bad weather, allergies and for covering and protecting injured areas. However, if your dog gets embarrassed by a bad haircut, he will likely be mortified by this form-fitting,

fur-flattening suit. And the print pattern is beyond hideous, but the simple solid colors allow dogs to maintain a bit of their dignity.

La Petite Maison
www.lapetitemaison.com
Payment: Credit Cards
Price Range: $$$
Despite the fact that they make more playhouses than dog-houses, La Petite Maison is too fabulous not to list. Forget about dark and dingy clapboard boxes. These custom-designed dog-houses can be made to match any home and to fit any dog—or you can choose from one of their designs, including the Swiss Chalet and French Chateau. Suddenly, being in the doghouse doesn't seem so bad.

Maxx's Closet
(877) MAXX-SCL
www.maxxscloset.com
Payment: Credit Card
Price Range: $$$
If you want to dress your dog, Maxx's Closet is the place to find the clothes. The Paris Chic collection would do Jackie-O proud—and even decked in Maxx's Weekend Wear, your dog will look done to the nines. All of the fashions are inspired, and modeled, by the eponymous Maxx, a sweet little Yorkie. The outfits come in all sizes, but this attire is definitely best left for delicate dogs.

Once Upon a Dog

www.onceuponadog.com
Payment: Credit Cards
Price Range: $$

If you're into alternative, then you've probably heard of quinoa —the main ingredient in Once Upon A Dog's healthy heart-shaped dog biscuits. First discovered by the Inca Empire — quinoa contains as close to perfect a protein balance as you will get from any common grain. These treats, which come in two sizes, are a wholesome and tasty option for dogs with allergies to corn and wheat.

Original Dog Biscuit

(800) 670-2312
www.originaldogbiscuit.com
Payment: Credit Cards
Price Range: $$/$$$

These dog biscuits—oatmeal raisin, peanut delight, veggie and apple crisp—are so yummy you'll probably want to eat them yourself, which you can since these all-natural organic treats are made with human-grade ingredients. If your dog gets tired of the same old snacks, the six-month membership in their Treat of the Month Club is a great value. Original also offers the inspirational Ultimutt Posters that would go well in any vet's, doctor's, dentist's or shrink's office.

Patio Park

(877) 206-5946
www.patiopark.com
Payment: Credit Cards
Price Range: $$$

If you're unable to take your dog outside, bring the outside to your dog with Patio Park. It's a small grass strip complete with mock fire hydrant and picket fence. Plastic liners and irrigation strips supposedly make this product safe for use in your home, but you might note that it's not called Living Room Park. The Patio Park makes a lot of sense for injured dogs or people who work odd hours and don't want to walk their dog late at night.

PawZessions

(805) 374-1949
2989 E Thousand Oaks Blvd
(west of Hampshire Rd)
Thousand Oaks, California 91362
www.pawzessions.com
Payment: Credit Cards
Price Range: $$/$$$
Pawzessions offers plenty of personalized necessities and niceties. The coolest pooch-centric offerings are the ceramic food dishes and water bowls, available in black and white or painted to your taste. If you're in need of knickknacks, the shabby-chic picture frames, preppy polka-dotted signs and the fabulously funky bone-shaped ceramic treat jars will definitely brighten your home. All items are available inscribed with the name of your four-legged favorite.

Pet Aromatics

(877) 738-2766
www.petaromatics.com
Payment: Credit Cards
Price Range: $$
Animal aromatherapy comes in several forms at Pet Aromatics: spritzes, candles and shampoos. Heavenly scents include Honeysuckle Hound, Rose Petal Pooch, Woodsy Woof and Canine Coconut. Alcohol-free spritzes are safe on your dog and your furniture. These soft, fresh scents are great for minor doggie smells, but if your dog's been skunked, they're not going to save you from the stink.

Pet Click

www.petclick.com
Payment: Credit Cards
Price Range: $$/$$$

All-natural dog food is just a click away on this straightforward site. Raw meat, vegan, European cuisine—you name it, they stock it. The one big drawback is the lack of serving-size information on the site. Unless you know your brands and quantities, especially with the raw foods, you will have to do some research. Fortunately, their customer-service line will answer just about any question you may have.

Pet Club

Payment: Credit Cards
Price Range: $

www.petclub.com

This J.C. Penny-sponsored community site has some great deals for bargain hunters—especially on pet-friendly lodgings. However, they are determined to be more than just a place to clip coupons; message boards, advice columns and game areas for kids make this family-oriented site a standout. And the ASPCA has given them two paws up.

Pet Elegance

(800) 942-0742
www.petelegance.com
Payment: Credit Cards
Price Range: $$$

If you're planning on putting your dog in your wedding party or want to throw them nuptials of their own, this is the place to find the proper threads, specifically tuxedos and bridal pearl bibs. They also have a rather creative collection of collar designs: daisy, plaid, faux leopard fur, gingham, nautical and the patriotic red, white and blue, as well as a specially designed greyhound collar. Tasty treats include: Dogstickers, Bacon Breakfast Croissant Cookies and Peanut Butter Yogart Bones—really healthy snacks that dogs love.

Pet Fly's

www.petflys.com

Petflys.com offers super-swanky dog carriers. Approved by most major airlines for cabin travel, the carriers feature wire windows, fur-lined bottom inserts and bold graphics.

Pet Food Direct

www.petfooddirect.com

Payment: Credit Cards

Price Range: $$/$$$

You won't find too many bargains, but this pet food outlet carries just about every brand of dog food—from the mainstream to the lesser-known all-natural brands. Check out their Pet Travel Central! section for some great finds; their Outward Hound food bag makes for easy transport of all your dog's dining essentials. They also have a large selection of poop-removal products that make this stinky task a little less unpleasant.

Pet Health Journal

(503) 342-1380

www.pethealthjournal.com

Payment: Credit Cards

Price Range: $$

For the uber-organized or those striving to be, this book allows you to systematically log and track all of your dog's vitals. Sections include vaccinations, appointments, medications, emergencies and pet-sitters. Putting it together may take some effort, but it sure beats lugging around an overstuffed file with scraps of paper and clippings falling out.

Pet Planet

www.petplanet.com

This site doesn't yet deliver everything it promises—and pet-loving singles will find it's slim pickings in the matchmaking section. Their city-specific databases are, at best, little better than the Yellow Pages, often producing no results for basic searches. Let's hope this one catches up to itself.

Pet Power

www.petpower.com

Payment: Credit Cards

Price Range: $$

Pet Power offers all sorts of all-natural options—all infused with bee pollen. Pet Power's Tranquility Formula—with L-tryptophan (think turkey), brewer's yeast, vitamin B-6, and of course, bee pollen—alleviates anxiety without putting your dog into a drug-induced coma. Their Cartilage Formula is a glucosamine concoction that contains lots of added nutrients.

Pet-tek

www.pet-tek.com

Payment: Credit Cards

Price Range: $$/$$$

Not too technical, this site is definitely no-frills functional. They have an amazing assortment of items that run from logical essentials to way-out-there, but still practical, gadgets. The all-natural dog food doesn't have to be refrigerated, making it great for road trips. While it may look like a trampoline, the

Flea-Free Dog Bed is for sleeping on. If you're into do-it-your-self grooming, this site supplies more information than most of us will ever need to know about canine styling. The PetSafe Spray Control Radio Fence offers an alternative electric-fence-style aversion shock therapy; instead of getting zapped, dogs get sprayed with smelly citronella.

PetVogue
www.PetVogue.com
Payment: Credit Cards
Price Range: $$$
The home page is retro '50s beauty-parlor chic but PetVogue is gadget central: wine-barrel dog houses, electric dog doors, lambswool-lined car seats, tennis-ball launchers and Pet Talk, which allows you to prerecord a message that will play for your pet while you are away. This is in addition to the requisite spoiled-dog standards: sweaters, jackets, Pucci bags and such. The topper is the Elizabethan wedding garb for all members of the wedding party—from the bride to the ring bearer. The only snag is the prices, and they may spoil your fun at this "boutique for spoiled pets."

Planet Dog
(800) 381-1516
www.planetdog.com
Payment: Credit Cards
Price Range: $$/$$$
For the Earth-minded pooch, the Planet Dog Gift Tote, which looks like it's right out of an L.L. Bean catalog, is the perfect gift. The Planet is best known for their Solar System balls that include the big Orbee and the little Lunee. The super-padded canvas beds and fuzzy fleece blankets are comfy from the start, while the hemp collars will only get softer and prettier with time. And for those who like everything perfectly in its place, the corner bed, pie-shaped with a perfect 90-degree angle, is a must-have.

Poop Happens

www.poophappensbag.com
Payment: Credit Cards
Price Range: $$$

If you can stomach actually putting your dog's filled poop bag inside your own bag, this may be just the item for you. The idea behind these utilitarian-chic bags is that they save you the embarrassment of carrying an unsightly and smelly bag around. But it seems hard to imagine that someone who is squeamish about being seen with a poop bag would be willing to stash the mortifying little mess into their own bag. And if all of that isn't enough, this bag can double as a water bowl. Someone call the germ police.

Post Modern Pets

www.postmodernpets.com
Payment: Credit Cards
Price Range: $$$

If your decor includes Eames and Le Corbusier, then a toile dog bed just won't do. Instead, try postmodern-pets.com, which features such trendsetting items as the Bau House and Alessi dog bowls. The site is divided into items for dogs, cats, birds and fish. And the design is as sleek as the proffered goods. Good taste has a price, however. Be prepared to shell out some moola for your pooch.

Purely Pets

(804) 748-7626
www.purelypets.com
Payment: Credit Cards
Price Range: $$$

If you're on the verge of going holistic, Purely Pets will definitely pave the way. Beginners can get their feet wet with the all-natural dry foods, while the more advanced can try out some of their shared recipes. The products are indexed by brand, by ailments, and from A to Z—making it very easy to search and compare. Pet nutritionist and Purely Pets founder Darleen Rudnick is available for consultations via phone or the Purely Pets private chat room—the cost is $35. If that's too steep, you can always take advantage of the health alerts on the site or subscribe to her newsletter.

R.C. Steele

(888) 839-9420
www.rcsteele.com
Payment: Credit Cards
Price Range: $/$$/$$$
Veterinarian R.C. Steele opened the doors of his shop in the '60s. Several decades later the enterprise is still booming,and online, which is simple, straightforward and stocked with reasonably priced solid essentials. Steele's dog-bed selection is stellar. Even their indulgences are budget friendly. The flannel pajamas are so snuggly.

Ruff Wear

www.ruffwear.com
Payment: Credit Cards
Price Range: $$/$$
Billed as gear for dogs on the go, Ruff Wear provides boots, collapsible bowls, packs, and so on for the active dog. If your idea of a trail hike involves backcountry passes and bear bags, then this site can outfit your dog accordingly. For instance, you can order a Kibble Kaddie or a Mutt Hutt—modeled on your own high-tech tent, but with a doggie door for nighttime nature calls.

Sit Stay

(800) SIT-STAY

www.sitstay.com

Payment: Credit Cards

Price Range: $$/$$$

The site looks more like msn.com than a dog-product site, but it's filled with a wide array of items—from figurines that your grandmother would love to cocktail-cool dog-bone-shaped ice-cube trays. Dogs respond well to the Bow Wow Botanicals Chinese formulas—Mellow Dog, Jumpin' Dog and Sneezy Dog—that are served treat-style, so there's no added pill-administering stress. For cold-weather outings, the Polartec North Paw coats are definitely North Face-inspired. The Canine Cooler gel dog bed will instantly cool off overheated dogs—just keep it in the freezer or ice chest until time to use.

Stylie Dog

(800) 213-3180

www.styliedog.com

Payment: Credit Cards

Price Range: $

The peppy Stylie Dog site offers an assortment of pooch-minded practicalities, from the leash pack, essentially a sporty Stylie Dog bag and leash, to the reflective leash and collar—think neon Stylie Dog—to the travel bowl.

Tails by the Bay

www.tailsbythebay.com

Payment: Credit Cards

Price Range: $$$

This site is tops for top-of-the-line clothes, furnishings and gifts, including—from the chic Metropolitan Dog Bed, to the pet-sized life jackets, to the hot-dog bun costume to go with your little hot dog. Check out the Tail's photo gallery to see pics of happy pets modeling their new threads.

Teddy's Dog Treats

www.teddysdogtreats.com
Payment: Credit Cards
Price Range: $$/$$$

This fine purveyor of dog treats offers several collections: Core, Christmas, Hanukkah, Love, New York, and so on. The name-sake of the company is an eight-year-old Dalmation named, of course, Teddy who is a cancer survivor. The company donates 8% of its profits to the American Cancer Society's Annual Dogwalk. The site also provides links to animal cancer organizations if you're interested in becoming more involved.

Three Dog Bakery

(800) 4TREATS
www.threedog.com
Payment: Credit Cards
Price Range: $/$$/$$$

Three Dog Bakery, with stores popping up all over the country, is tops for healthy, yummy dog treats. Their online Dogalogue has some great offerings, including Gift Boxers, Monthly Dogliveries and custom-made cakes. And if you want to treat your canine to some home cooking, get their *Three Dog Bakery Cookbook*.

Trixie & Peanut

www.trixieandpeanut.com
Payment: Credit Cards
Price Range: $$$

As much fun to browse as it is to buy from, this site has everything from basic balls to lavish pet carriers and clothing. If you're in the market for Nail Pawlish or a bridesmaid dress for your pampered pooch, check out this website. There's even a link for "all things perfectly pink." Site founder Susan Bing is a graphic designer, and it shows. The site is easy to navigate and products are clearly displayed.

Uptown Pets

www.uptownpets.com
Payment: Credit Cards
Price Range: $$$

At Uptown Pets, dress-up isn't just frills and frouf. Harley-Davidson dog collars and scarves are definitely downtown cool. Burberry coats are an instant classic for the preppy set, and the Magic Carpet dog beds are totally bohemian chic. You can also get their astrologist to do your dog's profile; just supply the date, time and location of your dog's birth. And if you believe in the healing properties of magnet-jewelry, this is where to get a necklace for your pet.

Waggin' Tails

www.waggintails.com
Payment: Credit Cards
Price Range: $$

All sorts of all-natural remedies here—from dental care to treats to the bitter-apple spray that's sour enough to stop your dog from chewing hot spots or furniture. They tell you the breed of dog their products have been tested on, so you're not relying on a St. Bernard to tell you what your Chihuahua will like. The Buddy Bowl is as spill-proof a bowl as you will find, making it great for the car. Plus they carry several brands and varieties of all-natural dog food.

Wagwear

www.wagwear.com

Payment: Credit Cards

Price Range: $$$

Casual cool goes cutting edge with Wagwear's simple textures and color combinations that define urban chic. The wool sweaters come in army green and orange, and baseball-jersey-inspired chocolate and gold. You will definitely want to get the fabulous fleece-lined suede collar that appeals to the sight as much as the touch. It's pretty much impossible to go wrong here. Wagwear is all the rage with the canine models in the magazine spreads.

Puppy Starter Kit

DOG LICENSING

As a resident in the San Francisco area you are required to license your dog within 30 days after they reach the age of four months. If you adopt a dog older than four months, you have 30 days to get them licensed.

The easiest way to get a dog license is to download the form off the Internet.

You will also need to pull together a few documents before animal control will issue you a dog license. Policies vary from city to city, but they all require the following:

A) A copy of your dog's current rabies vaccination certificate
B) A copy of your dog's spay or neuter certificate
C) A check or money order. (If you haven't gotten your dog spayed or neutered, be prepared to pay significantly more than the $20 to $30 you would otherwise be charged.)

Following is a list of agencies where you can get a dog license throughout the Bay Area.

Please note: If you are a resident of a city that does not fall under the jurisdiction of animal control for your county, you can usually obtain a license online from your city's website.

SAN FRANCISCO PROPER

Ocean Avenue Veterinary Hospital

(415) 586-5327
1001 Ocean Ave
San Francisco, California 94112

Office of the Treasurer and Tax Collector
(415) 554-6449
City Hall
1 Dr. Carlton B. Goodlett Pl, Room 110
San Francisco, California 94102

San Francisco Animal Care and Control
(415) 554-6364
1200 15th St
San Francisco, California 94103

NORTH BAY

Marin County Animals Services
(415) 883-4621 x220
Attn: Licensing
171 Bel Marin Keys Blvd
Novato, California 94949

Napa County Animal Shelter
(707) 253-4381
942 Hartle Ct
Napa, California 94559

Napa County Treasurer's Office
(707) 253-4327
1195 3rd St
Napa, California 94559

Sonoma County Animal Regulation
(707) 565-7100
1247 Century Ct
Santa Rosa, California 95403

Yountville Town Hall
(707) 944-8851
6550 Yount St
Yountville, California 94559

EAST BAY

Alameda City Animal Control

(510) 337-8565
1590 Fortmann Way
Alameda, California 94501

Antioch Animal Shelter

(925) 779-6989
300 L St
Antioch, California 94509

City Finance Dept

(510) 528-5730
1000 San Pablo Ave
Albany, California 94706

City Finance Dept

(510) 644-6470
2020 Center St
Berkeley, California 94704

City Hall

(925) 960-4000
1052 S Livermore Ave
Livermore, California 94550

City Hall Cashier's Window

(510) 790-7264
37101 Newark Blvd
Newark, California 94560

City Hall Utilities Dept Desk

(925) 484-8038
200 Old Bernal Ave
Pleasanton, California 94566

East County Animal Shelter

(925) 803-7040
4595 Gleason Dr
Dublin, California 94568

Emeryville Police Dept
(510) 420-3006
Animal Services
403 Highland Ave
Piedmont, California 94611

Finance Dept of City Hall
(510) 577-3200
835 E 14th St
San Leandro, California 94577

Hayward Animal Services
(510) 293-7200
16 Barnes Ct
Hayward, California 94544

License and Collections Department
(510) 981-7200
1947 Center St
Berkeley, California 94704

Martinez Animal Control
(925) 646-2995
4849 Imhoff Pl
Martinez, California 94553

Oakland Animal Services
(510) 535-5615
1101 29th Ave
Oakland, California 94601

Tri-City Animal Shelter
(510) 790-6640
1950 Stevenson Blvd
Fremont, California 94538

West County Animal Shelter
(510) 667-7707
2700 Fairmont Dr
San Lorenzo, California 94577

PENINSULA

Animal Services & Placement Center

(650) 496-5971

3281 E Bayshore Frontage Rd
Palo Alto, California 94303

San Mateo County Animal Licensing

(650) 363-4220

455 County Center, 1st Floor
Redwood City, California 94063

SOUTH BAY

City of San Jose

Department of Parks, Recreation & Neighborhood Services

(408) 277-4661

4 N 2nd St, Ste 600
San Jose, California 95113

Division of Animal Care & Control

(408) 776-7300

605 Tennant Ave, Ste G
Morgan Hill, California 95037

Silicon Valley Animal Control Authority

(408) 764-0344

Animal Licensing
2324 Walsh Ave
Santa Clara, California 95051
www.svaca.com

CARMEL & MONTEREY

Monterey County Animal Services Center

(831) 769-8850

160 Hitchcock Rd
Salinas, California 93908

SF LOW-COST SPAY/NEUTER CLINICS

SF PROPER

San Francisco SPCA
(415) 554-3084
Spay & Neuter Clinic
2500 16th St
San Francisco, California 94103

NORTH BAY

Animal Birth Control Clinic
(415) 456-7515
738 A St
San Rafael, California 94901

Humane Society of Napa County
(707) 252-7442
3265 California Blvd
Napa, California 94558

Humane Society of Sonoma County
(707) 542-0882 x204
P.O. Box 1296
Santa Rosa, California 95402
www.sonomahumane.org

Marin Humane Society
(415) 883-3383
171 Bel Marin Keys Blvd
Novato, California 94949

Sonoma County Animal Regulation
(707) 565-7100
1247 Century Ct
Santa Rosa, California 95403
www.theanimalshelter.org

Up Valley Spay/Neuter Network

(707) 942-9066
P.O. Box 841
Calistoga, California 94515

EAST BAY

Friends of Fairmont Animal Shelter (FOFAS)

(510) 816-0954
2700 Fairmont Dr
San Leandro, California 94578

Hayward Friends of Animals Humane Society (HFofA)

(510) 582-7561
P.O. Box 3986
Hayward, California 94540

Oakland SPCA Spay/Neuter Clinic

(510) 639-7387
410 Hegenberger Loop
Oakland, California 94621
www.eastbayspca.org

PENINSULA

Palo Alto Animal Services Low-Cost Clinic

(650) 496-5933

Peninsula Humane Society

(650) 340-7025
12 Airport Rd
San Mateo, California 94401
www.peninsulahumanesociety.org

SOUTH BAY

Animal Birth Control
(408) 244-8351

Humane Society of Santa Clara Valley
(408) 727-3383
2530 Lafayette St
Santa Clara, California 95050
www.hssv.org

CARMEL/MONTEREY

SPCA of Monterey County
(831) 373-2631
1002 Hwy 68
Monterey, California 93940

Lost Dog Help

Having a pet disappear is a very scary thing. However, there are some immediate steps you can take that will significantly increase the chances of their safe return. This section includes a list of suggestions to get you started on your search, as well as a list of local shelters and resources.

• Stay calm and make a plan.
• Enlist the help of as many people as possible; delegate as many tasks as possible.
• Divide up the areas and then fan out and search the streets.
• Call, or have someone else call, vets and animal hospitals in the area.
• Make, or have someone else make, flyers that include the following:
    1) A picture, preferably a color copy, of your pet.
    2) Identifying characteristics, such as age, weight and markings. Some people believe that if you state that your pet needs daily medication, they are more likely to be returned.
    3) The offering of a monetary reward for the return of your pet.
    4) Go, or send someone, to the shelters:
    5) Look through all of the kennels for your dog.
    6) Show pictures and/or flyers (which should also save a picture) to the staff and volunteers.
    7) Post flyers on the bulletin board(s).
• Check, or have someone check, posted pictures of found dogs on shelter and dog-rescue organization websites. If you spot your dog:
    1) Copy down the identification/impound number posted with your dog's picture
    2) Call the shelter:
    3) Give them the identification/impound number.
    4) Ask them what sort of proof of ownership you need to show them.
    5) Go immediately (or as soon as they open) to the shelter to collect your dog and take them home.
• If you do not find your dog's picture posted on a shelter website, they may still be there. Return to the shelters at least every few days to look for them.

- Post flyers or signs in the following places:
  - Local shelters.
  - Veterinarians' offices, animal hospitals and animal-emergency clinics.
  - Grooming salons.
  - Pet-supply stores.
  - Dog parks.
  - Anywhere that dog-conscious people might frequent, such as neighboorhood coffee shops, bookstores, etc.
- Consider hiring a pet detective.

AREA SHELTERS

SF Proper

San Francisco Animal Care and Control

(415) 554-6364
1200 15th St
(@ Harrison St)
San Francisco, California 94103
www.ci.sf.ca.us/site/acc_index.asp
Hours: Mon, Tue, Thu, Fri 12 P.M. - 6 P.M.,
Wed 11 A.M. - 7 P.M.

San Francisco SPCA

(415) 554-3000
2500 16th St
(@ Harrison St)
San Francisco, California, 94103
www.sfspca.org
Hours: Mon - Sun 11 A.M. - 6 P.M.

North Bay

Healdsburg Animal Shelter

(707) 431-3386
570 Westside Rd
Healdsburg, California 95448
www.healdsburgshelter.org
Hours: Tue - Sat 11 A.M. - 4 P.M., Sun 12 P.M. - 4 P.M.
Payment: Checks

Humane Society of Sonoma County

(707) 542-0882
5345 Hwy 12 W
Santa Rosa, California 95407
www.sonomahumane.org
Hours: Tue - Sat 12 P.M. - 5:30 P.M., Mon - Sun 12 P.M. - 3:30 P.M.

Marin Humane Society

(415) 883-4621
171 Bel Marin Keys Blvd
Novato, California 94949
www.marinhumanesociety.org
Hours: Tue - Sun 10 A.M. - 5:30 P.M., Wed 10 A.M. - 7 P.M.

Petaluma Animal Shelter

(707) 778-4396
840 Hopper St
Petaluma, California 94952
www.petalumaanimalshelter.org
Hours: Tue - Fri 12 P.M. - 6 P.M., Sat 11 A.M. - 6 P.M.

Rohnert Park Animal Shelter

(707) 584-1582
301 Jay Rogers Ln
Rohnert Park, California 94928
www.rpanimalshelter.org
Hours: Wed 1 P.M. - 6:30 P.M., Thu - Sat 1 P.M. - 5:30 P.M.,
Sun 1 P.M. - 4:30 P.M.

Sonoma County Animal Shelter

(707) 524-7100
1247 Century Ct
Santa Rosa, California 95403
www.theanimalshelter.org
Hours: Mon, Sat 12 P.M. - 5 P.M.,Tue - Fri 12 P.M. - 7 P.M.

East Bay

Alameda City Animal Shelter

(510) 337-8565
1590 Fortman Way
Alameda, California 94501
Hours: Every Day on, Sat 7 A.M. - 5 P.M.

Animal Care Services

(510) 981-6600
2013 2nd St
Berkeley, California 94710
Hours: Mon, Tue, Thu, Fri, Sat 10 A.M. - 4 P.M.,
Wed 10 A.M. - 7 P.M., Sun 11 A.M. - 3 P.M.

Antioch Animal Services

(925) 779-6989
300 L St
Antioch, California 94509
www.ci.antioch.ca.us/CityGov/Police/AntiochAnimalSvcs
Hours: Mon, Wed, Fri, Sat 10 A.M. - 4 P.M.,
Tue, Thu 10 A.M. - 8 P.M.

Berkeley East Bay Humane Society

(510) 845-7735
2700 9th St
Berkeley, California 94710
www.berkeleyhumane.org
Hours: Tue - Sun 11 A.M. - 7 P.M.

Contra Costa Humane Society

(925) 279-2247
609 Gregory Ln #140
Pleasant Hill, California 94523
www.cchumane.org

East Bay SPCA

(510) 569-1606
8323 Baldwin St
Oakland, California 94621
www.eastbayspca.org

Hayward Animal Shelter

(510) 293-7200
16 Barnes Ct
Hayward, California 94544
Hours: Tue 12 P.M. - 7 P.M., Wed - Fri 12 P.M. - 6 P.M.,
Sat 11 A.M. - 5 P.M.

Martinez Shelter
(925) 646-2995
4849 Imhoff Pl
Martinez, California 94553
Hours: Tue - Sat 10 A.M. - 5 P.M., Wed 10 A.M. - 7 P.M.

Oakland Animal Services
(510) 535-5605
1101 29th Ave
Oakland, California 94601
www.oaklandanimalshelter.org
Hours: Tue, Wed, Fri 12 P.M. - 6 P.M., Thu 12 P.M. - 7 P.M.,
Sat 12 P.M. - 4 P.M.

Oakland SPCA
(510) 569-0702
8323 Baldwin St
Oakland, California 94621
Hours: Tue, Wed 10 A.M. - 8 P.M.,
Thu - Sat 10 A.M. - 6:30 P.M., Sun 10 A.M. - 4:30 P.M.

Pinole Shelter
(510) 374-3966
651 Pinole Shores Dr
Pinole, California 94564
Hours: Tue - Sat 10 A.M. - 5 P.M., Wed 10 A.M. - 7 P.M.

Tri-City Animal Shelter
(510) 790-6640
1950 Stevenson Blvd
Fremont, California 94538
Hours: Tue - Fri 12 P.M. - 5 P.M., Sat 11 A.M. - 4 P.M.

Peninsula

Peninsula Humane Society
(650) 340-7022
12 Airport Blvd
San Mateo, California 94401
www.peninsulahumanesociety.com
Hours: Mon - Fri 11 A.M. - 7 P.M., Sat - Sun 11 A.M. - 6 P.M.

South Bay

Humane Society Silicon Valley
(408) 727-3383
2530 Lafayette St
Santa Clara, California 95050
www.hssv.org
Hours: Mon - Fri 10:30 A.M. - 8 P.M.,
Sat - Sun 10 A.M. - 6 P.M.

Palo Alto Animal Services
(650) 496-5971
3281 E Bayshore Rd
Palo Alto, California 94303
Hours: Mon - Sat 11 A.M. - 5:30 P.M.

Monterey/Carmel

SPCA of Monterey
(831) 373-2631
1002 Hwy 68
Monterey, California 93940
www.spcamc.org
Hours: Mon - Fri 11 A.M. - 5 P.M., Sat - Sun 11 A.M. - 4 P.M

When Dogs Go To Heaven

Losing a pet is a very sad, sometimes devastating, experience. Many people do not realize how much they will be affected until it happens. If you are too overcome with grief to deal with the logistics, many veterinarians' offices will take care of everything for you, including picking up your pet and having him cremated or buried. It may seem like a morbid thing to do, but it might be a good idea to ask your vet in advance what her policies are. Then, when the need arises, you will know whether you can count on her and what to expect.

If you prefer to take care of everything yourself, this section contains information, listed in the order it is most frequently needed:

HOSPICE

Nikki Hospice Foundation for Pets, The

(707) 557-8595
400 New Bedford Dr
(@ Sandy Neck Way)
Vallejo, California 94591
www.csum.edu/pethospice
Payment: Credit Cards, Checks
Price Range: $$

The first program of its kind in the country, the Nikki Hospice Foundation for Pets was named for its founder's late tabby cat. Nikki seeks to connect pet owners who do not want to euthanize their terminally ill pets with vets willing to facilitate a more natural, pain-managed death at home. In addition to developing a national vet database, Nikki has created the Tatiana Pet Memorial Fund, which provides owners with pet-burial information.

EUTHANASIA

The decision to put an animal to sleep is one of the most difficult decisions a person must make. The fact that it may be the most compassionate thing to do does not make it any easier. You may want to consult with your vet, and perhaps someone else that you trust, and ask them to help you determine if it is the right time and the right thing to do for your pet.

When the time comes, many people prefer to have a vet come to their house so that their animal can spend their final moments in the comfort of their home, not a veterinarian's office. If your vet does not offer this service, ask them to recommend someone for you. In many instances, the vet will give the animal a sedative prior to the euthanasia injection. When you speak to her, ask her if she does this. If she doesn't , ask her to prescribe a sedative for your dog and give it to him prior to her arrival.

FINAL ARRANGEMENTS

Bubbling Well Pet Memorial Park

(707) 255-3456
(800) 794-PETS (7387)
2462 Atlas Peak Rd
(Atlas Peak Rd exit, off Hwy 212)
Napa, California 94558
www.bubbling-well.com
Hours: Mon - Fri 8 A.M. - 4:30 P.M., Sat - Sun 9 A.M. - 3 P.M.
Closed: Holidays
Payment: Credit Cards, Checks
Price Range: $$
More than 10,000 pets have been laid to rest in this lovely mountaintop park among verdant lawns; flowing pools; olive, oak and manzanita grove; and cypress trees. Bubbling Well offers markers, plots and ceremonies to fit many budgets, including a low-cost country burial. Their website also offers a comprehensive list of resources for grief and loss support.

Monterey Bay Pet Memorial Park

(831) 722-8722
885 Strawberry Rd
(between Watsonville & Hwy 101)
Royal Oaks, California 95076
www.lovedpet.com
Hours: Mon - Fri 9 A.M. - 5 P.M., Sat - Sun 10 A.M. - 4 P.M.
Payment: Credit Cards, Checks
Price Range: $$

Losing a pet is never easy. Monterey Bay Memorial Park helps ease the pain. If you choose burial, your pup will be laid to rest in a private plot marked with a hand-carved headstone. The park's Garden of Wee Ones is reserved for toy dogs and petite pets. If you prefer cremation, you have the option of being present, and you can have your pet's likeness engraved on the urn. The park charges a modest annual maintenance fee.

Pet's Rest Cemetery and Crematory

(650) 755-2201
1905 Hillside Blvd
Colma, California 94014
www.petsrest.com
Hours: Mon - Fri 9 A.M. - 5 P.M., Sat 9 A.M. - 1 P.M.
Payment: Credit Cards, Checks
Price Range: $$

Of Colma's 17 cemeteries, the legendary Pet's Rest is the only one dedicated to pet burials. Founded in 1947, more than 13,000 animals have been buried here, among them dogs, cats, cheetahs and monkeys. Plots for small pets are $500; a pine box will run you another $90. A small granite marker is included in the price of the funeral, and owners are invited to be present both at a viewing in the chapel—fittingly, a former bee house—and at the actual internment.

Renaissance Charters

(415) 433-8800
San Francisco, California
www.renaissancecharters.com
Payment: Cash Only
Price Range: $$

If you're looking for a touching way to honor the memory of your animal companion, consider hiring Renaissance Charters to scatter his ashes under the Golden Gate Bridge. They'll take care of all the details: a minister, flowers and a keepsake certificate marking the longitude and latitude where they scattered your pet's ashes. Although you can't personally accompany your pup's ashes onto the boat, Renaissance can arrange for you to view the service from the bridge or the shore.

PET LOSS—BOOKS

Coping with Sorrow on the Loss of Your Pet
by Moira Anderson. 2nd Ed. Loveland, CO, Alpine Publications 1996

Loss of a Pet, The
by Wallace Sife, Ph.D. rev. ed. NY Howell Book House 1998

Pet Loss: A Thoughtful Guide for Adults and Children
by Herbert Nieberg, Ph.D. NY, Harper & Row 1996

PET LOSS—HOTLINES

University of California, Davis School of Veterinary Medicine
(800) 565-1526
Hours: 6:30 p.m. - 9:30 p.m. PST
Terri Austin, PhD
(408) 648-6283

U.C. Davis
(530) 752-4200
School of Veterinary Medicine
Davis, CA

Colorado State University
(303) 221-4535
College of Veterinary Medicine
Fort Collins, CO

University of Minnesota
(612) 624-4747
College of Veterinary Medicine
St. Paul, MN

Animal Medical Center, The
(212) 838-8100
New York, NY

Washington State University
(509) 335-1297
College of Veterinary Medicine
Pullman, WA

University of Pennsylvania
(215) 898-4529
School of Veterinary Medicine
Philadelphia, PA

PET LOSS—INTERNET SUPPORT

Association for Pet Loss and Bereavement, The
(718) 382-0960
www.aplb.org
The Association for Pet Loss and Bereavement (APLB) was
founded in 1987 by psychologist Wallace Sife—author of The
Loss of a Pet—after he lost his own dog and realized there was
nowhere to turn to process his grief. Today APLB is a nationwide
database with everything from cemeteries and support groups to
lawyers specializing in pet-related wrongful-action cases.

PET LOSS—SUPPORT GROUPS
& COUNSELORS

Pet Loss Support Group
(415) 554-3050
SF SPCA
243 Alabama St
(@ 16th St)
San Francisco, California 94103
www.sfspca.org/special_programs/petloss.shtml
Payment: No Charge
The Pet Loss Support Group is led by noted pet-loss counselor
Dr. Betty Carmack: She focuses on the grief, depression and
anger associated with the loss of a beloved pet. The group

meets on the first Tuesday evening of every month from 7:30
P.M. to 9 P.M. at the SF SPCA. There is no charge for the group
and you don't need to register in advance. For additional read-
ing, check out Dr. Carmack's recent book, *Grieving the Death
of a Pet*, which is available at the SF SPCA and bookstores.

Bloom, Elizabeth, DHM
(415) 924-3004
65 Golden Hind Passage
Corte Madera, California 94925

Kram, Beverly, LMFCC
(408) 557-8336
52 Harold Ave., Ste. K
San Jose, California

Carmack, Betty, RN, Ed.D.
(415) 334-5036
Grief Counseling for Pet Owners
449 Melrose St
San Francisco, California 94127
www.sfspca.org/special_programs/petloss.shtml

de Lovinfosse, Anne, Ph.D.
Pet Loss Support Group and Individual Counseling
(415) 456-5502
San Rafael, California

Sorensen, Jane, RN, MFCC; Lake, Roger, ChT
(707) 527-9330
Redwood Empire Veterinary Medical Association
c/o Montgomery Village Veterinary Clinic
775 Farmers Ln
Santa Rosa, California 95405
($10 per individual, $15 for couples/families)
cheribross@aol.com

Spector-Northrup, Audrey, MA, MFCC
(510) 704-5502
Albany, California
($20-$25 per workshop)

Nobori, Carol
(415) 569-0702
Oakland Humane Society
8323 Baldwin
Oakland, California 94621

Soares, Cecelia, DVM, MS
(925) 932-0607
Walnut Creek, California

Alameda/Contra Costa Pet Loss Support Group
Contra Costa Veterinary Medical Association
(925) 932-0607
2nd and 4th Tuesday of each month 6:30 P.M. - 8:30 P.M.
www.tlr-arf.org/Resources/caring/pet_loss.html

Leake, Mary
Peninsula Humane Society Pet Loss Support Group
(650) 340-7022 x344
12 Airport Blvd
San Mateo, California
mleake@peninsulahumanesociety.org

Ronen, Helaine, MSW
Humane Society of Santa Clara Valley
(408) 727-3383 x869
2530 Lafayette St
Santa Clara, California 95050

Richard, Julie D., RN, MPH
Pet Loss Workshops and Presentations
P.O. Box 62
Carmel, California 93921

Wagner, Teresa
Matters of the Heart
(408) 375-9389
74 Twin Oaks Dr
Monterey, California 93940
wagnertl@aol.com

Index

C

R